Judah, Past and Future

Judah, Past and Future

L.D.S. Teachings Concerning God's Covenant People

Howard H. Barron

INTERNATIONAL STANDARD BOOK NUMBER
0-88290-121-4

LIBRARY OF CONGRESS CATALOG CARD NUMBER
79-89350

Printed in the
United States of America
by

**Horizon Publishers
& Distributors
P.O. Box 490
50 South 500 West
Bountiful, Utah 84010**

ACKNOWLEDGMENTS

Writing this book has been a rich and faith-promoting experience. Voluminous materials have been carefully searched to obtain statements from the sermons and writings of prominent men in the Church which most clearly explain the subject areas being investigated. Because of the large volume of excellent material collected, one of the most challenging tasks has been to carefully edit the material in order to prevent this volume's becoming too large and unwieldy.

Grateful acknowledgment and deep appreciation is expressed to the numerous authors whose writings are quoted in this compilation. Their materials are exceptional. Without their contributions, perhaps much that is presented here may have been overlooked and forgotten.

Sincere appreciation is expressed to Dr. Ellis T. Rasmussen, Dean of the College of Religion, Brigham Young University; Dr. Larry C. Porter, Chairman of the Church History and Doctrine Department; Mrs. Rene Mortensen, Administrative Assistant in the College of Religious Instruction; and several excellent typists who assisted so cheerfully and did superior workmanship.

Grateful appreciation and acknowledgment is expressed to Deseret Book Company for their kindness in granting permission to use material from several of their copyrighted publications.

The staff of the LDS *Church Section* of the Deseret News also made materials available and to them I am also grateful for their assistance, as I am to all others from which materials were obtained. In some instances it was impossible to identify the author by name.

A very special thanks is extended to the Historical Department of the Church of Jesus Christ of Latter-day Saints and especially to Dr. Donald T. Schmidt, Church Librarian and his excellent staff; also to the Brigham Young University Library staff; and especially to Professor Chad Flake of Special Collections and his secretary DeAnna Stall, for their wholehearted generosity in the use of books, periodicals, journals, diaries, microfilms, etc.

Grateful recognition is expressed to several student research assistants; namely, Rex J. Allen, Cathy Gileadi and Dean Wheelwright for their efforts and encouragement.

Appreciation is also expressed to my good friend and president of Horizon Publishers, Duane S. Crowther. His keen insight, knowledge, and expertise of the subject matter of this volume has made his suggestions invaluable toward the improvement of the project. I am extremely grateful for his direction and help in getting this book published.

I am especially indebted to my precious wife, LaVerda, for her expertise and invaluable help in editing the final draft of the manuscript.

Above all, I am most thankful for the inspiration and guidance received from above. Without my Heavenly Father's assistance, no achievement would be possible. Hopefully this volume will help contribute to a better understanding of our Heavenly Father's dealings with His children, and if this be so, the compiler will be most grateful.

PREFACE

It is the hope of the compiler that this book will help the reader to understand more clearly the story of Judah. Their experiences are among the most exciting, colorful, and perhaps the most talked about of any people in the world. As the ancient covenant people of the Lord, they stand in a unique position among all the children of God. Volumes have been written concerning the Jews, and countless library shelves are bulging with dozens upon dozens of books about them written by eminent theologians, historians and philosophers. What, then, is the justification for another book about Judah? The book is probably unique among all the accounts of Judah in that its primary objective is to capture the powerful vision of the Jews as foreseen by the prophets, both ancient and modern, and by the modern-day descendants of Joseph. God has called upon modern Joseph, armed with the stick of Ephraim, to save modern Judah.

The prophets and inspired writers of the restored Church of Jesus Christ of Latter-day Saints have spoken fluently and eloquently of Judah. Through their efforts, the procession of Jewish history from antiquity to the present has been examined. The interactions between modern Joseph (the Mormons) and modern Judah (the Jews) has revealed the dramatic and colorful story of two brothers and the nations they sired. Indeed "the first shall be last and the last the first." It was first Judah then Joseph; now it is Joseph then Judah. The prophetic future envisions a united house of Israel where Judah and Joseph will reign triumphant with the Messiah as their King.

The following words of the Lord to the great modern-day prophet, seer and revelator, Joseph Smith, Jr., revealed the worldwide nature of these final events upon the earth:

..."For verily the voice of the Lord is unto all men, and there is none to escape; and there is no eye that shall not see, neither ear that shall not hear, neither heart that shall not be penetrated. And the rebellious shall be pierced with much sorrow; for their iniquities shall be spoken upon the housetops, and their secret acts shall be revealed. And the voice of warning shall be unto all people, by the mouths of my disciples, whom I have chosen in these last days. And they shall go forth and none shall stay them, for I the Lord have commanded them." (D&C 1:2-5)

For ease of reading, the compiler has prepared topical headings for the material presented. Another purpose of the topical guide is to help tie the material more closely together and to provide greater continuity of thought.

Table of Contents

List of Abbreviations

BYU...................... Brigham Young University

DNCS....... Church News Section of Deseret News

CR........................ L.D.S. Conference Report

JD........ Journal of (Brigham Young's) Discourses

HC................... History of the (L.D.S.) Church

DNW........................ Deseret News Weekly

MS................................. Millenial Star

WFWS......... Writings from the Western Standard

UGHM .... Utah Genealogical & Historical Magazine

TS............................. Times and Seasons

FOREWORD

> ...I am the Almighty God, walk before me and be thou perfect. And I will make my covenant between me and thee... And I will make thee exceedingly fruitful, and I will make nations of thee, and kings shall come out of thee. (Genesis 17:1, 2, 6.)
>
> ...And in thy seed after thee...shall all the families of the earth be blessed, even with the blessings of the Gospel, which are the blessings of salvation, even of life eternal.... (Abraham 2:11.)

As this wondrous covenant was made between Abraham and his God, how very close to that infinite source of all prophetic utterance must the spirit of Abraham have been. Could he envision, from that lofty station, the tortuous path his posterity would follow to reach their promised glory? Could he see Isaac, Jacob, Judah and Joseph succeeding him as patriarchs and prophets? Did Abraham's inspired vision reach down through the millenia to see his seed thrust, time and again, from sumptuous glory to unimaginable suffering; ravaged and scattered, reunited, then driven again?

Certainly no more dramatic or volatile story could ever be enacted than that of Abraham's posterity, especially the saga of the Jews. Nor has that history gone unsung. Thousands of writers and researchers have, with deft pens, painted the warm harmonies and stark contrasts of Judah's past. Hundreds more thoughtfully search the enigmatic moods of today's nation of Israel. And a few writers, standing on the shoulders of the ancient prophets, have even dared to whisper of Judah's final gathering and consumate glory. The Jewish story fills a multitude of volumes and touches every land and people on earth.

This particular work, however, is unique among all the accounts of Judah. When Abraham beheld the heavens and gazed across time to the ultimate exaltation of his seed, he saw with prophetic clarity. In this day mighty prophets have again been called by that same God who spoke to Abraham, Moses and Jeremiah. And, as all true prophets of the Lord have done from ancient times, these modern mouthpieces of Jehovah have consecrated much of their effort to the gathering and the restoration of the Jews. Indeed, no group of people, save the Jews themselves, has ever been so concerned with the modern Israel state as have been and are these latter-day prophets. This book seeks to capture the powerful vision of the Jews offered by the prophets of modern Joseph; to view Judah's history and future as did Abraham—through the sparkling window of inspiration.

Man Should Know Past, Present, and Future to Have Unrestricted Vision

Elder Anthony W. Ivins explained the need to understand God's workings with his chosen people in all dispensations of time when he said, "To properly comprehend the great plan of human redemption, designed by the Father for the blessing of his children, it is necessary that we be familiar with his hand-dealings with...his children.... It is not sufficient that we familiarize ourselves alone with the dispensation in which we live, important though that may be. We must know something of the past, as history has written it, the present as we see and understand it, and the future as the prophets have declared it. Without this grouping of the past, the present and the future, our vision will be restricted, and incomplete." (*CR,* p. 43, April, 1925.)

Mormons and Jews Have Much in Common

It is easy for members of The Church of Jesus Christ of Latter-day Saints to identify with the Jewish people. They, like the Mormons, have been subjected to misunderstanding, ridicule, slander, persecution, mobbings, and beatings. Like the Mormons, the Jews have been driven from their homes and various homelands. A prominent churchman has written, "If the Jewish people really understood, they would realize that no other people, organization, or church, has as much in common with them as do the Mormons."

We will speak of Judah and of Joseph, blood brothers, sons of mighty Israel. Judah was the elder and probably received priesthood power and lessons of truth from his father long before young Joseph. Judah was a mighty man, a proud man. Joseph, considerably younger, received these precious gifts after his brethren, and yet it was he, alone, who seemed to obey with exactness. For his obedience, Joseph was sold into Egypt by guilt-ridden brothers. A branch of Israel was sent "over the wall," and hidden in a "nethermost part of the vineyard." In time, through faith and obedience, Joseph brought forth that hidden, fruit-laden branch. It was Joseph, who came forth to save the rest of Israel's house when its "roots" literally became withered and its other branches were fruitless.

Today these dramatic scenes are played again before the preceptive observer. The stage has grown to worldwide proportions and the brothers have become nations of millions. Judah first received the word, then Joseph. Now Joseph turns, in the final great scenes, to save and nurture Judah. God has uncovered the branch "over the wall," and has blessed the hidden corner of the vineyard. He has called a modern Joseph, armed with the stick of Ephraim, to save a modern Judah.

Through Joseph Smith, the Prophet, Jehovah has now established his great storehouses of spiritual food, and the Latter-day Saints, the people of Joseph, cry unto Judah and all of scattered Israel: "Leave the parched and fruitless world. Come fill yourselves with the true Bread and the Living Water. Come up to the House of the Lord."

Indeed, the first shall be last and the last the first, so first Judah then Joseph; now Joseph then Judah.

Through these pages we will trace the dynamic relationship of two brothers, Judah and Joseph, and the peoples they sired. The compiler has taken as sources the revealed scriptures and the writings of the leaders and inspired writers of The Church of Jesus Christ of Latter-day Saints, the true gospel restored in these latter-days for the benefit of both Jew and Gentile. The compiler has sought to present these thoughts in such a way as to aid the reader in better understanding the vital, prophetic inter-relationship between Judah and Joseph. Only then can we begin to understand Judah—past, present, and future.

Section 1
Judah's Past

Israel and Judah in Old Testament Times

In The Meridian of Time

The Scattering and Scourging of Judah

Chapter 1

Israel and Judah in Old Testament Times

> And I will make of thee a great nation, and I will bless thee above measure, and make thy name great among all nations, and thou shalt be a blessing unto thy seed after thee, that in their hands they shall bear this ministry and Priesthood unto all nations;
>
> And I will bless them through thy name; for as many as receive this Gospel shall be called after thy name, and shall be accounted thy seed, and shall rise up and bless thee, as their father;
>
> And I will bless them that bless thee, and curse them that curse thee; and in thee (that is, in thy Priesthood) and in thy seed (that is thy Priesthood), for I give unto thee a promise that this right shall continue in thee, and in thy seed after thee (that is to say, the literal seed, or the seed of the body) shall all the families of the earth be blessed, even with the blessings of the Gospel, which are the blessings of salvation, even of life eternal. (Abraham 2:9-11.)

If we now, through our special window, are to watch the procession of Jewish history, this turbulent river of people and events, we must begin at its headwaters. Here we find a clear spring bubbling forth in the desert. It is Abraham, a man of righteousness amid evil, an enlightened mind among dark traditions. Through him Jehovah pours a new dispensation of truth upon the world with promises of blessings and power and glory to the sons of the great patriarch if they but remain worthy.

Through this chapter we will glimpse this fountain of truth and blessings, the man Abraham. We will feel somewhat of his trials and joy. We will watch Isaac and Israel, Joseph and his brethren, and their sons and grandsons as the procession swells from a handful of people to include millions. The setting shifts from Canaan to

Egypt and back again. Israel is divided, scattered. And while most of the sons of Abraham are lost to the four winds, Judah finally returns to his home, supported by the arm of a benevolent Gentile.

The Lord's Covenant With Abraham

To properly comprehend the occurrences of the past century one must be familiar with the covenant entered into by the Lord with Abraham and the history of the Israelitish people from that time until the present. The Lord declared that covenant to be eternal, everlasting, which means that it would not end until the promises made had been realized. In part the covenant declared that through Abraham and his seed all nations of the world should be blessed.

It is through the descendants of Abraham that the Holy Bible has come down to us, the book which has done more to civilize and stabilize the world than all others which have been published. It has given to us the fundamentals of our system of government and the laws under which its affairs are administered. From the family of Abraham the Lord has raised up his ancient and modern prophets, and most important of all, Jesus Christ, his Only Begotten Son, through whom redemption from death and salvation in the kingdom of our Father is made possible to mankind. What have we that is of indispensable value to humanity which has not come to us through the Israelitish race? (Anthony W. Ivins, *CR,* p. 15, April 1930.)

Purpose of Abraham's Call

Abraham was a dweller in Ur of the Chaldees, a city of Mesopotamia, which means, "between the rivers." The rivers in question were the Tigris and the Euphrates. God said to Abraham: Get thee out of thy country, and from thy kindred, and from thy father's house, unto a land that I will shew thee: and I will make of thee a great nation, and I will bless thee, and make thy name great; and thou shalt be a blessing; and I will bless them that bless thee, and curse him that curseth thee: and in thee shall all families of the earth be blessed." Genesis 12:1-3. The land referred to was Canaan, now Palestine. Abraham, in order to reach that land, had to pass over the river, Euphrates. Hence he was called by the Canaanites a "Hebrew," which signifies, "one from beyond the river."

What was the purpose of Abraham's call? Why was he taken out of his own country and from his father's house and promised that he should become a great nation? It was because Mesopotamia was steeped in the sin of idolatry, and the time had arrived for the founding of the lineage through which the Lord Jesus Christ, the Savior, would come into the world. Abraham was required to separate himself from his idolatrous surroundings, that he might establish such a lineage. The strict laws given to Israel, Abraham's descendants, had as their object the preservation in purity of the lineage of our Lord, the "Lamb without spot or blemish." (Orson F. Whitney, *MS* 86:611-612, March 9, 1924.)

The Promise to Abraham

It was about 122 years after the deluge that the Lord called Abram, who at that time was seventy-five years of age, and a direct descendant of Shem, the chosen son of Noah, commanding him to go out from the country of his kindred, and from his father's house, into a land which he promised to give him, and to his posterity after him, for an everlasting inheritance. In obedience to the word of the Lord, Abram went from Haran, to which place he had been taken by his father, from Ur of Chaldea, and pitched his tent in the land of Canaan. Twenty-four years later the Lord spoke to him as follows:

> And when Abram was ninety years old and nine, the Lord appeared to Abram, and said unto him: I am the Almighty God; walk before me, and be thou perfect.
>
> And I will make my covenant between me and thee, and will multiply thee exceedingly.
>
> And Abram fell on his face: and God talked with him, saying,
>
> As for me, behold my covenant is with thee, and thou shalt be a father of many nations.
>
> Neither shall thy name be called any more Abram, but thy name shall be Abraham; for a father of many nations I have made thee.
>
> And I will make thee exceeding fruitful, and I will make nations of thee, and kings shall come out of thee. (Genesis 17:1-6.)

We have here a promise made by the Lord, which, judged by human standards, was impossible of fulfillment. Abraham was an hundred years old, and his wife, Sarah, ninety years of age, a supposedly barren woman, but the Lord had spoken, and his word never fails. Isaac was born, and the Lord repeated to him the promise made to his father. (Anthony W. Ivins, *CR,* p. 43, April 1925.)

The Sacrifice of Isaac

Before Jehovah gave to Abraham the fulness of his blessing, He put him to a test that few men would have been able to bear. He had given him in his old age and in the old age of his wife, Sarah, a son, even Isaac, through whom the promise was to be realized that he should become a great nation. But when Isaac was grown to manhood, the Lord said to Abraham: "Take now thy son, thine only son Isaac"—the only son of promise—"and offer him for a burnt offering upon one of the mountains which I will tell thee of." Now, if ever a man had the right to hesitate, to argue and contend with the Almighty, that man was Abraham. God had set the seal of condemnation upon the first murderer, Cain, and in the days of Noah had instituted the law. "Who so sheddeth man's blood, by man shall his blood be shed." Yet after giving a son of promise to Abraham, He required him to slay that son, to shed his blood, and offer him up as a burnt offering. It was a thunderbolt from a clear sky.

Abraham was about to offer his son, no doubt his heart was bleeding but he was humble and obedient, and was about to carry out the divine behest, when that same Being who had told him to slay his son sent His angel to say: "Lay not thine hand upon the lad." Did that make God a changeable Being? No. He has the right to command and to countermand, and no man has the right to call Him in question. He approved of Abraham's course, and said: "because thou hast done this thing, and hast not withheld thy son, thine only son:...in blessing I will bless thee, and in multiplying I will multiply thy seed as the stars of the heaven, and as the sand which is upon the sea shore:...and in thy seed shall all the nations of the earth be blessed." (Orson F. Whitney, *MS* 86:612, March 9, 1924.)

Jacob Married His Cousins—Leah, Rachel, Bilhah and Zilpah

Great censure has been placed on Jacob, (which name means Supplanter) for his apparent duplicity in obtaining the blessing which he did from his father, the patriarch Isaac; but it was of the Lord, and Jacob obeyed his mother Rebekah, who was determined that Jacob should have a wife of the pure Shemite stock, as she knew the consequences of disregarding such a course. She was weary of the ways of the wives of Esau, and their Canaanitish customs (Gen., 27:46). So also was Isaac. He therefore sent Jacob to Haran to her brother Laban, where Jacob remained 14 years. During that time he married Leah and Rachel, the two daughters of Laban, his cousins. Thus we see how this same stock intermarried for three generations.

Jacob also married the two maids of Leah and Rachel, who were named Bilhah and Zilpah, and sons were born by them. Some may think that Jacob polluted his race by marrying these two maids of his wives, and that they were of an inferior race. A little light is thrown on these two women in the following extract, taken from the "Testaments of the Twelve Patriarchs" written between the years 107-137 B.C. by a Pharisee savant. Here in the "Testament of Naphtali" the latter speaks of his mother Bilhah, Rachel's maid:

> Now my mother was Bilhah, daughter of Rotheus the brother of Deborah, Rebekah's nurse (Gen. 35:8), who was born in one and the self same day with Rachel. And Rotheus was of the family of Abraham, a Chaldean, godfearing, freeborn, and noble. And he was taken captive and bought by Laban; and he gave him Euna, his handmaid to wife, and she bare a daughter and called her name Zilpah, after the name of the village in which he had been taken captive. And next she bore Bilhah.

A very interesting episode this, showing the purity of the race of these two handmaids, who were of the race as Abraham and Shem. Thus the twelve sons of Jacob, now called Israel or a Prince of God (see Genesis 32:24-32) were chosen seed of Abraham, and the purity of the race was preserved. (Hatton Carpenter, *UGHM* 21:164-166, October 1930.)

Egypt Was Not the Heritage of Israel

Isaac, in turn, became the father of Jacob, through whose lineage, and the twelve sons who were born to him, the foundation was laid for the twelve tribes of Israel, the progenitors of a mighty nation.

...twelve sons were born to Jacob, six of whom Reuben, Simeon, Levi, Judah, Issachar and Zebulon, were the sons of Leah, his first wife. Joseph and Benjamin the sons of Rachel; Dan and Naphtali the sons of Bilhah, the handmaid of Rachel; and Gad and Asher, the sons of Zilpah, the handmaid of Leah.

...Joseph, was sold by his brethren to passing Ishmaelites who carried the boy into Egypt, and sold him to Potiphar, a captain of the king's guard. He was cast into prison, and finally released and made the vice-regent of the king, the most powerful personage, except the Pharaoh, in all Egypt. Famine came to the land, which made it necessary for Jacob to send his sons to Egypt to procure food, where these men discovered that the governor of all the land was their younger brother, whom they had sold into slavery, and after returning to Canaan brought down their father and all of their possessions into Egypt, and were established in the land of Goshen, where they became a numerous people.

But Egypt was not the heritage of Israel. Naturally they would have remained there and been absorbed by the Egyptians, but the Lord had decreed otherwise. He had given them Palestine as the land of their inheritance, and their return to that land was inevitable, even though it were against their will. (Anthony W. Ivins, *CR,* p. 44, April 1925.)

The Sojourn in Egypt: Israel Multiplies Exceedingly

According to one chronological record, Jacob and his whole household numbering 70 souls, went from Palestine to Egypt in 1706 B.C. In 1491 B.C. the children of Israel returned under Moses, or 215 years after Jacob entered that country. Hebrew records give the period between the entrance and the exodus as 400 years. Whether the greater or lesser period of time is the correct one has very little bearing upon the statement that at the time of the exodus they were a numerous people and were in a position to muster 603,550 men who were twenty years of age and upwards, capable of bearing arms. (Numbers 1:45-6.) Accepting the general method employed in history in census taking of counting four persons for each one capable of bearing arms, we have more than two million people who entered Palestine. And here they were to fulfill the promise given to Abraham by the Lord that they should become as numerous as the stars of the heaven and the sand upon the seashore. (Joseph Littke, *UGHM* 25:2, January 1934.)

Israel Tainted with Egyptian Philosophy

Israel, when Moses found her, had been ground under the heel of Egyptian aggression for more than four hundred years, during which she lost faith in God, and became tainted with Egyptian philosophy. Moses struggled hard in his endeavor to instill faith in God, but was unsuccessful, the result of which was that heaven's decree against them was voiced by Moses in the following words:

> And the Lord shall scatter you among the nations, and ye shall be left few in number among the heathen, whither the Lord shall lead you. (Deuteronomy 4:27) (Octave F. Ursenbach, *Liahona,* 19:427, April 25, 1922)

The Conquest of Palestine

The history of the Israelitish people, from the time they crossed the river Jordan, under Joshua, and subdued Jericho, until the establishment of the kingdom, under Saul, about four hundred years later, is one of almost constant war and contention, which resulted in the subjugation of neighboring kingdoms and peoples, until Israel, under David, became the possessor of Palestine from Dan on the north to Beersheba on the south.

It was under Solomon that Israel reached the zenith of power and glory as a nation and kingdom. One hundred and twenty years had elapsed from the establishment of the kingdom, under Saul, until the division of the nation, which occurred during the reign of Rehoboam, the son of Solomon. Five hundred years in all, since the return from Egypt. Years of conflict among themselves and with other peoples, years of faithlessness on the part of Israel, and suffering because of their transgression and indifference to the words of the prophets whom the Lord sent among them to call them back into the old way of righteousness, but they said, we will not walk therein. When the watchmen whom the Lord placed on the towers of Zion sounded the warning trumpet they said, we will not hearken. (Anthony W. Ivins, *CR,* p. 45, April, 1925)

Glory of Solomon's Reign

As long as they hearkened to His word, God did prosper them; He did bless their land; He did send them the early and the latter rains; He did multiply them and strengthen them in the land; He did set them on high; He did make them His covenant people, and they became famous throughout the known world. The glory of Solomon reached to the uttermost parts of the earth. The kings and queens of the earth heard of his greatness and of his wisdom. They took pilgrimages to Jerusalem to see for themselves and to verify the reports they had heard of the greatness of the children of Israel. The Queen of Sheba went and saw Solomon in his glory. She heard of the wisdom that fell from his lips and beheld the greatness of his kingdom, and she said to the king: "It was a true report that I heard in mine own land of thy acts and of thy wisdom. Howbeit I believed not the words, until I came, and mine eyes had seen it; and behold, the half was not told me; thy wisdom and prosperity exceedeth the fame which I heard. Happy are thy men, happy are these thy servants, which stand continually before thee, and that hear thy wisdom." (Joseph F. Smith. *CR,* p. 45, October, 1899)

The Separation Into Two Kingdoms: Israel and Judah

They lived as a united nation under one government for about 475 years. Then they began to dissent among themselves. Their union was brought to a breaking point at the death of King Solomon, when Solomon's son Rehoboam was made king of Israel at Sechem; while Jeroboam, son of Nebat, an Ephraimite, who had earlier been forced to flee to Egypt because Solomon sought his life, now returned to assume leadership of the Ten Tribes. He, and all the congregation, came to Rehoboam and asked him to make the grievous yoke of his father lighter, saying, if he did this, they then would be willing to serve him; but Rehoboam's answer was: "And now whereas my father did lade you with a heavy yoke, I will add to your yoke: my father hath chastised you with whips, but I will chastise you with scorpions." (Kings 12:1-4, 11.) Then the people answered: "What portion have we in David? neither have we inheritance in the son of Jesse: to your tents, O Israel: now see to thine own house, David. So Israel departed unto their tents." (I Kings 12:16) (Joseph C. Littke, *UGHM* 25:3-4, January 1934)

Israel's Influence Extended Into Spain

It is evident from biblical and chronological records that Israel had extended its boundaries far beyond the promised land during the reign of King Solomon. Their bounds reached even as far as Spain, as is evident from the fact that King Solomon sent his chief tax collector to Spain to collect taxes for the king, but he was killed. A tombstone found in Zaragoze, Spain bore the following inscription: "This is the tomb of Adoriram, the servant of King Solomon, who came to collect tribute and died here." The following passages in the Bible substantiate this: I Kings 4:6; 12:18.

But as already mentioned the house of Israel after the death of King Solomon and at the time of the succession of his son Rehoboam, was divided into two kingdoms. In one the chief tribe was Judah, and in the other, Ephraim.

According to Israelitish custom the two kingdoms thenceforth were known as Judah and Ephraim, assuming the name of the ruling dynasty as that of their national identity. This is borne out by numerous Biblical passages such as Isaiah 7:2: "Syria is confederate with Ephraim": and all the people shall know, even Ephraim, and the inhabitants of Samaria. The envy of Ephraim also shall depart, and the adversaries shall be cut off; Ephraim shall not envy Judah and Judah shall not vex Ephraim. (Joseph C. Littke, *UGHM* 25:3-4, January, 1934.)

The Dissolution of Israel

The dissolution of Israel, as a great nation, commenced when the ten tribes, under the leadership of Jeroboam, the son of Nebat, broke away from Judah and Benjamin and established the kingdom of Israel, with Samaria as its capital city, while Judah and Benjamin, with a part at least of the tribes of Simeon and Dan retained Jerusalem as the capital city of their kingdom.

Both nations rapidly relapsed into idolatry, Israel to the worship of the golden calf of the Egyptians, while Judah, to a great extent, turned to the worship of Bel of the Babylonians, and the idolatrous gods of the nations with which they were surrounded.

In this condition Israel continued until about seven hundred years before Christ, when the Assyrian armies, under Sennacherib overcame the Israelitish armies, captured Samaria, carried the Ten Tribes captive into Assyria, at the head of the Euphrates, and brought people from their own country whom they established in the cities of northern Palestine, and the identity of Israel as a distinct people, was lost to the world.

Judah continued to maintain a semblance of power for more than one hundred years after the fall of Israel, when they suffered the same fate. Judea was overrun by the Babylonian armies under Nebuchadnessar, Jerusalem taken, the temple desecrated, and despoiled of its wealth, and Judah carried captive into Babylon, as their brethren has been carried into Assyria. (Anthony W. Ivins, *CR*, p. 45-46, April, 1925)

First Scattering of Israel Foreseen

A prophetic picture of the afflictions which the Lord would heap upon Israel is drawn by Moses in the twenty-sixth chapter of Leviticus. If persistently disobedient, they were to be scattered among all nations and suffer great afflictions in the lands of their enemies.

The Ten Tribes Carried into Captivity

The prophet Abijah said to the wife of Jeroboam, "The Lord shall smite Israel, as a reed is shaken in the water, and he shall root up Israel out of this good land, which he gave to their fathers, and shall scatter them beyond the river." (I Kings 14:15.) This prophecy was fulfilled when the ten tribes were carried into captivity by the king of Assyria 721 B.C. (2 Kings 17.) In the Apocrypha, the prophet Esdras states that these ten tribes went a year and a half journey into the north country. (2 Esdras 13:39-45.) That many remained is evident from verses 48 and 49 of the same chapter.

Josephus Wrote About Scattered Israel

The great historian of Israel, Josephus, who wrote nearly 800 years after the captivity of the ten tribes, corroborates this view of the subject. Speaking of the return of the Jews under Esdras, he says: "Many of them took their effects with them, and came to Babylon as very desirous of going down to Jerusalem, but then the entire body of the people of Israel remained in that country, wherefore there are but two tribes in Asia and Europe subject to the Romans, while the ten tribes are beyond the Euphrates till now, and are an immense multitude, and not to be estimated by numbers." (Antiquities, Book 11:C, 5.) For over twenty-six centuries these scattered tribes of Israel, which Josephus 1800 years ago, declared were an immense multitude in Asia, have continued to intermingle with the nations of the earth.

The Second Scattering of Israel

The second great scattering of Israel was brought about by the Babylonish captivity. The Lord said through the prophet Jeremiah, "I will give all Judah into the hand of the king of Babylon." (20:4.) There is an account of the fulfillment of this prophecy in 2 Kings, chapters 24 and 25. Jerusalem was desolated and only the poor left to till the land.

The Jews, like the ten tribes before them, were scattered among the nations of Asia. In Ezra, Chap. 2, we have an account of those who returned to build the waste places of Judah, but multitudes of them remained in their scattered condition, as is evident from the book of Esther. Some nine years after the completion of the term of their captivity they were scattered from India to Ethiopia, through the 127 provinces of the Persian empire. (8:9)

Jeremiah prophesied the entire desolation of Judah: "Judah shall be carried away captive all of it, it shall be wholly carried away captive." (13:19). It was nearly 600 years from the consummation of the Babylonish captivity to the fulfillment of this prophecy, by the final destruction of the Jews, as a nation, by the Romans when a remnant of some 97,000 were sold into slavery in the cities of the Roman empire, and were scattered wherever the caprice of their masters led them.

Two Colonies Left Jerusalem for the Western Hemisphere

...B.C. 600 a colony left Jerusalem, under Lehi, to people the western hemisphere. Eleven years after, it was followed by another under the direction of Mulek. Their descendants have scattered over the American continent from Cape Horn to the Arctic Sea.

This branch of the house of Israel may truly be said to be scattered over half the globe. The Book of Mormon, and the monumental ruins they have left on the land, give us all the information we have of them down to the year 1492, A.D., when Christopher Columbus discovered America.

Since that time, their history forms a part of the general history of the continent, which is a record of the fulfillment of many of the prophecies in the Bible and the Book of Mormon, concerning the scattering of Israel. (Franklin D. Richards and James A. Little, *Principles of the Gospel,* published by The Church of Jesus Christ of Latter-day Saints, 1943, pp. 84-86, 88.)

The Fate of the House of Israel Foretold

The fate which befell the House of Israel had been plainly outlined by the prophets whom the Lord had sent to warn them that the penalty of disobedience would be the dissolution of the nation, and that they would be taken from the land of their inheritance, and scattered among the strange and unbelieving nations of the world. A final fulfillment of this prophecy occurred when, about one hundred years after the birth of the Redeemer, Judea was trodden down by the Roman armies under Vespasian and his son Titus, Jerusalem taken, the temple destroyed, and the Jews scattered among the nations of the world, where they have remained until the present day. (Anthony W. Ivins, *CR,* p. 46, April 1925.)

"Dispersion of Israel Foretold—Biblical Predictions"

The following summaries of Bible and Book of Mormon passages concerning the dispersion of Israel was prepared by Elder James E. Talmage and presented in his book, *The Articles of Faith:*

Prediction that the descendants of Joseph should be as branches that run over the wall—Gen. 49:22.

And I will scatter you among the heathen—this conditioned on the wickedness of the people—Lev. 26:33; see also Deut. 4:27.

Israel to flee before their enemies, and to be removed into all the kingdoms of the earth—Deut. 28:25. The people to become an astonishment, a proverb, and a byword, among all nations, whither the Lord would lead them—verse 37. And the Lord shall scatter thee among all people, from the one end of the earth even unto the other—verse 64.

Because of their wickedness the Lord would smite Israel, and root them up out of the good land, and scatter them beyond the river—I Kings 14:15.

The Lord removed Israel out of his sight, as he had said by all his servants the prophets. So was Israel carried away out of their own land to Assyria—2 Kings 17:23.

To the kingdom of Judah the Lord spake: And I will cast you out of my sight, as I have cast out all your brethren, even the whole seed of Ephraim—Jer. 7:15. Judah shall be carried away captive all of it, it shall be wholly carried away captive—13:19; see also 15:1-4. Judah to be delivered, to be removed to all the kingdoms of the earth, to be a curse, and an astonishment, and a hissing, and a reproach, among all the nations whither the Lord would drive them—29:16-19.

And I will scatter thee among the heathen, and disperse thee in the countries—Ezek. 22:15.

I will sift the house of Israel, among all nations, like as corn is sifted in a sieve, yet shall not the least grain fall upon the earth—Amos 9:9.

And I will sow them among the people: and they shall remember me in far countries—Zech. 10:9.

Woes to fall upon the people in the day of visitation, and in the desolation which would come from far—Jer. 5:15.

Israel shall surely go into captivity—Amos 7:17.

The people who remained until the time of Christ were to be further scattered: Shall be led away captive into all nations: and Jerusalem shall be trodden down of the Gentiles, until the times of the Gentiles be fulfilled—Luke 21:24.

Book of Mormon Prophecies of the Dispersion

Lehi predicted the Babylonian captivity, and that the people should be scattered on all the face of the earth, and recognized the bringing of himself and his colony to the western continent as part of the decreed scattering—1 Nephi 10:3, 12-14.

Scattering of the descendants of Lehi shown in vision to Nephi—1 Nephi 13:14, 15.

Scattering of the Jews following the crucifixion of Christ foretold by Jacob—2 Nephi 10:5, 6; compare verse 22.

The Voice from heaven proclaimed further scattering unless the people would repent—3 Nephi 10:7.

The Gentiles to contribute to the scattering of the house of Israel—3 Nephi 20:27; see also Mormon 5:9, 20.

The Dispersion Successively Accomplished

The kingdom of Israel removed, and none but those of Judah left; all the seed of Israel delivered into the hand of spoilers—2 Kings 17:20.

And the king of Assyria did carry away Israel into Assyria—2 Kings 18:9-11.

The Lord gave Jacob for a spoil, and Israel to the robbers, because of the sins of the people—Isa. 42:24.

Zion a wilderness and Jerusalem a desolation—Isa. 64:10, 11.

I lifted up mine hand unto them also in the wilderness, that I would scatter them among the heathen, and disperse them through the countries—Ezek. 20:23, 24; see also 36:19; compare 34:5, 6.

And them that had escaped from the sword carried he away to Babylon—2 Chron. 36:17-20.

But I scattered them with a whirlwind among all the nations whom they knew not—Zech. 7:13, 14; compare Joel 3:2; James 1:1.

Nephi proclaimed part of the dispersion already accomplished and predicted further scattering—1 Nephi 22:3-5, 7, 8.

The Lord revealed to Jacob that the Jews had been carried away captive—2 Nephi 6:8.

Consider the allegory of the olive-tree, and the pruning of the vineyard—Jacob, chapters 5, 6. (James E. Talmage, *Articles of Faith,* The Church of Jesus Christ of Latter-day Saints, 1949, pp. 326-327.)

The Capture of Babylon and the Magnaminity of Cyrus

Jerusalem was redeemed after being in bondage seventy years. The Lord had told the prophet Jeremiah that Jerusalem would be destroyed and its people would be in bondage seventy years.

One hundred years before the birth of Cyrus, the general who captured Babylon, the Lord revealed to the Prophet Isaiah that Cyrus should be his servant and say unto Jerusalem that the city should be rebuilt. Babylon at that time was the greatest city in all the world, and was thought to be impregnable. Cyrus was not a Jew. Cyrus did not understand the Old Testament, nor did he know of the part he was to play in the freeing of the captive Jews and rebuilding Jerusalem.

Cyrus Freed the Jews in Babylonia

While Cyrus was besieging the city of Babylon the great king, Belshazzar of Babylon and his associates were using the sacred vessels that had been taken from the house of the Lord in Jerusalem to drink from. It was a great debauch, and suddenly in the midst of it was seen a hand writing on the wall these words, "Me-ne, Me'ne, Tekel, U-phar-sin," and they could not read it.

The Queen said to the King, "There is a Hebrew prophet among us. He can tell you what it means."

And so they went out and brought Daniel in and when Daniel saw the handwriting on the wall he could read it. It was not difficult for him. He was the servant of the Lord. He had the priesthood and he had honored it in a most marvelous way all down through his life.

The king and others felt perfectly secure, feeling that with food and provisions, and a river of water running through the city, not anything could come in to disturb them, and yet on that wall were written the words, which, when interpreted, read, "You have been weighed in the balance and found wanting, and your kingdom will be divided among the Medes and the Persians." At that very hour "my servant Cyrus" had diverted the river that went through the city from its channel and his army entered under the wall, which wall was so high that it could not be scaled or destroyed with any means or weapons that they had, and so wide that several chariots could ride abreast on the top.

When that gentile, if we may use that term, that alien to those that had had the priesthood and the blessings of the Lord, the descendants of Abraham, Isaac and Jacob, realized that the Lord had given him Babylon, he issued a proclamation freeing the Jewish captives and returning them to rebuild their city of Jerusalem. He not only took his own army and his own people but he gave them means to use in payment to the workers. (George Albert Smith, *CR,* p. 182-183, October, 1948.)

Return of the Jews and Rebuilding of Jerusalem

After the fall of the Babylonian kingdom to the armies of Media and Persia, King Cyrus permitted the Jews to return from Babylon to Palestine and rebuild their city and temple which had been destroyed by Nebuchadnezzar. With great enthusiasm this work was undertaken, and it appears that the Jews who returned from the Babylonian captivity showed greater faith in the God of their fathers than had been manifested before they were carried away. (Anthony W. Ivins, *CR,* p. 46, April, 1925.)

A Time Without Prophets—The Apocrypha

Approximately four hundred years separates the writings of the last of the Old Testament prophets and the New Testament as recorded in the King James Version of the Bible. The obvious question that comes to mind is why such a gap should exist. One answer, proposed by Dr. Robert J. Matthews in *The Ensign* (October 1973, p. 77) is that there were "no inspired prophets among the Jewish people in Palestine."

To be sure, there do exist certain writings that claim their origin in this time. Known collectively as the *Apocrypha,* they consist of a wide variety of genre, from doctrinal essays to poetry to history. As the Bible was formed from the vast amount of "sacred" writings, each group responsible for forming the accepted works, the "canon," was faced with what to do with the Apocrypha. They were variously included and excluded, even with one version such as the King James, included until 1830 and then discontinued.

As he was working on the revision of the Bible, Joseph Smith, the Prophet, came upon the Apocrypha still contained in the King

James Version he was using. In response to his inquiries of the Lord on the matter he received the following instructions:

> Verily, thus saith the Lord unto you concerning the Apocrypha—There are many things contained therein that are true, and it is mostly translated correctly;
>
> There are many things contained therein that are not true, which are interpolations by the hands of men.
>
> Verily, I say unto you, that it is not needful that the Apocrypha should be translated.
>
> Therefore, whoso readeth it, let him understand, for the Spirit manifesteth truth;
>
> And whoso is enlightened by the Spirit shall obtain benefit therefrom;
>
> And whoso receiveth not by the Spirit, cannot be benefited. Therefore it is not needful that it should be translated. Amen. (D&C 91:1-6.)

Four Hundred Years—Malachi to Matthew

With the preceding admonition in mind, let us try and paint a picture of those four hundred years from Malachi to Matthew, using both secular sources and the two historical books of the Apocrypha, 1 and 2 Maccabees. The following discussion is a summary of material presented in two very highly regarded sources: *Encyclopaedia Judaica,* Jerusalem: The Macmillan Co., 1971, Vol. 7, pp. 1455-1458. Hastings, James. *A Dictionary of the Bible,* New York: Charles Scribners Sons, 1900, Vol. 3, pp. 181-187.

The Persians, who allowed the Jews to return to Jerusalem in the 5th century B.C. ruled the area of Palestine until conquest of the majority of the ten-known world in the last decades of the 4th century by Alexander the Great. After forging a mighty empire, Alexander died in 323 B.C. leaving no heir. His domain in the east was taken over by one of his generals and became known as the Seleucid Kingdom. Although life was not free of problems, the Jews lived fairly well until 175 B.C. when Antiochus IV came to the throne in Syria. He forbade the practice of the Jewish religion under pain of death and sought to force the people into the Greek paganisms.

Rising in revolt about 170 B.C. was a priestly family known alternately as the Hasmoneans and the Maccabees. Beginning with the patriarch of the family, Mattathias ben Johanan, the Maccabees served as a rallying point for all the Jews who sought relief from the Greek servitude.

Under Mattathias' son Judah Maccabee, the Syrian forces were gradually repelled. As this family gained prominence in military affairs they also were given prominent positions in both the Jewish religious and secular hierarchy. Simeon was made a hereditary high priest in 140 B.C. while his descendent Aristobulus I in 104 B.C. named himself king.

During the reign of Yannai (103-76 B.C.) the Hasmonean kingdom ran from the borders of Egypt to the Syrian frontier and from the Mediterranean Sea well into the Transjordan. Jewish freedom and culture had been successfully preserved.

The Hasmonean kingdom was unable, however, in 63 B.C. to resist the annexation of the whole area by the Roman general Pompey. Rome was just too big and powerful to make resistance a viable alternative. The Maccabees were allowed to rule for a while and the blood line lasted down through to the Christian era through the marriage of the Maccabeean Mariamne to Herod, grandfather of Herod Agrippa I.

Chapter 2

In the Meridian of Time

"Wherefore, as I said unto you, it must needs be expedient that Christ—for in the last night the angel spake unto me that this should be his name—should come among the Jews, among those who are the more wicked part of the world; and they shall crucify him—for thus it behooveth our God, and there is none other nation on earth that would crucify their God." (2 Nephi 10:3.)

As we watch the Abrahamic dispensation slowly closes, the procession seems to falter, to change course, to flow without direction. No more prophets cry in Jerusalem's streets. The Jewish shepherds seem content to wrap themselves in traditions and rules, attempting to thus warm hearts turned cold toward Israel's true God. They seek a Messiah, not to free them from ignorance and sin but from gentile oppression, from Roman chains which seem so much heavier than ignorance. Indeed, it is time for the Messiah. A man some say is a prophet is preaching in the desert that the time is near. But when he comes, the nation is too caked with tradition, too clogged with laws to feel or hear. The dazzling light blinds rather than enlightens them, for they will not see. And as they scream "Crucify him, crucify him," the new gospel dispensation is opened, but not to the Jews. They will have to wait, now, for another chance.

The Jews Anxiously Awaited the Messiah

The first thing he [Christ] calls their attention to, among the things that had been transpiring, was, that a great many deceivers should come and profess to be Christ, saying, "I am Christ, but do not go after them, take care and not be deceived by them."

The reason for this was that the Jews were looking for a Messiah, and for a deliverance from the Roman yoke, and for their national independence to be restored to them; and for their city, and temple, and nation, to be the seat of government for all nations, a universal theocracy.

Jews Rejected the True Messiah

They were looking for this, and they had rejected the true Messiah, and were about to kill him, and were looking for another to fulfill what all men were in the expectation of; for the old Prophets had told them that such a day would come, in relation to that nation, and their city Jerusalem, and the temple; that the throne of God would be there; that the tabernacle of God would be there; that there would be one king and one Lord, and his name one; that all the nations of the earth would come up to worship—the nations they were acquainted with in that country.

They had reason to look for that day, because the old Prophets had foretold it, and John the Baptist came along as a special Prophet, and nearly all that people had received him as a Prophet, professedly, though in reality, some of them received him, and he told them some of those things were about to be fulfilled.

He had told them about their king, about the Lamb of God, about the Messiah, and that they must repent and be baptized for the remission of their sins, and make his paths strait.

With this double assurance, first the testimony of their old Prophets, and secondly the renewed testimony of a new Prophet, to immediately prepare for the fulfillment of some of the old prophecies; with this double assurance they were looking for somebody to do something, and that pretty largely too; and as they had rejected the true king—the true Messiah, of course they would be looking for somebody, that ambitious spirits would enter, and they would rise up and tell the people, "I am he you look for; set me up, and I will deliver you from the Roman yoke, I will break your fetters, and bring about the restoration of your national independence." (Parley P. Pratt *JD* 3:129-130, October 7, 1855)

Misunderstanding Regarding the Messiah's Mission

There has been a time spoken of by all the holy prophets since the world was, when God should govern his people, and the Jews, when the Messiah came, expected that he was come to reign over

Israel as a temporal king, that he was going to take possession of his kingdom to overthrow all other kingdoms, empires, dynasties and powers, and declare himself the king of Israel and of the world. But they did not understand many things associated therewith, and they do not now; and the world does not, and we ourselves understand very little about them. But the Scriptures say that "till heaven and earth pass, one jot or one tittle shall in no wise pass from the law till all be fulfilled." (John Taylor, *JD* 21:64, January 4, 1880)

The Jews Observe the Letter of the Law of Moses, But Not the Spirit

They [the Jews] were a people who spoke highly of religion, who built synagogues and places of worship, who honored the Sabbath day, who wore long phylacteries, on which were written select passages from Scripture, who had the word of God written on their very doorposts, who prayed at the corners of the streets, who fasted, and apparently, sought in every way to glorify God. They believed in Abraham and Moses, and in the covenants which God made with them. They believed and practiced the law which Moses had revealed unto them, and so strict were they in observing many of its principles, that they were ready on one occasion to have a woman slain for the violation of the commandment respecting adultery; and at another time their wrath was kindled against the disciples because they plucked some ears of corn on the Sabbath day to appease their hunger. They considered that act a violation of the Sabbath, and their righteous souls were shocked thereat. They were shocked even at the idea of Jesus eating with unwashed hands, and at him, who professed to be a teacher, associating with publicans and sinners. They thought it was beneath the dignity of a man of God to condescend to associate with the low and degraded. This was the kind of people that existed when Paul wrote...[about them],... yet with all their professions and with all their apparent sanctity they were utterly destitute of the knowledge and power of God. They drew near to God with their lips, but their hearts were far from him. They made a great parade of their religion, but they dwelt on the glories of the past, on the evidences of God's favor which their nation and religion had formerly received. But did they themselves possess the spirit of prophecy, and the faith which Paul describes? If they had they would have recognized Jesus when he came amongst them, and they would have gladly received him and his teachings, and would have obeyed and practiced in their lives the principles of his Gospel. But as I have said, they were utterly destitute of the spirit of God, they were darkened in their minds, and instead of receiving Jesus and his teachings, they hounded him until they got him into their power and then they slew him, and they treated his apostles in the same manner. (George Q. Cannon, *JD* 15:368, March 23, 1873.)

Christ Spoke with Authority

Among the Jews, the Scribes and Pharisees would teach the people in this way—"Now, if this is to be, then the inference is so-and-so; and if this proposition be true, then the conclusion is certain." But when Jesus spoke to the people and taught them, he made no vain propositions and drew no milk-and-water conclusions: but he spoke and it was done; and the contrast was so great between the teaching of the Jewish Rabbies (sic) and the teachings of the Saviour, that they could not but notice it. "Why," said they, "he speaks as one having authority, and not as the Scribes." He, having this Priesthood, and having communion with God, our heavenly Father, manifested the wisdom of the heavens; and this difference is manifested and felt in this generation when the servants of God proclaim to the inhabitants of the earth that God has spoken, and that he again reveals his will to man. (Orson Hyde, *JD* 8:23, March 23, 1860.)

Jews to be Remembered Despite Iniquity

Now, the Jews boasted that they were the literal descendants of Abraham; and, notwithstanding their unrighteousness, stubbornness of heart, blindness of mind, and unbelief, they considered themselves heirs to all the promises made unto Abraham, and a distinguished and honored people. Jesus came to them, and taught and instructed them, and would have saved them, but they would not allow him to be their Savior; hence he said, "O Jerusalem, Jerusalem, thou that killest the prophets, and stonest them which are sent unto thee, how often would I have gathered thy children together, even as a hen gathereth her chickens under her wings, and ye would not." The Savior began to reason with them on one occasion; they answered and said unto him, Abraham is our father. Jesus saith unto them, "If ye were Abraham's children, ye would do the works of Abraham. Ye are of your father the devil, and the lusts of your father ye will do; he was a murderer from the beginning, and abode not in the truth, because there is no truth in him," etc. [Nevertheless] they are the people to whom the promises were made, of whom it is said they should be remembered for ever, and that too with loving kindness and favor. It was understood that they would be chastened if they went astray, but the Lord would always remember them on account of their fathers. (Orson Hyde, *JD* 11:152, October 7, 1865.)

Why the Jewish Rabbis and Teachers Persecuted Christ and His Followers

Why was it that the Jewish Rabbis and teachers of the law, those men who looked so contemptuously upon the poor despised Nazarene and his equally contemptible followers, the fishermen, whom he had gathered together as his disciples from the sea coast of Galilee; men who had studied the prophecies, men who claimed to have Abraham for their father, men who claimed to be well-disposed towards every agency which tended to bring to pass the fulfillment of prophecy and execute the terms thereof—why was it that they of all men should be the men from whom the Savior and his disciples met the severest opposition? Has it ever occurred to us that this is a strange inconsistency? If this position had been developed among a people and had been exerted by a class of men and women who were unbelievers in revelation, who were professedly infidel to the doctrines of prophets, to the teachings of patriarchs, to the spirit and revelations of Evangelists and of Apostles, we would not be surprised; but to find that the most powerful agencies that had been brought to bear for the suppression of Christianity, for the overthrow of its doctrines, for the retardation of its success throughout the land, were fostered by men who, from their professed adherence to the scriptures of divine truth, to the writings of Moses and the Prophets which they claimed to be in possession of, should have been its warmest friends; it should have received from them the most effective support; but on the contrary, it received from them the most heartless and unprincipled opposition. And it appears that there was but one solution to the problem, and that solution in their minds was this: This man is a promoter of sedition, we must have him taken out of the way, and so clamorous became the demand for the surrender of the great teacher and founder of Christianity, Jesus of Nazareth, that the populace cried, "away with him, away with him, crucify him, crucify him."

The Trial of Jesus of Nazareth

...And why did they want to get rid of him? Why did they wish to dispose of him in this way? What had he done to them? What doctrines had he taught that were in opposition even to the law or to good morality? None whatever. He was acquitted before the highest tribunal of his land, and one of our ablest jurists, Alexander Innis, in reviewing the trial of Jesus of Nazareth, concluded that in the light of the nineteenth century, in the advanced state of the science of jurisprudence, the crucifixion of Jesus Christ was a judicial murder. He went about continually doing good. He berated men for their sins, to be sure. He chastised them for their iniquity. He did call them hypocrites, he did call them some uncomplimentary names, but they richly deserved it, and any man who is acquainted with the history of the times, with the morality of that age, with the depths of degradation to which men and women had sunken, and the almost extinction of the first conception of morality, knows full well that his accusations were only too just, that there was no other cause for their ire being raised against him other than it was true, and they could not endure it. (George A. Bywater, *JD* 23:253-254, August 27, 1882.)

The Jews were in possession of many laws and regulations given to their fathers, and they were taught the true and the living God, but darkness covered their minds, and many of them walked in darkness at noonday, and enjoyed not the true light, as it was in Christ, pertaining to themselves and to their Heavenly Father. (Erastus Snow, *JD* 19:266, March 3, 1878.)

Because of Spiritual Blindness,
Jews Did Not Understand Scriptures

When the Jewish church was in a state of apostasy, and was about to be broken off because of their unbelief;...they supposed themselves to be a wise people, to have great understanding in spiritual things: and, therefore, they could not receive the light that come [sic] immediately from heaven, because they were too much blinded by their own superstition and bigotry, having all confidence in the imagined light and wisdom of their age and nation. But instead of so great light and wisdom as they imagined, how dark and benighed [sic] was [sic] their minds while they received not a ray of light from heaven to interrupt their darkness! They were called blind Pharisees, and their leaders "blind leaders of the blind." Indeed, nothing was now wanting to render impossible their escape from this dilemma, but an established opinion that there could be no revelations from heaven in their days. They erred from the truth because they were not dictated by the spirit of truth, but formed opinions of their own according to the depravity of the human heart; and disagreeing in their opinions, they split into sects and parties: but still supposed themselves to be an enlightened people, that they had a perfect knowledge of their scriptures, and that their scriptures were sufficient for their instructions. Yet they did not understand their scriptures, because they had not the teaching of the Holy Spirit. Their scriptures had taught them "that Christ cometh of the seed of David, and out of the town of Bethlehem where David was," John's gospel 7:24, therefore they rejected him that came out of Galilee. For they stumbled at the stumbling stone because there was no light in themselves, for where there is no light from heaven, the darkness is total. And although the Lord sent them apostles, evangelists, prophets, and teachers, men inspired of God, yet, this people knowing that they received no revelations from heaven, immediately to themselves, and disbelieving others who did, might have concluded like the present day Gentiles, that there was [sic] no revelations from heaven in their days. (Signed "B," *TS* 2:367-368, April 1, 1841.)

Jews Sought Signs Because of Unbelief

The position of those to whom Joseph [Smith] taught the Gospel was very similar to that of the Jews in Paul's day, only the former were more blessed than the Jews were unto whom Jesus came. They had the Prophets and Apostles, that is, they had their words. They had the record of the Gospel as taught by Jesus and his Apostles, with the account of the miracles wrought by them; they had a form of godliness, and they thought they were on the road of salvation. But they did not believe in miracles, they did not believe that God was a God of revelation, hence they would not receive the testimony of the Prophet Joseph, but they wanted miracles to convince them. In this they made a great mistake, as many others have done in other ages of the world in relation to this matter. It is written of Jesus that he did not do many mighty works in Galilee because of the unbelief of the people; and he said it was a wicked and adulterous generation that demanded a sign, and none should be given them. (George Q. Cannon, *JD* 15:370, March 23, 1873.)

The Greater Condemnation of the Jews for Having Denied the Savior

Hence it was that so great a responsibility rested upon the generation in which our Savior lived, for, says he, "That upon you may come all the righteous blood shed upon the earth, from the blood of righteous Abel unto the blood of Zacharias, son of Barachias, whom ye slew between the temple and the altar. Verily I say unto you, all these things shall come upon this generation." (Matthew 23:35, 36.) Hence as they possessed greater privileges than any other generation, not only pertaining to themselves, but to their dead, their sin was greater, as they not only neglected their own salvation but that of their progenitors, and hence their blood was required at their hands. (Joseph Smith, *HC* 4:599, April 15, 1842.)

Despite Christ's Death, Work to Continue

...Was there a cessation of the work of God, when Jesus was suffering upon the cross? No, the work was still going on.... But the High Priests of the Jewish faith, and all those who were foremost in the crucifixion of the Savior, believed they had accomplished their purpose in putting to death Him whom they feared would take away their name and nation, and doubtless felt satisfied with their work, especially as He failed to come down from the cross, when they cried out, if He be the Son of God let Him come down from the cross. (Lorenzo Snow, *JD* 23:152, April 7, 1882.)

Gospel Taken from the Jews after Their Rejection of the Christ

He came, as he, himself, expressed it, to his own, but his own received him not. They looked upon him as a base impostor, as a Sabbath-breaker, a gluttonous man and a wine-bibber. Instead of being a moral character, in their estimation, he was a friend of publicans and sinners, and associated with them instead of with those who professed to be religious. They persecuted, hated, and reviled him; and finally succeeded, in fulfillment [sic] of prophecy, in crucifying him.

Jesus, before he was crucified, said unto the Jews, "I say unto you that the kingdom of God shall be taken from you, and shall be given to a people who shall bring forth the fruits thereof." As much as to say, "You once enjoyed the fruits of the kingdom; you once had in your midst inspired men, prophets, great and holy men who spoke as they were moved upon by the Holy Ghost; you once enjoyed all the blessings and gifts of the kingdom of God; in the days of your righteousness you enjoyed these fruits in abundance. But, alas! you have departed from the laws of that kingdom; you have forsaken the religion of your fathers; you have turned your hearts away, you have apostatized from the truth, and the fruits that were enjoyed by your fathers no longer exist among you. Your fathers were in possession of all the miraculous fruits and blessings and gifts of the kingdom. They could prophecy [sic] and see visions; they could hear the voice of the Lord speaking to them; they could enjoy the power and gift of the Holy Spirit; work miracles in the name of the Lord; heal the sick; cast out devils and perform all these miracles that are recorded in the Old Testament; and those were the fruits of that kingdom which you, the Jewish nation, once enjoyed; but because you have rejected your Messiah, rejected the testimony of the prophets concerning him; rejected the testimony given in the law of Moses, and those great types pointing to the Messiah, you, in turn, shall be rejected, the kingdom shall be taken from you, and it shall be given to a nation who shall bring forth the fruits thereof." (Orson Pratt, *JD* 14:59-60, March 26, 1871.)

Chapter 3

The Scattering and Scourging of Judah

> And because they turn their hearts aside, saith the prophet, and have despised the Holy One of Israel, they shall wander in the flesh, and perish, and become a hiss and a by-word, and be hated among all nations. (1 Nephi 19:14.)

How often disobedience brings dissolution! Time after time, Judah has been dispersed, and flung to the ends of the earth. Jeremiah saw his people scattered by the Babylonians. The Romans uprooted the very foundation of Judah's hopes and destroyed her dreams in the meridian of time. From country to country, from century to century, nations and churches inflicted unimaginable persecutions and suffering upon the Jews, right up to the present day. World War II brought the horrors of the holocaust. The horrors of Dachau and Auschwitz may never be forgotten.

Yet through our window of modern inspiration we will see some reason behind a world's hatred for a single race. Might it be that only through dispersion and persecution could this mighty race remain unique? Could it be that the drivings and the scourgings will finally drive them home to glory? Can we doubt the promises made far behind us where the spring bubbled up and the river began?

The World Has Persecuted the Jews

I have been thinking of the history of the world and the blessing that has come to men and women who dwell in the flesh, in the birth of our Lord and Master, Jesus Christ; and while I have been rejoicing in the thought of what has been accomplished by reason of His coming into the world, living so pure a life and preparing the way for the resurrection, I am reminded that the race of people from which He sprang is in ignorance today, comparatively, of the divine mission of the Lord. I am reminded of the terrible circumstances that have surrounded the Hebrews since Christianity became a power in the world. They have been driven from place to place and in many lands they have been almost slaves—these people who were of the same blood as our Lord and Master. The world has heaped upon the Jewish race untold privation and suffering, and most unfortunate of all is the fact that it has been done under the guise of Christianity in many cases. It has been the so-called Christians that have brought distress and trouble to the Hebrew race. (George Albert Smith, *Liahona,* 5:837-839, January 18, 1908.)

Israel Suffered from the Penalty of Disobedience

The fate which befell the House of Israel had been plainly outlined by the prophets whom the Lord had sent to warn them that the penalty of disobedience would be the dissolution of the nation, and that they would be taken from the land of their inheritance, and scattered among the strange and unbelieving nations of the world. A final fulfillment of this prophecy occurred when, about one hundred years after the birth of the Redeemer, Judea was trodden down by the Roman armies under Vespasian and his son Titus, Jerusalem taken, the temple destroyed, and the Jews scattered among the nations of the world, where they have remained until the present day.

The prophets Zechariah and Ezekiel had declared that the shepherds would neglect the flock, and that the sheep would be scattered, and become the prey of strange nations. To all human appearance, judged by every law of human reasoning, the promise made to Abraham had failed, he had been promised that Palestine should be the everlasting heritage of his children, and now they held dominion over no part of it. The end, it appeared, had come, the words of the prophets had been literally fulfilled, the promise made by the Lord if ever to be realized was still future. (Anthony Ivins, *CR,* p. 46, April 1925.)

Zedekiah's Eyes Were Put Out and He Was Carried a Prisoner Into Babylon

...Zedekiah was the last king of Judea, that long after the Ten Tribes had been carried away by Shalmaneser, Nebuchadnezzar came up from Babylon and subdued the Jews, and made this reigning king prisoner. It was during Zedekiah's reign that Lehi and his colony left Jerusalem, led away by God our Father, in order that He might preserve that people from that which He knew was to come; for Lehi prophesied, the Book of Mormon tells us, that Jerusalem would be destroyed, that there would be great suffering, that the people would be carried into captivity. Zedekiah had a number of sons. The Bible tells us that they were all put to death before their father, that his eyes were put out, and that he was carried down Into Babylon where he lived in darkness the remainder of his days. But one of those sons escaped the Babylonians and brought a small colony to this continent. It was God that brought them here, not Mulek. He did it, of course, but the Lord directed him, just as He always uses men to do the things that He has to do.

The Prophet Jeremiah Was the Great-Grandfather of Zedekiah's Two Daughters

Zedekiah, at the time, had two daughters. The Prophet Jeremiah was the great-grandfather of these two girls. His granddaughter was the wife of Zedekiah, the king. These two beautiful girls were left, and in order that they might be protected against the Babylonians, they were placed in the cave of Jeremiah, the prophet. He became their guardian, the custodian of their welfare. Because of his fear that they might fall into the hands of the Babylonians, which would have been an abomination to an Israelitish maiden, Jeremiah took them down into Egypt, it is said, to the same place where Joseph and Mary went with Christ, our Lord, at the time of the execution of the decree of Herod by which the children of Bethlehem were put to death. They abode there, at a place called Taphanes, the ruins of which are now well known. The natives refer to it to this day as the palace of the Jew's daughter, or the house of the old Prophet. See Jeremiah 41:10-15, and 43:1-7.

Babylonian Armies Invaded Egypt

After the conquest of Palestine, the Babylonian armies invaded Egypt and it became evident that they would be victorious over the Egyptians. Just at this time we lose sight of Jeremiah and these two girls, so far as the Bible is concerned. At that time the ships of Tyre were sailing the Mediterranean. The tribe of Dan, one of the sons of Jacob, was the seafaring nation. Their ships brought in from the

British Isles the tin used to make the brass that went into the temple of Solomon. Just at that time a ship landed upon the coast of Spain, from which an old man and his secretary and two young women disembarked. They remained for a short period in that country, where one of the girls married into the reigning house of Spain, but the old man, who is referred to in Ireland as Ollamh Fodhla (the old prophet), in their traditions and the songs which they still sing of him, passed across the channel and landed on the coast of Ireland, taking with him the elder of the two girls, whose name was Tamar Tephi, which translated from Hebrew into English means The Beautiful Palm, or the Beautiful Wanderer.

Tamar Tephi Promised in Marriage if King Accepted Her Religion

Eochaidh was then reigning king of Ireland. (There were ten kings at that time on this little island. When there was an invasion from the outside, they all joined together and had one king, who was acknowledged their leader. When there was no danger from the outside, they fought against each other. The Irish haven't entirely gotten over that habit yet.) Eochaidh solicited the hand of Tamar Tephi in marriage, to which the old prophet consented, provided the king would accept the religion which he brought. He brought with him a small chest, strongly bound, which was very jealously guarded and the contents of which were unknown. The king of Ireland agreed to this, the marriage ceremony was performed, and the religion of Ollamh Fodhla, which corresponded almost exactly to the service to God under the law of Moses, was established in Ireland. After a time this king went over and effected the conquest of the southern part of Scotland. Both he and his queen finally died and were buried at Tara in Ireland. A great monument stands there today over their grave.

The Lord Preserved that Lineage

Why am I telling you this story? It is because modern genealogists now at work upon the collection and definite establishment of genealogical records, trace both the Tudor and the Stuart lines of kings, from the present King George of England, directly back to the girl, Tamar Tephi. So it would seem that, unknown to men at the time, the Lord preserved that lineage. It exists today, and I do not believe that it will ever cease to exist until the Israelitish people are redeemed and the covenant entered into between Abraham and the Lord realized. It doesn't matter to us whether that story is true or not, but it is true according to the very best information that it is possible to obtain upon the subject. We know definitely and well that the lineage of both of these kingly lines, the Tudors, and the Stuarts of Scotland, trace back to this girl. So the Lord has kept the royal blood, the house of Israel, until today; and when the final determination of it all is made, we will find out that He has been watching over those people, that He has been directing them, that He has been helping them, that it is He and not their numerical strength that has made Great Britain, Scandinavia, and Germany the dominant powers of the world. (Anthony W. Ivins, *Utah Genealogical Magazine,* pp. 6-8, January 1932.)

Children of Abraham Called to Prepare the Way for the Coming Forth of the Fullness of the Everlasting Gospel

Now the same spirit of revelation that sought out the Prophet Joseph [Smith] from the loins of Joseph who was sold into Egypt, and that raised him up in this dispensation to receive the keys of the Priesthood and to lay the foundation of this great work in the earth, has also called the children of Abraham from among the kingdoms and countries of the earth to first hear and then embrace the everlasting Gospel; and the remnants of the seed of Ephraim who were scattered from Palestine and who colonized the shores of the Caspian Sea and thence made their way into the north of Europe, western Scandinavia and northern Germany, penetrating Scotland and England, and conquering those nations and reigning as monarchs of Great Britain, and mingling their seed with the Anglo-Saxon race, and spreading over the waters a fruitful vine, as predicted by Jacob, whose branches should run over the wall. Their blood has permeated European society, and it coursed in the veins of the early colonists of America. And when the books shall be opened and the lineage of all men is known, it will be found that they have been first and foremost in everything noble among men in the various nations in breaking off the shackles of kingcraft and priestcraft and oppression of every kind, and the foremost among men in upholding and maintaining the principles of liberty and freedom upon this continent and establishing a representative government, and thus preparing the way for the coming forth of the fullness of the everlasting Gospel. And it is the foremost of those spirits whom the Lord has prepared to receive the Gospel when it was presented to them, and who did not wait for the Elders to hunt them from the hills and corners of the earth, but they were hunting for the Elders, impelled by a spirit which then they could not understand; and for this reason were they among the first Elders of the Church; they and the fathers having been watched over from the days that God promised those blessings upon Isaac and Jacob and Joseph and Ephraim. And these are they that will be found in the front ranks of all that is noble and good in their day and time, and who will be found among those whose efforts are directed in establishing upon the earth those heaven-born principles which tend directly to blessing and salvation, to ameliorating the condition of their fellowmen, and elevating them in the scale of their being; and among those also who receive the fullness of the Everlasting Gospel, and the keys of Priesthood in the last days through whom God determined to gather up again unto himself a peculiar people, a holy nation, a pure seed that shall stand upon Mount Zion as saviors, not only to the house of Israel but also to the house of Esau. (Erastus Snow, *JD* 23:186-187, May 6, 1882.)

Many Prophecies Have Been Fulfilled—
Particularly Those of the Scattering and Scourging

As Latter-day Saints we accept the words of the ancient Prophets and believe that they will be fulfilled literally? Has Jerusalem become a heap of ruins literally? Were the seed of Abraham in bondage and oppressed by the Egyptians literally? Were they delivered and brought out of that land with a high hand and with great power literally? Did God bring them literally into the land of Canaan, which he promised to Abraham? Have they been broken up and scattered from that land literally? Did the Savior come, born of a virgin, as the Prophets predicted, literally? Did he suffer for our sins and endure all that the Prophets had spoken of him literally? Did his enemies cast lots for his vesture and divide his garments among themselves literally? Were "the shepherd smitten and the sheep scattered" when Jesus was crucified literally? Yes, in all these particulars, history records, with the greatest minutiae, the literal fulfillment of prophecy. Was the house of the Lord thrown down and the very foundation thereof ploughed as a field, literally? Yes, then what reason have we to expect other than a literal fulfillment of the next part of the same prophecy, which foretells the establishment of the Lord's house in the tops of the mountains, the gathering of people from all nations thereunto, that the Lord will rebuke strong nations afar off, and that the nations will beat their swords into ploughshares, their spears into pruning hooks, that they will live at peace and learn war no more, and the Lord will reign over them, from henceforth, even forever? (Erastus Snow, *JD* 16:204, September 14, 1873.)

Judgments of Christ Descended Upon the Jews

This has been the course the Almighty has pursued in every age when his judgments have been poured out upon the people—he has sent Prophets to warn them and to tell them how they might escape the calamities threatened. This was so with the Jews, unto whom the Son of God came. He proclaimed the Gospel unto them, and warned them of coming judgments, and he sent his disciples through all Jewry, doing the same.

...[Many heard] the Savior's pathetic lament over Jerusalem, when he said he would have gathered her people as a hen gathereth her chickens under her wing, but they would not receive him as a messenger of salvation, as the heir and Son of God, empowered to impart unto them principles, obedience to which would have secured them life here and hereafter. He also pronounced a woe upon many cities of that land, and said that if the mighty works which had been done in them had been done in Sodom and Gomorrah, their people would have repented. But the Jews hardened their hearts, and not only rejected his testimony, but they shed his blood, and invoked condemnation on their own heads for doing so. History tells us that the judgments which Christ and his Apostles had declared did descend upon the Jewish nation. (George Q. Cannon, *JD* 15:112-113, July 14, 1872.)

Persecution of the Jews by the Romans

Titus, the Roman general, laid seige to that city and overcame the Jews, eleven hundred thousand of whom were killed, and ninety-seven thousand taken into captivity, many of the latter being afterwards persecuted and killed by their enemies; thus a poor, miserable remnant were scattered abroad among all the various nations and kingdoms of the earth. Jerusalem, their beloved city, where their temple was built, where the name of the Lord was placed, and from which they had been warned by the mouth of the prophets, where the voice of inspiration had been heard; where Jesus himself who spake as never man spake, ministered for many months. That city was delivered up to the Gentiles, and overcome by them; the stones of their beautiful temple were torn down to the very foundation, and the city passed into the hands of the Gentiles. (Orson Pratt, *JD* 14:59-60, March 26, 1871.)

A Day of Vengeance Fell Upon Jerusalem

Josephus vividly described how the city (Jerusalem) was blockaded—none could escape. Besides this there were several factions within the city; Jews were at war with Jews under different leaders. This made a desolating war within, while the enemy was encamped without; and besides all this, famine overtook them, and pestilence caused by want, and by being crowded and shut up in the city, and by the dead bodies with no place to bury them.

Hence with sword, famine, pestilence, etc., Jerusalem began to be desolated. "Now when you see this, understand that the desolation thereof is nigh. Then let them which are in Judea flee to the mountains; and let them which are in the midst of it depart out, and let not them that are in the countries enter therein."

Jesus Warned the Jews to Gather to the Mountains

Some of our Sectarian friends tell us that Jesus Christ did not preach a gathering; he only preached the Gospel, and then let the people live right where they had a mind to. But here is a positive revelation from the Son of God, to those that would give heed to his warning voice, to actually remove to the mountains in order to escape the war, the troubles, and pestilence that awaited the Jews and Jerusalem.

Now if we had all the history of those times; if we only had what the Apostles have written, in full, instead of a little of it, we should have the particular place where they did go, and where they lived, you would have an account of the organization of a gathered people taking care of themselves, while war desolated the nation. We have not got this part of ancient history, but we will have it, for there is nothing secret but what will be revealed—hid but what will be brought to light.

When God sees fit, we will have the record of the fulfillment of this gathering; of every man, woman, and child that heeded the warning of the blessed Jesus. About seventy years after the birth of Christ, which was about the date that the Roman army compassed Jerusalem, I warrant you they left Judea and Jerusalem, and gathered into the mountains to take care of themselves.

"Let them which are in the midst of it depart out, and let not them that are in the country enter thereinto." We are given to understand that there was a little time after the Roman army had laid siege to Jerusalem, in consequence of a certain movement of that army, that gave a chance to the people in the city that were wide awake, to gather. If they would give heed to the warning voice of Jesus, or to the words of his Apostles, not to come down from the house top, or stop to get their bed, but run with all their might, they could escape. A little moment of relaxation, an advantageous position of the army, made escape possible to those who would not stop to take their clothes out of the house, their bed, or anything else, but flee at once.

"For these be the days of vengeance." Vengeance on what? On the people of the Jews and on all the people of Jerusalem that had rejected the Gospel, that had rejected and killed the true Messiah and persecuted and killed the Apostles, and his disciples.

"These be the days of vengeance." What for? That all things that were written may be fulfilled, not spiritualized, nor transformed, nor done away, but absolutely fulfilled.

...read Moses and the Prophets and see if they do not predict the horrors of war to that age, desolation, even to the eating of their own children for mere want, because of the pressure of the famine; "even the tender and delicate women," says Moses, "who would not venture to put the soles of their feet on the ground for tenderness and delicacy, should eat their own children in the siege and the straitness whereby your enemies shall distress you in all your gates, if you will not hearken to my words." (Parley P. Pratt, *JD* 3:131-133, October 7, 1855.)

A Tale of Horror Among the Jews

The history of their sufferings is a continued tale of horror. Revolt is natural to the oppressed; and their frequent seditions were productive of renewed privations and distress. Emperors, Kings, and Caliphs, all united in subjecting them to the same "iron yoke." Constantine, after having suppressed a revolt which they raised, and having commanded their ears to be cut off, dispersed them as fugitives and vagabonds into different countries whither they carried in terror to their kindred, the mark of their sufferings and infamy. In the fifth century, they were expelled from Alexandria, which had long been their safest place of resort. Justinian, from whose principles of legislation a wiser and more human policy ought to have emanated, yielded to none of his predecessors in hostility and severity against them. He abolished their synagogues, prohibited them even from entering into caves for the exercise of their worship, rendered their testimony inadmissable, and deprived them of the natural right of bequeathing their property; and when such oppressive enactments led to insurrectionary movements among the Jews, their property was confiscated—many of them beheaded—and so bloody an execution of them prevailed, that as it is expressly.related, "all the Jews of that century trembled." Gregory the Great afforded them a temporary respite from oppression, which only rendered their spoilation more complete, and their sufferings more acute, under the cruel persecutions of Heraclias. That emperor, unable to satiate his hatred against them by inflicting a variety of punishments on those who resided in his own dominions, and by finally expelling them from his empire, exerting so effectually against them his influence in other countries, that they suffered under a general and simultaneous persecution from Asia to the farthest extremities of Europe.

The Church of Rome Treated the Jews as Heretics

...The Canons of different councils pronounced excommunication against those who should favor or uphold the Jews against Christians; enjoined all Christians neither to eat, nor hold communion with them; prohibited them from bearing public offices, or having Christian slaves appointed, to be distinguished by a mark, decreed that their children should be taken from them, and brought up in monasteries; and what is equally descriptive of the low estimation in which they were subjected, there was often a necessity even for those who otherwise oppressed them, to ordain that it was not lawful to take the life of a Jew without any cause. (Alfred Morris Myres, *The Jews Both One In Christ,* p. 249, quoted in *TS,* 4:85-89, February 1, 1843.)

The Jews Were Persecuted Throughout Most of Europe

In their wanderings, their fortunes varied—sometimes in Europe they were declared heretics, and the burdens and responsibilities of citizenship were imposed upon them whilst its rights were denied; at other times, for a brief period, they would enjoy all the privileges possessed by other citizens, until in the days of Charlemagne their limited prosperity seemed to reach its zenith.

From that date their fortunes gradually declined, until the right to live was denied them, and in almost every country in Europe they were trampled under foot and butchered with little more considerations than as many sheep....

...In France, Spain, and Britain they were subjected to every conceivable indignity and outrage. Intercourse with them was forbidden, their debtors forgiven by legal enactment, a Christian might kill a Jew without risk of punishment.... At about the same period the continent of Europe from Switzerland to Silesia was literally drenched with Jews' blood.

In Spain and Portugal, up to the 13th century, they enjoyed greater privileges than in most other portions of Europe; but from that period, the same spirit of hatred that burned elsewhere towards this unfortunate people, began to be manifest in Spain, and eventually culminated in acts of the greatest ferocity. In the after part of the 14th century, of 7,000 Jewish families residing in Seville, between three and four thousand were put to death, the remainder being spared only upon making profession of the Christian faith. In other large cities similar scenes were enacted—many thousands who preferred death rather than apostacy from their ancient faith being mercilessly slaughtered.

In the 13th century Henry III, after depriving them of their wealth by every means that avarice and injustice could devise, sold all the Jews in England for 10,000 marks to his brother, giving the latter full control of their persons and property, for this sum. (As quoted from Deseret Evening News, *MS* 30:341-342, May 30, 1868.)

Persecutions of the Jews by the Russians

In 1893 W. B. Dougal wrote the latest move of the Russian government is in a twofold direction. In the first place it is ascertained that Russia intends to expel all Jewish artisans from those towns in Russia proper, in which they have hitherto been permitted to reside, if members of a trade union. Secondly, the expulsion of the Jews from the interior of Russia is being prosecuted with renewed vigor. These measures are being accompanied by a host of smaller restrictions and annoyances which render the life of the Jews in that country a daily martyrdom. Having done his best to make an enemy of the Jew, the Czar, by the pure inertia of evil, probably had no choice but to treat him as one. When lies were needed to justify a policy of official corruption, it was the Jew who was slandered; and when suspicion became necessary, the weight of it fell upon the poor Israelite. Now that the Russian government, ground down by intolerable taxation, and stunted in its industrial development by despotic institutions, is threatened with another famine, it does not seem strange that she should accuse the poor Jews of the conditions of her own creating, or that the very qualities bred in the Jew by her policy—the qualities of thrift, prudence and foresight—should be cited against him as evidence of his native weakness. (W. B. Dougal, *MS* 55:164-165, March 6, 1893.)

Cannon Reported in 1897 that the Jews are Living in the Most Awful Squalor and Misery Conceivable Within the Confines of the Jewish Pale of Russia....

The inhabitants of these congested districts—I refer particularly to the pale—are not only suffering from dire privations, but their vitality and that of their children is gradually being undermined, and the race is threatened with both physical and moral degeneration. Ill-fed, ill-housed, anemic mothers can give birth only to puny, sickly children. It is for the salvation of these poor people that there arises the necessity of prompt action. All but the wilfully blind must surely see that if the present condition of things lasts, in a few years from now the Jews of the Russian pale will be past regeneration.

It is further argued that this feeling of distrust and hatred towards Israel is deepening in intensity and extending its limits. (George Q. Cannon, *MS* 59:644-645, October 14, 1897.)

Hitler Used as an Instrument in the Hand of God

At the general conference of The Church of Jesus Christ of Latter-day Saints on April 4, 1938, in Salt Lake City, Elder Melvin J. Ballard of the Council of the Twelve Apostles said:

I look to the Jew. Notwithstanding all his distress and peril through the ages that have passed, he seems to be in another peril, and yet I see the hand of God in it. He was to go to his native land, to the land of promise for Judah, to the Holy Land, and they are going, though many of them are going as our fathers came west—willingly because they had to. Even Hitler is used as an instrument, in the hands of God, of driving them where the Lord wants them.

Oh you, our half brothers, oh, that I could speak to you and your hearts could feel it and know that God has not forsaken you! Your hour is coming. Your deliverance is at hand. Do not complain, but be patient, and go where the Lord wants you, for he yet will redeem you. Your hour is dawning. Let there be no doubt about it.

A German-Jewish Rabbi Testified After World War II

In his book, entitled "Behind the Silken Curtain," by Bartley C. Crum, a member of the Anglo-American Committee on Palestine, which was appointed by President Harry S. Truman of the United States, there appears the following report by committee members who visited Palestine in 1945. To show how effective the Nazis had been in destroying the German-Jewish rabbis and synagogues the following is quoted:

> In Frankfort, a patriarchal old gentleman was introduced to us by Judge Rifkind: "Gentlemen," he said, "this is Rabbi Leopold Neuhaus. I thought you might wish to speak to him as your first witness, for he is the only surviving German-Jewish rabbi in Germany. We have been able to find no other."
>
> Rabbi Neuhaus nodded, and looked at us with resignation. He had been first arrested by the Nazis in 1938, when all the synagogues in Germany and in German-occupied territory were set afire.
>
> Had he any explanation why he alone survived, I asked.
>
> "Ah, yes," he said. He drew from his clothes a worn, tattered letter upon which the signature "von Hindenburg" was still visible. In World War I he had assisted the German Army in Prussia: this had come to the notice of Hindenburg, who had written him this warm letter of appreciation. Because he was able to show it to the Nazis, it had saved his life numerous times.

The report of the above mentioned committee revealed that the great majority of the remaining Jews in Europe desired to go to Palestine. Those who wanted to remain were primarily the aged, who felt they were too old to leave and desired to die in peace. (Bartley C. Crum, *Behind the Silken Curtain*, New York, Simon and Schuster, 1947, pp. 81-82.)

Prophecies from the Book of Mormon Which Describe the Scattering of Israel and the Jews

(1) And it came to pass that as he read, he was filled with the Spirit of the Lord.

And he read, saying: Wo, wo unto Jerusalem, for I have seen thine abominations! Yea, and many things did my father read concerning Jerusalem—that it should be destroyed, and the inhabitants thereof; many should perish by the sword, and many should be carried away captive into Babylon.

And it came to pass that when my father had read and seen many great and marvelous things, he did exclaim many things unto the Lord; such as: Great and marvelous are thy works, O Lord God Almighty! Thy throne is high in the heavens, and thy power, and goodness, and mercy are over all the inhabitants of the earth, and, because thou art merciful, thou wilt not suffer those who come unto thee that they shall perish! (I Nephi 1:12-14.)

(2) Therefore, I would that ye should know, that after the Lord had shown so many marvelous things unto my father, Lehi, yea, concerning the destruction of Jerusalem, behold he went forth among the people, and began to prophesy and to declare unto them concerning the things which he had both seen and heard.

And it came to pass that the Jews did mock him because of the things which he testified of them; for he truly testified of their wickedness and their abominations; and he testified that the things which he saw and heard, and also the things which he read in the book, manifested plainly of the coming of a Messiah, and also the redemption of the world.

And when the Jews heard these things they were angry with him; yea, even as with the prophets of old, whom they had cast out, and stoned, and slain; and they also sought his life, that they might take it away. But behold, I, Nephi, will show unto you that the tender mercies of the Lord are over all those whom he hath chosen, because of their faith, to make them mighty even unto the power of deliverance. (I Nephi 1:18-20.)

(3) Yea, even my father spake much concerning the Gentiles, and also concerning the house of Israel, that they should be compared like unto an olive-tree, whose branches should be broken off and should be scattered upon all the face of the earth.

Wherefore, he said it must needs be that we should be led with one accord into the land of promise, unto the fulfilling of the word of the Lord, that we should be scattered upon all the face of the earth.

And after the house of Israel should be scattered they should be gathered together again; or, in fine, after the Gentiles had received the fulness of the Gospel, the natural branches of the olive-tree, or the remnants of the house of Israel, should be grafted in, or come to the knowledge of the true Messiah, their Lord and their Redeemer. (I Nephi 10:14.)

(4) And this is what our father meaneth; and he meaneth that it will not come to pass until after they are scattered by the Gentiles; and he meaneth that it shall come by way of the Gentiles, that the Lord may show his power unto the Gentiles, for the very cause that he shall be rejected of the Jews, or of the house of Israel. (I Nephi 15:17.)

(5) And because they turn their hearts aside, saith the prophet, and have despised the Holy One of Israel, they shall wander in the flesh, and perish, and become a hiss and a by-word, and be hated among all nations.

Nevertheless, when that day cometh, saith the prophet, that they no more turn aside their hearts against the Holy One of Israel, then will he remember the covenants which he made to their fathers.

Yea, then will he remember the isles of the sea; yea, and all the people who are of the house of Israel, will I gather in, saith the Lord, according to the words of the prophet Zenos, from the four quarters of the earth. (I Nephi 19:14-16.)

(6) That he has spoken unto the Jews, by the mouth of his holy prophets, even from the beginning down, from generation to generation, until the time comes that they shall be restored to the true church and fold of God; when they shall be gathered home to the lands of their inheritance, and shall be established in all their lands of promise. (2 Nephi 9:2.)

(7) And behold it shall come to pass that after the Messiah hath risen from the dead, and hath manifested himself unto his people, unto as many as will believe on his name, behold, Jerusalem shall be destroyed again; for wo unto them that fight against God and the people of his church.

Wherefore, the Jews shall be scattered among all nations; yea, and also Babylon shall be destroyed; wherefore, the Jews shall be scattered by other nations.

And after they have been scattered, and the Lord God hath scourged them by other nations for the space of many generations, yea, even down from generation to generation until they shall be persuaded to believe in Christ, the Son of God, and the atonement, which is infinite for all mankind—and when that day shall come that they shall believe in Christ, and worship the Father in his name, with pure hearts and clean hands, and look not forward any more for another Messiah, then, at that time, the day will come that it must needs be expedient that they should believe these things. (2 Nephi 25:14-16.)

(8) And it shall come to pass that the Jews which are scattered also shall begin to believe in Christ; and they shall begin to gather in upon the face of the land; and as many as shall believe in Christ shall also become a delightsome people. (2 Nephi 30:7.)

(9) And as surely as the Lord liveth, will he gather in from the four quarters of the earth all the remnant of the seed of Jacob, who are scattered abroad upon all the face of the earth. (3 Nephi 5:24.)

(10) And after that ye were blessed then fulfilleth the Father the covenant which he made with Abraham, saying: In thy seed shall all the kindreds of the earth be blessed—unto the pouring out of the Holy Ghost through me upon the Gentiles, which blessing upon the Gentiles shall make them mighty above all, unto the scattering of my people, O house of Israel. (3 Nephi 21:27.)

Section 2

From Joseph To Judah

A New Dispensation

From Joseph to Judah:
Mormon Missions to the Jews

The Times of the Gentiles

The Gathering, Object of All Prophecy

Zionism, Prophecy Fulfilled

The Miracle of Judah's Identity

Chapter 4

A New Dispensation

> And it shall come to pass in that day, that the Lord shall set his hand again the second time to recover the remnant of his people, which shall be left from Assyria, and from Egypt, and from Pathros, and from Cush, and from Elam, and from Shinar, and from Hamath, and the islands of the sea. And He shall set up an ensign for the nations, and shall assemble the outcasts of Israel, and gather together the dispersed of Judah from the four corners of the earth. (Isaiah 11:11, 12.)

We will shift our view now, if only a little, to capture the gathering and growth of modern Joseph, blood brother to the scattered Judah. We need not lean far, though, from our visions of Judah, for the brilliant light which filled the wooded grove in the Spring of 1820 surely shined on all of Israel. If we now turn to the Restoration of the Gospel and the Prophet Joseph Smith, we do not forget the Jews but learn how God remembers them, how He has established for them an ensign in the wilderness and called, for them, prophets to help them back to Zion. Indeed, never has one man spoken with more power, love or hope to Judah than did Joseph Smith. His own prophetic statements, the endless works of his brethren, and the *Book of Mormon* he gave the world have done and will do more to bring the Jews to eternal glory than any other efforts. For as Joseph once saved and succored his wayward brother, so will modern Joseph sustain the establishment of modern Israel.

Our Day is the Time of the Restitution of the Jews

The dealings of God with the human family have been the subjects of prophecy and revelation, and more especially with the descendants of Shem, the offspring of Abraham, Isaac and Jacob, and not only the Chosen People, but the nations with which they were identified, and with whom they were more or less connected and allied in a national capacity. All these things have been the subjects of prophecy; but the burden of prophecy, from the beginning of the world down to the present time, seems to center upon our day—the time of the restitution of all things spoken of so frequently by the Prophets of God. By reference to the 3rd chapter of the Acts of the Apostles, we find that the Apostle Peter, talking to the wondering Jews assembled together gazing upon him and his brother John, at the time he healed the lame man at the beautiful gate of the Temple, and told them concerning Jesus, whom they had crucified, and whom the Father had raised from the dead, of which they were his witnesses, told them that this same Jesus had been taken up into heaven, and would remain at the right hand of God until the time of the restitution of all things spoken of by all the Prophets since the world began. Then he, Jesus, will descend again. From this scripture we understand that Peter and his brother Apostles comprehended the doctrine of the restitution of all things, and that it should take place in the latter days preparatory to the second advent of the Savior. (Erastus Snow, *JD* 16:201, September 14, 1873.)

What is a Standard?

The prophet says, "Behold thus saith the Lord God, I will lift up mine hand to the Gentiles, and they shall bring thy sons in their arms, and thy daughters upon their shoulders, and I will lift up my standard to the Gentiles."

[The Standard is] the same as an ensign—an ensign that is to be lifted up upon the mountains, upon a land afar off. It is the standard of the Almighty, the same standard that was spoken of in connection with the great highway that was to be cast up over the continent. (Orson Pratt, *JD* 16:85, June 15, 1873.)

Jews Shall Set up an Ensign for the Nations

But as a still further testimony of the power that will be made manifest in the restitution of Israel, let me refer you to another passage, which is contained in the 11th chapter of Isaiah. "He shall set up an ensign for the nations, and shall assemble the outcasts of Israel, and gather together the dispersed of Judah from the four corners of the earth." Here is a declaration that the two great kingdoms of Israel—its "outcasts," the ten tribes, scattered seven hundred and twenty years before Christ, and the "dispersed of Judah," dispersed among nations, shall be gathered. But before he gathers them he will set up an ensign—an ensign is to be raised in the latter-days especially for the gathering of Israel.

...But in regard to this ensign, the Lord has never said that he will lift it up before the time comes to gather Israel. And now let us inquire where will it be lifted up; in what part of the earth will he commence the great work? He must begin it among the gentiles,... and as Isaiah tells us in the 49th chapter—a standard or ensign, to which the people will gather, will be reared among the Gentiles. Recollect this is something to be commenced among the Gentiles, not among the Jewish nation, not away yonder in Palestine or Jerusalem. "Thus saith the Lord God, behold I will lift up mine hand to the Gentiles and set up my standard to the people"—the same ensign that Isaiah speaks of in the eleventh chapter—for a standard and an ensign are synonymous terms.

To show still more fully the place where this ensign or standard is to be raised,...refer...to the 18th chapter of Isaiah, wherein you will find these words, "Woe to the land shadowing with wings, which is beyond the rivers of Ethiopia." In the 3rd verse of that chapter, after uttering the prediction concerning the judgment to come upon that land beyond the rivers of Ethiopia from Palestine—a land that has the appearance of a shadowing with wings, like North and South America, the prophet says, "All ye inhabitants of the world and dwellers on the earth, see ye, when he lifted up an ensign on the mountains, and when he bloweth with a trumpet, hear ye"—something that the Lord considered worthy of the attention of all the people of the earth. It was not to be sounded to one nation alone, not a work like that of ancient days—to be done among the Egyptian nation alone, but *"all* ye inhabitants of the world and dwellers on the earth, see ye, when he lifts up an ensign on the mountains, and when he bloweth a trumpet, hear ye."

...You Latter-day Saints have rallied to these mountains from all the various nations and kingdoms of Europe; from Australia, Southern Africa, Hindostan and other parts of the earth. Here the "standard" has been lifted up, the "ensign" has been raised; the angel has come, the voice of inspiration is again heard; the Church of the living God is again reared; Zion is rising in the earth; the times of the Gentiles will soon be fulfilled, and when the epoch arrives, all the inhabitants of the earth will be required to see, understand and listen to that which God is doing in the midst of the mountains. He is raising up a people there that are called his Church, his kingdom, that never is to be destroyed, but is to continue forever. (Orson Pratt, *JD* 14:58-70, March 26, 1871.)

Why Build a Highway in the Desert?

Not only is Israel to be saved; but "prepare ye the way of the Lord, make straight in the desert an highway for our God."

...We...read about the highway through the Red Sea, and through the seven streams of the river of Egypt that is to be cast up like it was in ancient days; but what need have we for a highway in the desert? It is for the ransomed of the Lord to pass over. What ransomed of the Lord? Those who are ransomed from among the nations, by the proclamation of the everlasting Gospel, those who listen to the angelic message that comes from heaven; they who have toiled with ox teams, mule teams and handcarts and wheelbarrows to get themselves here, to lay a foundation of the work of God in the midst of this desert. They need a highway here, that the balance who are to come hereafter, and they will come by hundreds of thousands, may come swiftly, and more speedily than by handcart conveyances. And this puts me in mind of another passage in regard to the highway connected with the proclamation of the Gospel to all the world.

Isaiah says, "Cast up, cast up an highway, gather out the stones, lift up a standard for the people, prepare ye the way of the people, for behold the Lord hath proclaimed unto the ends of the world, say ye to the daughter of Zion, behold thy salvation cometh; behold his reward is with him and his work is before him. They shall call them a holy people, the redeemed of the Lord; and they shall be called, sought out, city not forsaken." What a curious work to take place in the latter days! A highway to be made, and the stones to be gathered out! When these men, sitting here on these seats, were working out in these rugged mountains for some two or three hundred miles fulfilling these prophecies, did you blast out the rocks and gather out the stones?

The Prophet Must Have Seen the Trains Crossing the Continent

Another thing connected with the prophecy says, "Go through, go through the gates; cast up an highway," etc. I have no doubt that the prophet saw the construction of this highway in vision, in fact, he must have seen it or he could not have predicted it to such a nicety. He must also have seen these trains crossing this great continent, "dodging" into what seemed to be holes in the mountains, and after watching a little while see them come out at the opposite side. He did not call them tunnels in those days, but said, "Go through the gates," etc. (Orson Pratt, *JD* 14:69, March 26, 1871.)

The Lord Will Reign in Mount Zion in the Top of the Mountains

"But in the last days it shall come to pass, that the mountain of the House of the Lord shall be established in the top of the mountains, and it shall be exalted above the hills; and people shall flow unto it. And many nations shall come, and say, come, and let us go up to the mountain of the Lord, and to the house of the God of Jacob; and he will teach us of his ways, and we will walk in his paths; for the law shall go forth of Zion, and the word of the Lord from Jerusalem. And he shall judge among many people, and rebuke strong nations afar off; and they shall beat their swords into plowshares, and their spears into pruning-hooks: nation shall not lift up sword against nation, neither shall they learn war anymore. But they shall sit every man under his vine, and under his fig tree; and none shall make them afraid: for the mouth of the Lord of hosts hath spoken it. For all people will walk every one in the name of the Lord our God for ever and ever. In that day, saith the Lord, will I assemble her that halteth, and I will gather her that is driven out, and her that halted a remnant, and her that was cast far oft a strong nation; and the Lord shall reign over them in Mount Zion from henceforth, ever for ever." (Micah 4:1-7.)

It is evident from the above that the righteous will be assembled upon the Lord's holy mountain, and that all nations shall lay down their weapons of war: and it is equally evident that the Lord will reign in Mount Zion. (Anonymous, *TS* 3:687, February 15, 1842.)

Gathered Israel to Build a House to the Lord in the Rocky Mountains

We have seen that Israel has been scattered, and the Lord has promised He would also gather them. He said His eye has been on them although in disgrace: (see Amos 8:9) "For lo, I will command, and I will sift the House of Israel among all nations, like as corn is sifted in a sieve, yet shall not the least grain fall upon the earth." See also 14 and 15 verses. Many more quotations can be given. However, Micah 4:1-2 speaks of the last days, and the gathering of Israel to erect a House to the Lord in the tops of the mountains, and many nations shall come to meet and visit in this gathering place. It must be a mountainous country: and where is that other than in these Rocky Mountains of Western America, the everlasting hills referred to by the Patriarch Jacob, the progenitor of the mighty race of Israel, who promised this land to his son Joseph and his seed. This promise Christ ratified to the Nephites when He visited them (3 Nephi 21:22), speaking of "this the remnant of Jacob unto whom I have given this land for their inheritance."

"Saint" Means Israel or those of Israel Settling in the Rocky Mountains

This portion of Israel settling in the valleys of the Rocky Mountains is known as the Latter-day Saints; the term "Saints" is not applied in the sense, as is commonly supposed, of a sanctified or holy being, who is almost too good for this earth. "Saint" in this case means *Israel,* and is another of those names under which Israel has ceased to be remembered among men. Psalms 148:14 states thus: "He also exalteth the horn of his people, the praise of all his *Saints,* even of the children of *Israel,* a people near unto Him." (J. Hatton Carpenter, *Utah Genealogical Magazine* 21:168-169, October 1930.)

Joseph Smith Chosen as the Prophet of the Restoration from the Beginning

"It was decreed in the counsels of eternity long before the foundations of the earth were laid, that he, Joseph Smith, should be the man, in the last dispensation of this world, to bring forth the word of God to this people, and receive the fulness of the keys and power of the Priesthood of the Son of God. The Lord had his eyes upon him, and upon his father, and upon his father's father, and upon their progenitors, clear back to Abraham, and from Abraham to the flood, and from the flood to Enoch and from Enoch to Adam. He has watched that family and that blood as it has circulated from its fountain to the birth of that man. He was foreordained in eternity to preside over this last dispensation...." (Brigham Young, *JD* 7:289-290.)

Joseph Smith—Prophesied about the Jews

Another notable fact, showing how clearly the youthful Prophet understood the hidden but foretold predictions of the prophets of the Lord, is shown in the first publication of the Church, other than that of the Book of Mormon which was published before the Church was organized, namely, the "Evening and Morning Star," printed in June 1832, in Independence, Missouri. In its first issue, setting forth its mission and the object of its publication, is the statement that it was to be "a messenger of truth in these the last days, to present to the world the revelations and commandments of God which have been given, and those which may be given, etc., and good tidings of great joy to all—but more especially to the House of Israel scattered abroad, that the day of their redemption is near, for the Lord has set his hand again the second time to restore them to the lands of their inheritance."

I would like to call your attention to the fact, that at the dedication of the Kirtland Temple in 1836, in the prayer of the Prophet Joseph (found in the Doctrine and Covenants), among other most significant things he said: "We therefore ask thee to have mercy upon the children of Jacob, that Jerusalem, from this hour, may begin to be redeemed; and the yoke of bondage may begin to be broken off from the House of David: and the children of Judah may begin to return to the lands which thou didst give to Abraham, their father." (James H. Moyle, *CR,* p. 27, April 8, 1932.)

Joseph—A Modern Moses to Deliver Israel

In verse 9 of II Nephi 3, Joseph of Egypt says... "And he shall be great like unto Moses, whom I have said I would raise up unto you, to deliver my people, O house of Israel." This is a most significant verse and it is readily apparent the role fulfilled by the Prophet Joseph Smith was most similar to that of Moses.

(1) Both saw and spoke with Jehovah. (2) Both were liberators who led multitudes in exodus for the sake of liberty from oppression. (3) Both were law-givers by divine inspiration. (4) Both were prophets and seers. (5) Both performed mighty miracles. (6) Both encountered opposition, from "friends" and enemies. (7) Both depended largely on a brother for success: Moses on Aaron; Joseph on Hyrum. (George Reynolds and Janne M. Sjodahl, *Commentary on the Book of Mormon,* Salt Lake City: Deseret News Press, 1955, 1, p. 253.)

The Fig Tree Prophecy Refers to the Second Coming of the Savior

Erastus Snow said: The rendering of this 24th chapter of Matthew is somewhat imperfect in King James' translation; the events connected with the destruction of Jerusalem and the dispersion of the Jews seem to be intermingled with the events that were to precede and accompany the second advent of the Savior. In the new translation of this chapter by the Prophet Joseph Smith, which may be found in the *Pearl of Great Price,* the difference is made very plain, and the figure of the fig tree and the second coming of the Son of Man and the generation referred to therein is made applicable, not to the period of the destruction of Jerusalem, but to the time of the second coming of the Son of Man. And the new translation reads, in speaking of the putting forth of the fig-tree and the signs that should precede the coming of the Son of Man, "Verily, I say unto you, this generation, in which these things shall be shewn forth, shall not pass away, till all I have told shall be fulfilled." From the reading of the new and correct rendering, it will be seen that, instead of the things spoken of being fulfilled in the generation in which the prophecy was made—which is the inference—the application is transferred at once from the generation in which the Savior was speaking to the generation who should witness the signs of the times therein set forth. (*JD* 20:180, 181, April 6, 1874.)

The Book of Mormon Will Have a Major Effect on Converting the Jews

Furthermore, when speaking of the Book of Mormon, the Lord says: "It contains a record of a fallen people, and the fullness of the Gospel of Jesus Christ to the Gentiles and to the Jews also." Again in a revelation to Martin Harris, one of the Three Witnesses to the Book of Mormon, the Lord said:

I command thee that thou shalt not covet thine own property, but impart it freely to the printing of the Book of Mormon, which contains the truth and the word of God, which is my word to the Gentile, that soon it may go to the Jews, of whom the Lamanites are a remnant, that they may believe the Gospel, and look not for a Messiah to come who has already come. (D&C 19:26-27.)

Hence we have reasons to believe that the Book of Mormon will be a powerful agent in converting many of the Jews to a belief in Jesus as the promised Messiah, as it has been a means of establishing many thousands of the Gentiles in that faith, leading them to receive the Gospel in its fullness.

Jews to be Persuaded that Jesus is the Christ by the Book of Mormon

Moreover, when the Prophet Mormon was about closing up his abridgement of the records of the ancient Nephites, he said in speaking of the words which he had written:

They shall go unto the unbelievers of the Jews; and for this intent shall they go, that they may be persuaded that Jesus is the Christ, the Son of the Living God, that the Father may bring about through His most beloved, His great and eternal purpose in restoring the Jews, or all the house of Israel to the land of their inheritance. (Mormon 5:14.)

Again it is predicted by the first Nephi, the prophet, speaking of the time when the Book of Mormon should go to the remnant of his people—the American Indians—that, it shall come to pass that the Jews which are scattered, also shall begin to believe in Christ; and they shall begin to gather in upon the face of the land; and as many as shall believe in Christ shall also become a delightsome people (2 Nephi 30:7).

And in many other places in the sacred volume it is recorded that this book shall be the means of converting the Jews to a belief that Jesus is the Son of God. (B.H. Roberts, *MS* 50:89-90, February 6, 1888.)

The Union of Two Records to Precede a Mighty Work

...Thus saith the Lord God, Behold I will take the children of Israel from among the heathen whither they be gone. I will gather them on every side, and bring them into their own land upon the mountains of Israel. They shall no more be two nations, neither shall they be divided into two kingdoms any more at all. But they shall dwell in the land which I have given to Jacob my servant, wherein your fathers have dwelt, and they shall dwell therein, even they and their children and their children's children for ever, saith the Lord."

Has that been fulfilled? No. When will the work commence that will bring it about? When the Lord takes the stick of Joseph, written upon for Joseph, and puts it with the Jewish record, written upon for Judah, and makes them one in his own hand, and not until then. You might raise millions of dollars, and form missionary societies for the amelioration of the condition of the Jews; you might form Christian societies and raise funds until they are ever so great, and go to the nations of the earth and try to convert Israel, but you can not do it. Why? Because God Almighty has decreed that that work shall be brought about after the union of the two records, and not until then. When he brings forth the record of the tribe of Joseph—his sacred writing and puts it with the record of the Jews—the Bible, then and not till then may we look for the restitution of the house of Israel; and not even then, until the times of the Gentiles are fulfilled.

The Book of Mormon to Further the Work of Gathering

We have been proclaiming for years this Book of Mormon, which we have declared has sprung forth from the earth by the power of the Almighty, for the benefit, first of the Gentile nations. The proclamation, according to the words of the book, must go forth to all people, nations and tongues under the whole heavens, called the Gentile nations, after which the Lord has promised in numerous places in this record that it should go to the remnants of the house of Israel. But that which the Lord intends to accomplish first by the bringing forth of this book, is the redemption of as many as will hearken to its words in all the Gentile nations of the earth, and to gather them together in one; for not only are the house of Israel and the house of Judah to be gathered back to their own lands, but all Christians throughout the whole earth are to be gathered in one in the latter days, according to a prophecy which you will find in the 43rd chapter of Isaiah: "I will bring them from the east, and gather them from the west. I will say to the north, Give up; and to the south, Keep not back: bring my sons from afar, and my daughters from the ends of the earth; even every one that is called by my name." This has reference to the sons and daughters of the living God, to the people called Saints; not particularly to the literal seed of the house of Israel, but to all those who believe in him, and who are called by his name. (Orson Pratt, *JD* 15:180, 189-190, September 22, 1872.)

The Book of Mormon is a Warning Unto All Nations

The Lord has brought forth the Book of Mormon in order that all the nations, kindreds, tongues and peoples on the face of the earth may be warned of the great events which are about to take place. This book contains prophecies which affect every nation under Heaven, prophecies that will be fulfilled on their heads. Can we read the future of this great American nation—our great republic? Yes, we can learn a great many features within its pages concerning this nation and government that we never should have learned without its aid or the spirit of revelation. (Orson Pratt, *JD* 13:129, April 10, 1870.)

The Lost Tribes of Israel Should Receive the Records of the Nephites and the Jews

...The ten tribes in the north country will have a record as well as the Jews, a Bible of their own, if you please. Indeed Jesus after having instructed the remnant of Joseph upon this land and revealed to them His gospel, said to them, "But now I go unto the Father, and also to show myself unto the lost tribes of Israel, for they are not lost unto the Father, for He knoweth whither He hath taken them." And it was predicted concerning them by one of the ancient American prophets, who lived in those days, that when God should bring these ten tribes from the north country, they would bring their records with them. And it should come to pass that they should have the records of the Nephites, and the Nephites should have the records of the Jews, and the Jews and the Nephites should have the records of the lost tribes of the house of Israel, and the lost tribes of Israel should have the records of the Nephites and the Jews. "It shall come to pass that I will gather my people together, and I will also gather my word in one." Not only the people are to be gathered from the distant portions of our globe, but their records, or bibles, will also be united in one. (Orson Pratt, *JD* 19:172, December 2, 1877.)

When the Book of Mormon Should be Published, Jews to Return and Believe in Jesus

When the Book of Mormon should be published, the Jews would begin to believe on His divine mission, they were to begin to gather in upon the land of their fathers, "yea the kings of the Gentiles shall be nursing fathers unto them and their queens shall become nursing mothers." "And the nations of the Gentiles shall be great in the eyes of me, said God in carrying them forth to the lands of their inheritance." So it is not a far distant day, my brethren and sisters when that great race of people that has done so much for us, the people beloved of the Lord, they of whom He spoke so tenderly and affectionately upon many occasions, they who turned their backs unwittingly upon the greatest privilege that could come to them—a knowledge of the gospel of our Lord—the time is not far distant when they will thus rejoice in the knowledge that God is our Father, that He is a personal being, that Jesus Christ, His Son, was the manifestation of God in the flesh, the Redeemer of the world, and that He is our elder brother. (George Albert Smith, *Liahona* 1:839, January 1908.)

Book of Mormon—Fulfills Isaiah's Prophecy in Chapter Twenty-Nine

That generation in which Judah was to be gathered was clearly designated by the Savior and it is not in the power of man to change that decree. He who would attempt it must fail, as evidenced by the tremendous efforts to wrench the Holy Land from the Mohammedans, who held such determined sway. Crusade after crusade, though waged in the name of Christ and the Cross, failed. For it was not the prerogative of those peoples to possess the Holy Land that was held in reserve for Judah. Moreover, the time for such deliverance was yet future. The time was spoken of by Isaiah when, in the last days, a wonderful sealed book was to be delivered. But to give Isaiah's words:

The Book Is Delivered to Him that is Not Learned

"And the vision of all is become unto you as the words of a book that is sealed, saying: Read this, I pray thee; and he saith, I cannot, for it is sealed. And the book is delivered to him that is not learned, saying: Read this, I pray thee; and he saith, I am not learned. Wherefore the Lord said: Forasmuch as this people draw near me with their mouth and with their lips do honor me, but have removed their heart far from me, and their fear toward me is taught by the precepts of men: Therefore, I will proceed to do a marvellous work among this people, even a marvellous work and a wonder, for the wisdom of their wise men shall perish, and the understanding of their prudent men shall be hid.... And Lebanon shall be turned into a fruitful field, and the fruitful field shall be esteemed as a forest. And in that day shall the deaf hear the words of the book, and the eyes of the blind see out of obscurity, and out of darkness." (Isaiah, ch. 29.)

How significant it is that the coming forth of the Book of Mormon fills that part of the prophecy in its minutest details, and in this generation in which it came, the deaf have heard and the blind have been given vision to see and read the book. This was to take place in the day in which Lebanon (Palestine) was to become fruitful and regain her primeval fertility and climate. (Octave F. Ursenbach, *Liahona* 19:427-430, April 25, 1922.)

The Book of Mormon is Filled with Many Prophecies About the Jews and Their Land

The Latter-day Saints, who always feel a deep interest in the return of the Jews to the holy land and the fulfillment of the prophecies connected therewith, cannot fail to watch the movements of that people.

We have been taught by the revelations which the Lord has given to us in these latter days, to expect the fulfillment of all prophecies of the ancient prophets concerning the return of the Jews, the re-building of Jerusalem, and the peopling of the holy land by the seed of Israel. The Book of Mormon is filled with predictions concerning this great event, and the faith of the Latter-day Saints has been aroused and is concentrated on these promises which the Lord has made. He has made covenants with His ancient servants concerning their posterity that cannot be broken; and it is exceedingly interesting to us who live in these days to witness the gradual fulfillment of the promises, and to watch the movement of the nations as they are bringing them to pass. (George Q. Cannon, *MS* 58:732, Dec. 3, 1896.)

Jews Admonished to Repent, Search the Prophets and the Scriptures

To the Jews we would say...seek the God of your fathers. Search the Prophets; for lo, your Messiah cometh speedily, and all the Saints with him.

After you have carefully reviewed your own prophets, search the New Testament with the same careful and prayerful attention, and then obtain a copy of the Book of Mormon, and search that with the same degree of candor and earnestness; and I think your minds will expand and you will be constrained to say, that Jesus of Nazareth is the Christ.

You will then know the truth, and be prepared for less surprise and a more glorious triumph on the Mount of Olives in the day of your returning king. (Parley P. Pratt, *MS* 14:468, September 18, 1852.)

Chapter 5

From Joseph to Judah: Mormon Missions to the Jews

Behold, I will send for many fishers, saith the Lord, and they shall fish them; and after will I send for many hunters, and they shall hunt them from every mountain, and from every hill, and out of the holes of the rocks. (Jeremiah 16:16.)

The pace quickened when the Church was organized in 1830, many Jews hardly dared dream of Judah's restoration to Palestine. They didn't seem to know that God's hand was set to gather them again. Yet just six years later the Prophet Moses returned in glory to this earth and delivered to Joseph Smith the keys of gathering. Shortly thereafter, an Apostle of the Lord knelt on the Mount of Olives and by the power of the priesthood and the proper keys called the Jews home. Other Apostles followed, and the powers of heaven honored those prayers. Joseph extended his brotherhood and hand to Judah.

A Visitation from Moses

On the occasion of the dedication of the temple in Kirtland, Ohio, in April, 1836, the Prophet Joseph Smith and associates were made the recipients of many glorious blessings, visions and manifestations. One of these was a visitation from Moses, the great leader and law-giver of ancient Israel, whose work on earth had been finished more than thirty-three centuries, and who bestowed upon the Prophet and his fellow laborer, Oliver Cowdery, "the keys of the gathering of Israel from the four parts of the earth, and the leading of the Ten Tribes from the north."

Pursuant to the commission thus conferred. Orson Hyde, one of the Twelve Apostles, was, in April, 1840, four years after the visitation of Moses, sent on a mission from Nauvoo, Illinois, to Palestine, for the especial purpose of dedicating that land, in the name of the Lord Jesus Christ, and by virtue of the authority of the Holy Priesthood which he held. for the return of the Jews. Should an explanation of this delay of four years be asked, a sufficient answer would be found in an account of the mobbings, drivings and persecutions which the Church, and especially the Prophet Joseph Smith and other leaders of it, were compelled to undergo during that period. (Editorial, *Liahona the Elders' Journal* 6:233, August 22, 1908.)

Orson Hyde was Converted to Mormonism After Much Studying and Prayer

Soon after the Prophet, Joseph Smith, restored the fulness of the gospel, his inquiring brilliant mind was occupied with the responsibility of teaching the gospel unto all the world. This "ordained plan of deity" allowed that "the Jews must return to Palestine." The ancient Book of Mormon prophets spoke of a future time "when the hearts of the Jews will be softened," and they will be persuaded after many years of persecution to "accept their once-rejected Messiah via the Ephraimite Mormons."

A young Campbellite preacher was attracted to the message of the Mormon elders, who were proselyting in the vicinity of Kirtland, Ohio, during 1830-31. In a few months, after much studying and prayer, their persuasive arguments in conjunction with the message of the Book of Mormon convinced Orson Hyde to become a Mormon. Later events in his life are best described in his own words:

"The circumstances which gave rise to this mission of Elder Hyde are quite peculiar and extraordinary; and in an American publication are thus described by himself:—"Something near eight years ago, Joseph Smith, a prophet and servant of the Most High God, did predict upon my head, that I should yet go to the city of Jerusalem, and be a watchman unto the house of Israel, and perform a work there which would greatly facilitate the gathering together of that people;...

Orson Beheld a Vision of the Lord

"In the early part of March last (1840), I retired to my bed one evening as usual, and while contemplating and enquiring out, in my own mind, the field of my ministerial labors for the then coming season, the vision of the Lord, like clouds of light, burst upon my view. The cities of London, Amsterdam, Constantinople, and Jerusalem all appeared in succession before me; and the Spirit said unto me, 'Here are many of the children of Abraham whom I will gather to the land that I give to their fathers, and here also is the field of your labors.'

"A strict observance of the movements of the Jews, and a careful examination of their faith relative to their expected Messiah—the setting up of his kingdom among them, and the overthrow of the present kingdoms and governments of the Gentiles, will serve to open the eyes of many...when faithfully laid before them, that the great day of the Lord comes not upon them unawares as a thief.

"Take, therefore, proper credentials from my people, your brethren, and also from the Governor of your State, with the seal of authority thereon, and go ye forth to the cities which have been shown unto you, and declare these words unto Judah, and say: 'Blow ye the trumpet in the land: cry, gather together; and say, assemble yourselves, and let us go into the defenced cities. Let the standard be reared towards Zion, Retire! stay not, for I will bring evil from the north and a great destruction. The lion is come up from his thicket, and the destroyer of the Gentiles is on his way, he is gone forth from his place to make thy land desolate, and thy cities shall be laid waste without inhabitant. Speak ye comfortably to Jerusalem, and cry unto her that her warfare is accomplished—that her iniquity is pardoned, for she has received at the Lord's hand double for all her sins. Let your warning voice be heard among the Gentiles as you pass, and call ye upon them in my name for aid and for assistance. With you it mattereth not whether it be little or much; but to me it belongeth to show favor unto them who show favor unto you. Murmur not, therefore, neither be ye sorrowful that the people are slow to hear your petition; but do as has been told you. All things shall work together for your good if you are humble and keep my commandments; for it must needs be that all men be left without excuse, that a righteous retribution may be awarded to all.'

"Many other things were shown and told me in the vision which continued open for a number of hours, that I did not close my eyes in sleep." (*A Sketch of the Travels and Ministry of Elder Orson Hyde,* Salt Lake City: Deseret News Office, 1869, pp. 3-4.)

General Conference of the Church Assembled at Nauvoo, Illinois

Members of the Church assembled in general conference at Nauvoo, Illinois, on April 6, 1840, were addressed by Elder Hyde, who explained..."that he had a great work to perform among the Jews; and that he had recently been moved upon by the spirit of the Lord to visit that people."

The prophet Joseph and Church authorities approved of Elder Hyde's mission and prepared the necessary credentials "to represent them as their envoy to the Jewish people."

"Orson Hyde's Credentials as a Missionary to Palestine."

"To all people unto whom these presents shall come, Greeting—

"Be it known that we, the constituted authorities of The Church of Jesus Christ of Latter-day Saints, assembled in Conference at Nauvoo, Hancock County, and state of Illinois, on the sixth day of April, in the year of our Lord, one thousand eight hundred and forty, considering an important event at hand, an event involving the interest and fate of the Gentile nations throughout the world.... The Jewish nations have been scattered abroad among the Gentiles for a long period; and in our estimation, the time of the commencement of their return to the Holy Land has already arrived. As this scattered and persecuted people are set among the Gentiles as a sign unto them of the second coming of the Messiah, and also of the overthrow of the present kingdoms and governments of the earth, by the potency of His Almighty arm in scattering famine and pestilence like the frosts and snows of winter, and sending the sword with nation against nation to bathe it in each other's blood; it is highly important,...that the present views and movements of the Jewish people be sought after and laid before the American people, for their consideration, their profit and their learning.

Elder Hyde Instructed to Converse with the Priests, Rulers, and Elders of the Jews

"And feeling it to be our duty to employ the most efficient means in our power to save the children of men from "the abomination that maketh desolate," we have, by the counsel of the Holy Spirit, appointed Elder Orson Hyde, the bearer of these presents, a faithful and worthy minister of Jesus Christ, to be our Agent and

Representative in foreign lands, to visit the cities of London, Amsterdam, Constantinople, and Jerusalem; and also other places that he may deem expedient; and converse with the priests, rulers, and elders of the Jews, and obtain from them all the information possible, and communicate the same to some principal paper for publication, that it may have a general circulation throughout the United States.

"As Mr. Hyde has willingly and cheerfully accepted the appointment to become our servant and the servant of the public in distant and foreign countries, for Christ's sake, we do confidently recommend him to all religious and Christian people, and to gentlemen and ladies making no profession, as a worthy member of society, possessing much zeal to promote the happiness of mankind, fully believing that they will be forward to render him all the pecuniary aid he needs to accomplish this laborious and hazardous mission for the general good of the human family.

"Ministers of every denomination upon whom Mr. Hyde shall call, are requested to hold up his hands, and aid him by their influence, with an assurance that such as do this shall have the prayers and blessings of a poor and afflicted people, whose blood has flowed to test the depths of their sincerity and to crimson the face of freedom's soil with martyr's blood.

"Mr. Hyde is instructed by this Conference to transmit to this country nothing but simple facts for publication, entirely disconnected with any peculiar views of theology, leaving each class to make their own comments and draw their own inferences.

"Given under our hands at the time and place before mentioned.

Joseph Smith, Jun., Chairman
Robert B. Thompson, Clerk"

(Joseph Smith, *History of The Church of Jesus Christ of Latter-day Saints,* Salt Lake City: Deseret News, 1948, Vol. 4, pp. 112-113. Hereafter cited as *HC.*)

Two Apostles Sent on Mission to Palestine

Within the month of April, 1840, two Mormon Apostles had commenced their mission to Palestine to dedicate the land and signal the day for the return of the Jews to the Holy Land.

"To the world, the very idea was imprudent—a tiny band of religionists on the western frontier of the United States announcing to the world the time had come for the gathering of the Jews." (*Deseret News,* Church News, May 12, 1973, p. 16.)

Hyde and Page Traveled Without Purse or Scrip

The financial situation of the missionaries required they travel without purse or scrip and therefore, required them to work and solicit financial assistance for their mission. At Philadelphia, Pennsylvania, Elder John E. Page lost the spirit of the mission and Orson continued on alone. It is to the credit of Orson Hyde that he had the faith and courage to continue on alone facing the hazards to life and health on sea and in distant foreign lands. On board ship Orson wrote "I have not time to tell you how many days I have been at sea, without food, or how many snails I have eaten; but if I had had plenty of them, I should have done very well."

During his travels Orson met many notable personalities, some of whom were amazed and interested in his mission. He enjoyed his travels through Europe and while waiting for his visa in Munich, learned to write and speak German fluently in eight days.

He encountered the most dangerous part of his mission in the unsettled and war torn Middle East. "At the time I was in Beyroot (sic), a battle was fought in the mountains of Lebanon, near that place, and about 800 killed."

Orson Climbed to the Top of the Mount of Olives

Tired and weary after several months' travel of nearly 10,000 miles, Orson's enthusiasm was revitalized as he finally arrived at the sacred city of Jerusalem. Here he carefully walked along the dark, narrow street avoiding the heavily loaded camels who traveled toward him. In the early morning hour, he passed through the ancient gate in the old decayed wall toward the brook, Kidron. As Orson crossed over the small brook and climbed up the gentle slope of the hill, the bright rays of sunshine encompassed the Mount of Olives. It was a magnificent sight as he gazed upon the surrounding countryside from the top of the mount.

Palestine Dedicated for the Return of the Jews on October 24, 1841

There alone, on Sunday, October 24, 1841, "in solemn silence, with pen, ink, and paper, just as I saw in the vision," Orson wrote and offered the prayer dedicating Palestine for the return of the Jews and for the building of a temple in the future. In our day, the prayer is in the process of being fulfilled as its contents indicate:

"On Sunday morning, October 24, a good while before day, I [Orson Hyde] arose from sleep, and went out of the city as soon as the gates were opened, crossed the brook Kedron, and went upon the Mount of Olives, and there, in solemn silence, with pen, ink, and paper, just as I saw in the vision, offered up the following prayer to Him who lives forever and ever—

Prayer of Orson Hyde on the Mount of Olives

'O Thou! who art from everlasting to everlasting, eternally and unchangeably the same, even the God who rules in the heavens above, and controls the destinies of men on the earth, wilt Thou not condescend, through thine infinite goodness and royal favor, to listen to the prayer of Thy servant which he this day offers up unto Thee in the name of Thy holy child Jesus, upon this land, where the Sun of Righteousness set in blood, and thine Anointed One expired.

'Be pleased, O Lord, to forgive all the follies, weaknesses, vanities, and sins of Thy servant, and strengthen him to resist all future temptations. Give him prudence and discernment that he may avoid the evil, and a heart to choose the good; give him fortitude to bear up under trying and adverse circumstances, and grace to endure all things for Thy name's sake, until the end shall come, when all the Saints shall rest in peace.

'Now, O Lord! Thy servant has been obedient to the heavenly vision which Thou gavest him in his native land; and under the shadow of Thine outstretched arm, he has safely arrived in this place to dedicate and consecrate this land unto Thee, for the gathering together of Judah's scattered remnants, according to the predictions of the holy Prophets—for the building up of Jerusalem again after it has been trodden down by the Gentiles so long, and for rearing a Temple in honor of Thy name. Everlasting thanks be ascribed unto Thee, O Father, Lord of heaven and earth, that Thou hast preserved Thy servant from the dangers of the seas, and from the plague and pestilence which have caused the land to mourn. The violence of man has also been restrained, and Thy providential care by night and by day has been exercised over Thine unworthy servant. Accept, therefore, O Lord, the tribute of a grateful heart for all past favors, and be pleased to continue Thy kindness and mercy towards a needy worm of the dust.

'O Thou, Who didst covenant with Abraham, Thy friend, and Who didst renew that covenant with Isaac, and confirm the same with Jacob with an oath, that Thou wouldst not only give them this land for an everlasting inheritance, but that Thou wouldst also remember their seed forever. Abraham, Isaac, and Jacob have long since closed their eyes in death, and made the grave their mansion. Their children are scattered and dispersed abroad among the nations of the Gentiles like sheep that have no shepherd, and are still looking forward for the fulfillment of those promises which Thou didst make concerning them; and even this land, which once poured forth nature's richest bounty, and flowed, as it were, with milk and honey, has, to a certain extent, been smitten with barrenness and sterility since it drank from murderous hands the blood of Him who never sinned.

'Grant, therefore, O Lord, in the name of Thy well-beloved Son, Jesus Christ, to remove the barrenness and sterility of this land, and let springs of living water break forth to water its thirsty soil. Let the vine and olive produce in their strength, and the fig-tree bloom and flourish. Let the land become abundantly fruitful when possessed by its rightful heirs; let it again flow with plenty to feed the returning prodigals who come home with a spirit of grace and supplication; upon it let the clouds distil virtue and richness, and let the fields smile with plenty. Let the flocks and the herds greatly increase and multiply upon the mountains and the hills; and let Thy great kindness conquer and subdue the unbelief of Thy people. Do Thou take from them their stony heart, and give them a heart of flesh; and may the Sun of Thy favor dispel the cold mists of darkness which have beclouded their atmosphere. Incline them to gather in upon this land according to Thy word. Let them come like clouds and like doves to their windows. Let the large ships of the nations bring them from the distant isles; and let kings become their nursing fathers, and queens with motherly fondness wipe the tear of sorrow from their eye.

'Thou, O Lord, did once move upon the heart of Cyrus to show favor unto Jerusalem and her children. Do Thou now also be pleased to inspire the hearts of kings and the powers of the earth to look with a friendly eye towards this place, and with a desire to see Thy righteous purposes executed in relation thereto. Let them know that it is Thy good pleasure to restore the kingdom unto Israel—raise up Jerusalem as its capital, and constitute her people a distinct nation and government, with David Thy servant, even a descendant from the loins of ancient David to be their king.

'Let that nation or that people who shall take an active part in behalf of Abraham's children, and in the raising up of Jerusalem, find favor in Thy sight. Let not their enemies prevail against them, neither let pestilence or famine overcome them, but let the glory of Israel overshadow them, and the power of the Highest protect them; while that nation or kingdom that will not serve Thee in this glorious work must perish, according to Thy word—'Yea, those nations shall be utterly wasted.'

'Though Thy servant is now far from his home, and from the land bedewed with his earliest tear, yet he remembers, O Lord, his friends who are there, and family, whom for Thy sake he has left. Though poverty and privation be our earthly lot, yet ah! do Thou richly endow us with an inheritance where moth and rust do not corrupt, and where thieves do not break through and steal.

'The hands that have fed, clothed, or shown favor unto the family of Thy servant in his absence, or that shall hereafter do so, let them not lose their reward, but let a special blessing rest upon them, and in Thy kingdom let them have an inheritance when Thou shalt come to be glorified in this society.

'Do Thou also look with favor upon all those through whose liberality I have been enabled to come to this land; and in the day when Thou shalt reward all people according to their works, let these also not be passed by or forgotten, but in time let them be in readiness to enjoy the glory of those mansions which Jesus has gone to prepare. Particularly do Thou bless the stranger in Philadelphia, whom I never saw, but who sent me gold, with a request that I should pray for him in Jerusalem. Now, O Lord, let blessings come upon him from an unexpected quarter, and let his basket be filled, and his storehouse abound with plenty, and let not the good things of the earth be his only portion, but let him be found among those to whom it shall be said, 'Thou hast been faithful over a few things, and I will make thee ruler over many.'

'O my Father in heaven! I now ask Thee in the name of Jesus to remember Zion, with all her Stakes, and with all her assemblies. She has been grievously afflicted and smitten; she has mourned; she has wept; her enemies have triumphed, and have said, 'Ah, where is thy God?' Her Priests and Prophets have groaned in chains and fetters within the gloomy walls of prisons, while many were slain, and now sleep in the arms of death. How long, O Lord, shall iniquity triumph, and sin go unpunished?

'Do Thou arise in the majesty of Thy strength, and make bare Thine arm in behalf of Thy people. Redress their wrongs, and turn their sorrow into joy. Pour the spirit of light and knowledge, grace and wisdom, into the hearts of her Prophets, and clothe her Priests with salvation. Let light and knowledge march forth through the empire of darkness, and may the honest in heart flow to their standard, and join in the march to go forth to meet the Bridegroom.

'Let a peculiar blessing rest upon the Presidency of Thy Church, for at them are the arrows of the enemy directed. Be Thou to them a sun and a shield, their strong tower and hiding place; and in the time of distress or danger be Thou near to deliver. Also the quorum of the Twelve, do Thou be pleased to stand by them for Thou knowest the obstacles which they have to encounter, the temptations to which they are exposed, and the privations which they must suffer. Give us [the Twelve], therefore, strength according to our day, and help us to bear a faithful testimony of Jesus and His Gospel, to finish with fidelity and honor the work which Thou hast given us to do, and then give us a place in Thy glorious kingdom. And let this blessing rest upon every faithful officer and member in Thy Church. And all the glory and honor will we ascribe unto God and the Lamb forever and ever. Amen.'

"On the top of Mount Olives I erected a pile of stones as a witness according to ancient custom. On what was anciently called Mount Zion [Moriah?], where the Temple stood, I erected another, and used the rod according to the prediction upon my head.

"I have found many Jews who listened with intense interest. The idea of the Jews being restored to Palestine is gaining ground in Europe almost every day. Jerusalem is strongly fortified with many cannon upon its walls. The wall is ten feet thick on the sides that would be most exposed, and four or five feet where the descent from the wall is almost perpendicular. The number of inhabitants within the walls is about twenty thousand. About seven thousand of this number are Jews, the balance being mostly Turks and Armenians. Many of the Jews who are old go to this place to die, and many are coming from Europe into this eastern world. The great wheel is unquestionably in motion, and the word of the Almighty has declared that it shall roll.

"I have not time to write particulars now, but suffice it to say that my mission has been quite as prosperous as I could expect.

"I am now about to go on board a fine ship for Trieste, and from thence I intend to proceed to Regensburg and there publish our faith in the German language. There are those who are ready and willing to assist me.

"I send you this letter by Captain Withers, an English gentleman, who goes direct to England, on board the Oriental steamer. He has come with me from Jerusalem. If I had money sufficient I should be almost tempted to take passage on board of her to England, but this I cannot do.

"On receipt of this, I wish you to write to me immediately, and direct to Regensburg, on the Danube, Bayern, or Bavaria. If you know anything of my family tell me.

"My best respects to yourself and your family, to Brothers Adams and Snow, and to all the Saints in England.

"May grace, mercy and peace, from God our Father, and from the Lord Jesus Christ, rest upon you all from this time, henceforth and for ever. Amen.

Your brother in Christ,
Orson Hyde"

"For the first time in 1800 years, an Apostle stood again on the Mount of Olives." After his prayer, Orson Hyde built two stone altars patterned after those of ancient Israel for memorials. The first memorial was on the Mount of Olives and the second on Mt. Moriah.

The significance of Orson Hyde's mission to Palestine is emphasized by the following statement of President B. H. Roberts: "The mission appointed to Elders Orson Hyde and John E. Page, of the quorum of the Twelve, to Jerusalem, was second in importance only to that appointed to the rest of the Twelve to Great Britain." (*HC* 4:xxxi.)

Importance of the Palestine Mission

The results from this mission may be answered by an investigation of the facts. Orson Hyde had traveled 20,000 miles to fulfill a mission call for his beloved Church, which was probably one of the longest and most hazardous missions undertaken in this dispensation. Many events have taken place and others are presently being fulfilled and will continue to be as the time scale of the restoration of Israel is completed in accordance "to the favor and blessing of God."

President B.H. Roberts explained:

"I have called the attention of my readers to this mission of Apostle Hyde to Jerusalem, because it doubtless has a greater significance than most people would be inclined to give to it. The rebuilding of Jerusalem is regarded by Mormonism as of as much importance as the establishment of Zion; the gathering of the dispersed of Judah is as much a part of the great latter-day work as the reassembling of the other tribes of Israel; and the commencement of that work was made by Apostle Hyde, when by the authority of his apostleship, he consecrated that land to the return of the house of Judah, to inhabit it, and rebuild their city according to the predictions of their prophets; and it will yet be said that Orson Hyde was called to lay the foundation of a great work—how great, men at present know not.[1] (Brigham H. Roberts, *The Contributor,* 8:161-162, March 1887.)

---

1. For additional information on the life and mission of Orson Hyde, the reader is referred to the author's book entitled, *Orson Hyde—Missionary, Apostle, Colonizer,* Horizon Publishers, Bountiful, Utah, 1977.

George A. Smith Called to Rededicate Palestine

"President George A. Smith:

Dear Sir: — As you are about to start on an extensive tour through Europe and Asia Minor, where you will doubtless be brought in contact with men of position and influence in society, we desire that you observe closely what openings now exist, or where they may be effected for the introduction of the Gospel into the various countries you shall visit.

"When you go to the Land of Palestine, we wish you to dedicate and consecrate that land to the Lord, that it may be blessed with fruitfulness, preparatory to the return of the Jews in fulfillment of prophecy, and the accomplishment of the purposes of our Heavenly Father.

"We pray that you may be preserved to travel in peace and safety, that you may be abundantly blessed with words of wisdom and free utterance in all your conversations pertaining to the Holy Gospel, dispelling prejudice, and sowing seeds of righteousness among the people.

Brigham Young
Daniel H. Wells"

(Brigham Young, *Correspondence of Palestine Tourists,* Salt Lake City, Utah, pp. 1-2, October 15, 1872.)

...The Latter-day Saints had been driven from the beautiful city which they had created in the wilderness on the east bank of the Mississippi to the heart of the Great American Desert, where they had again established themselves in comfortable and prosperous homes. Even in the midst of their deepest poverty and sufferings they never lost interest in the welfare of the Jews, and when at length they found themselves in a position to do so, they made a second move, of great importance and significance from their standpoint, towards the political and spiritual redemption of that race.

George A. Smith, counselor to Brigham Young in the First Presidency of The Church of Jesus Christ of Latter-day Saints, accompanied by a party of elders and sisters, left Salt Lake City, Utah, in October 1872, bound for Palestine. The object of the expedition was to again supplicate the blessings of the Lord of Hosts upon that land, beseech Him to speedily gather to it His ancient covenant people, and again solemnly dedicate it for this purpose. (Anonymous, Future of the Jews, *Liahona* 6:233-236, August 22, 1908.)

George A. Smith and Party on the Mount of Olives

Sunday morning, March 2nd, 1873, President Smith made arrangements with our dragoman, and had a tent, table, seats and carpet taken up on the Mount of Olives, to which all the brethren of the company and myself repaired on horseback. After dismounting on the summit, and committing our animals to the care of servants, we visited the Church of Ascension, a small cathedral, said to stand on the spot from which Jesus ascended. By this time the tent was prepared, which we entered, and after an opening prayer by Brother Carrington, we united in service in the order of the Holy Priesthood, President Smith leading in humble, fervent supplication, dedicating the land of Palestine for the gathering of the Jews and the rebuilding of Jerusalem, and returning heartfelt thanks and gratitude to God for the fulness of the Gospel and the blessings bestowed on the Latter-day Saints. Other brethren led in turn, and we had a very interesting season; to me it seemed the crowning point of the whole tour, realizing as I [Eliza R. Snow] did that we were worshipping on the summit of the sacred Mount, once the frequent resort of the Prince of Life. (Eliza R. Snow, "Letter 65," *Correspondence of Palestine Tourists,* Nazareth, March 9, 1873, p. 260.)

George A. Smith Described Conditions in Palestine and the Fulfillment of Many Prophecies

I have visited the land of Palestine, on which God revealed himself to Abraham, Isaac and Jacob. He promised that land to them and their seed for ever. It was to this land that Moses led the children of Israel, and upon which God promised them very great blessings if they would live in obedience to his laws and commandments.

Any one who will attentively read the 27th, 28th, 29th and 30th chapters of Deuteronomy, will see foreshadowed, in plain language, the entire history of the children of Israel from the days of Moses to the present time; and in Palestine he will see the fulfillment of many of the prophecies contained in those chapters, with a minutiae that is really astonishing. Some men say they are infidels because that country is barren, sterile, rocky—a vast limestone quarry, and could never have sustained such a population as the Bible represents it to have done. Others are infidel because they believe that so many kingdoms that are said to have once existed on that land could not have existed in so small a compass. But these querists and unbelievers do not realize that the barrenness, desolation, scanty population and condition of affairs which now exist there is a fulfillment, to the very letter, of the prophecies of Moses, the holy Prophets and of Jesus and the Apostles. God required certain things of Israel. If they complied, it was all right with them; if they failed, the catalogue of curses contained in the chapters I have referred to was pronounced upon their heads. Read the Bible and you will find that when they were obedient, they were blessed, their lands were blessed, their armies were blessed, they were a great nation, they were able to resist the power of neighboring nations, they were courted, they were looked up to, neighboring nations paid them tribute. But when they refused to do that which the law of God required at their hands, they lost this power—they fell into the hands of their enemies, they quarrelled among themselves, they fell into darkness, married the daughters of aliens, worshipped strange gods, and they were finally broken up. Many of them were sold as slaves, some of them were compelled to eat their own children to save them from starvation, in the midst of the straits and sieges to which they were forced by their enemies. They were scattered to the four winds of heaven, they were sold in the slave market of Egypt, until they could not be bought, that is, there was no man to buy them. All these terrible judgments fell upon the Jewish nation, yet they were not utterly destroyed, a remnant was all the time preserved, and today, in every nation under heaven is found a remnant of the seed of Israel, retaining the Hebrew language, many of their ancient manners and customs, their old law written on parchment, which is read in their synagogues every Sabbath day. In nearly all the countries in which they have been scattered they have been subject to the most extreme abuse. They have been in constant fear, they have been permitted to reside only in certain quarters, and have had imposed upon them the most fearful exactions....

Where are the inhabitants of Babylon and Nineveh? The city of Babylon was fifteen miles square, sixty in circuit. According to Herodotus, it was surrounded with a wall three hundred and fifty feet high, and eighty-seven thick, flanked with over two hundred towers, and contained palaces and hanging gardens that were the wonder of the world. It is almost doubtful now, where this once famous city stood, and the vicinity in which it is believed to have stood, is a vast marsh, rendering it difficult of access to any who may wish to visit it. And the Babylonians, where are they? Their descendants are so mixed up with the rest of the world, that none of them can be identified. You may trace other great nations of antiquity, and they have gone in the same way. But the Jews are still a distinct race, and they are a living record of the truth of the revelations of God.

There are a few thousand Jews in Jerusalem. They have synagogues and they are permitted to go to a portion of the old wall, which they suppose to be a remnant of the outside enclosure of Solomon's temple, and wail. A great many people who visit Jerusalem, go to witness their wailing. These Jews are graciously accorded the privilege, by the rulers of that country—the Turks—to wail over the desolation of Israel, provided they do not make so much noise as to disturb the neighborhood.

There are several other places, such as Mount Gerizim, a place in Samaria, considered holy, where a small sect of the ancient Samaritans meet annually. And in Tiberium, on the lake of Galilee, two or three thousand Jews live. It is the Tiberias of Herod the Tetrarch; they consider that a holy place. The Jews are broken up into sects and parties, and in almost every town in Palestine, you find a few of them, oppressed, poor and despised, there, as elsewhere, living monuments of the fulfillment of prophecy....

An Interview with Chief Jewish Rabbi, Abraham Askenasi

While I was passing through Palestine, I had some very serious reflections as to the causes which had operated to reduce the country to its present barren condition, and why the descendants of Jacob were so oppressed, and, as an independent nation, blotted out. In an interview with the venerable Chief Rabbi, Abram Askenasi, I enquired for the ten tribes. Said he, "We have no idea where they are, but we believe they will be found, and will return and inherit their land." While traveling in Palestine I reflected a good deal on the fate of Israel. I asked myself, why they were persecuted, scattered, peeled and hidden from the face of men, and why were the tribes of Judah and Benjamin still scattered? Some of them can go to Jerusalem occasionally and visit, but only a very few thousand live, in a scattered condition, in the land of their fathers, and they are in bondage, under tutors, governors, and rulers, and have in reality no power of themselves. Rabbi Askenasi said they had more liberty than heretofore. The Christian Powers have...taken a course which has modified the action of the Turks toward them. They were now permitted to buy land, but they were poor and could buy but little, and he wished the Jews of all nations to contribute to enable the Jews of Jerusalem to extend the area of their possessions. They had purchased a piece of land in Jerusalem, and were building on it a home for widows and orphans.

Children of Israel Failed to Obey the Law of God

Now I saw this degradation with which Israel [was] visited. Where did it begin? It was simply because the children of Israel failed to obey the law of God. If we search the Bible, we shall find many references by the Prophets to this subject, which are very plain and clear. In the third chapter of Malachi, and eighth verse, the Prophet, speaking of the condition of Israel in his day, uses this singular language, or rather the Lord, speaking through the Prophet, says—"Will a man rob God? Yet ye have robbed me. But ye say, Wherein have we robbed thee? In tithes and offerings. Ye are cursed with a curse: for ye have robbed me, even this whole nation."

Now, God required of Israel tithes and offerings. He blessed them with land and with abundant rains. He made their land exceedingly fertile; he blessed them with flocks, with herds, and with everything on the face of the earth seemingly that they could desire. He gave them wealth in every direction; he gave them power over their neighbors—they were the head and not the tail. In return for all this, what did he require of them? He required them to pay tithes and make offerings. Tithes meant one-tenth of all their increase. One-tenth of all this the Lord required them to place in the hands of the Levites and those whom he had selected to look after the general welfare. In addition to this tenth he also required certain offerings. You may trace the history of the Jewish nation through and you will find that when the people paid their tithes and offerings, and thereby acknowledged their dependence upon and allegiance to the God of heaven, they were prospered and blessed continually. While they did this they were not running after other gods, making golden calves, setting up idols, or worshipping the gods of their heathen neighbors. (George A. Smith, *JD,* June 27, 1873, pp. 103-106.)

It isn't the intent of this chapter to give a lengthy account of the missions to the Near East. A few missions were selected to give the reader an awareness of the great interest of the Church in sharing the gospel with the children of Israel.

Mormon Missionaries in the Near East

Perhaps as early as 1884 Mormon missionaries were having limited success in their proselyting efforts in the Near East. They had aspirations of establishing a Mormon colony in Palestine for their Turkish and Armenian converts and any others. This plan of temporal and spiritual development was never fulfilled. The "decaying Ottoman Empire" festering with its numerous political and social restrictions was a great hindrance to the Mormon proselyting program. It also hampered the spiritual growth and development of the few converts and emigration was unthinkable except for the wealthy, who could afford to bribe the corrupt officials to permit them to leave the country.

Elder Anthon H. Lund Called on Special Mission to the Near East

The newspaper account stated that Apostle, Anthon H. Lund would depart on a special mission to Palestine and other parts of Asia Minor on December 30, 1897. Elder F. F. Hintze, a former missionary in the Turkish mission would accompany him. The article explained the primary purpose of the mission was to persuade the Turkish government to grant permission for a gathering place for the Saints in Turkey. (*Deseret News,* December 29, 1897, p. 4.)

Francis M. Lyman and Sylvester Q. Cannon Visited the Holy Land

In a letter dated March 16, 1902, addressed to President Joseph F. Smith, Elder Lyman described his visit in Egypt, Beirut, Jaffa, Jericho, and other interesting sites. Like Orson Hyde, George A. Smith, Lorenzo Snow, and Anthon H. Lund, he was impressed to offer a prayer on the Mount of Olives. On their knees in the solemnity of a young cypress forest Elders Lyman, Cannon and Herman prayed for the redemption of Judah, Jerusalem, and the fulfillment of the words of Isaiah, the Savior and "other ancient prophets."

They blessed the land, the people, and that a way be "opened up for the preaching of the Gospel in all nations." (Albert R. Lyman, *Francis Marion Lyman,* edited and published by Melvin A. Lyman, M.D.; Delta, Utah, 1958. Also Francis M. Lyman, *Journal History,* p. 12, March 16, 1902.)

James E. Talmage Visited Palestine

During the visit of Elder Talmage to the Holy Land in 1927, he was accompanied by Joseph W. Booth, President of the Armenian Mission. While in Haifa, they visited the cemetery where Elders John A. Clark and Adolph Haag were buried. They had died over thirty years previous to this time, while serving as missionaries in Palestine.

On Mount Carmel, Tuesday morning the 18th of October, President Talmage knelt on bended knees and dedicated the city of Haifa "for a central place of mission labour, and confirmed all the former dedicatory prayers pertaining to the Holy Land, including Syria and adjacent country." (Joseph W. Booth, *MS,* November 17, 1927, from a letter written by Joseph W. Booth, President of the Armenian Mission, on October 23, 1927.)

John A. Widtsoe Toured the Holy Land in 1933

Human history has been tremendously influenced by inhabitants of the tiny land of Palestine. It is the homeland of Abraham, who made a covenant with the Lord of Heaven. It is a promised land and was once a mighty center and fountain of spiritual truth and oratory by the ancient prophets of God. It is becoming a land of fulfillment as "the Jewry of the world have set their hands to the redemption of their homeland." Their determination and undaunted courage in building up their homeland "is one of the most interesting experiments of modern times."

Elder Widtsoe in common with those who had preceded him on previous missions possessed the same feelings of love and concern for the covenant people of the Lord in this mighty land. Jerusalem like all the rest of the world needs the enlightening and strengthening influence of the Gospel of Jesus of Nazareth. With the pleading echo of the message of the Savior in his soul, Elder Widtsoe wrote, "We gathered under a noble olive tree, on the mount where the Master often taught, and prayed to God that the restored truth might be prospered for the good of men in the Promised Land. (John A. Widtsoe, *Deseret News,* July 29, 1933.)

The Lord Has Watched Over the Nations for His Purposes

...There are nations in which that blood predominates, nations which the Lord has magnified which He has made the foundation for Christian development and decent government in modern times. His hand has been over that family, that race, wherever they have been, wherever they are now or may be. God our Father is watching over them and they will be redeemed and will come to Zion, this land of Zion. You know what we say in our articles of faith: "We believe in the literal gathering of Israel and in the restoration of the Ten Tribes; that Zion will be built upon this continent; that the earth will be renewed and receive its paradisiacal glory; and that Christ (our Lord) will reign personally upon the earth," over His people, and will bring with Him a period of peace, fraternity and good will, the like of which this earth of ours has never before known.

That is what the Lord contemplates doing through the Church and its members. He will accomplish it, and He will use nations to do it, just as he used people who were not at that time identified with His church (for it did not exist upon the earth), to lay the foundations of this government of which we form a part—the best in the world, notwithstanding all of its shortcomings and weaknesses.

Abraham's Children are in Every Country and Must be Searched Out and Taught the Gospel

We are all of Abrahamic descent, and people of Abrahamic descent are in every country in the world today. They were scattered broadcast. They went into China. Records have been discovered which definitely tell us that a part of those people, after they left Assyria, after they broke away from the captivity in which the Assyrians had held them for centuries and went into other lands, some of them spread out and went over into China. There is a part of China today in which the inhabitants are recognized as Jews by students who have made a study of the question. They are Chinese, of course, but they are Jews in their habits, they are Jews in their appearance, and the roots of their language are Jewish to the present time. They are known as China Jews. Records have been found, dug up from the tombs, that tell us definitely that some of these people did go into China. It is another interesting thing to know that some philosopher or student in Japan...has set up a claim that a part of the Japanese people are descended from the Ten

Tribes of Israel. That is a thing which has not yet been generally recognized or admitted, but it may be true.

Israelitish People to be a Dominant Factor in the World

...I have...become...familiar with the history and story of the Israelitish people from the day that the Lord entered into covenant with Abraham until the present...God will make them the dominant factor in this world of ours, and it appears that the time is very near when those things are going to be done, if we are to judge by the signs which He gave us, and depend upon the word of Christ our Lord entirely rather than the words or conclusions of scholars and men. We know just what is going to happen before His coming, and we know that many of those things are happening, and we know that He tells us that when we see these things we may know that His coming is near at hand, even at the doors. Another thing which He tells us, which is not so pleasing, is that these things which we are experiencing now are just beginning of sorrows, so we may be prepared for tribulations, for trials, all that our souls can stand. Then will come the day of redemption. (Anthony W. Ivins, *Utah Genealogical and Historical Magazine,* 23:1-9, October 1, 1931.)

Latter-day Saints Possess a Good Attitude Toward the Jewish People

There should be no ill-will, and I am sure there is none, in the heart of any true Latter-day Saint, toward the Jewish people. By the authority of the Holy Priesthood of God, that has again been restored to the earth, and by the ministration, under the direction of the Prophet of God, Apostles of the Lord Jesus Christ have been to the Holy Land and have dedicated that country for the return of the Jews: and we believe that in the due time of the Lord they shall be in the favor of God again. And let no Latter-day Saint be guilty of taking any part in any crusade against these people. I believe in no other part of the world is there as good a feeling in the hearts of mankind towards the Jewish people as among the Latter-day Saints. (Heber J. Grant, *CR,* p. 124, April 4, 1921.)

Chapter 6

The Times of the Gentiles

And this I have told you concerning Jerusalem; and when that day shall come, shall a remnant be scattered among all nations; But they shall be gathered again; but they shall remain until the times of the Gentiles be fulfilled. And in that day shall be heard of wars and rumors of wars, and the whole earth shall be in commotion, and men's hearts shall fail them, and they shall say that Christ delayeth his coming until the end of the earth. And the love of men shall wax cold, and iniquity shall abound. And when the times of the Gentiles is come in, a light shall break forth among them that sit in darkness, and it shall be the fulness of my gospel; But they receive it not; for they perceive not the light, and they turn their hearts from me because of the precepts of man. And in that generation shall the times of the Gentiles be fulfilled. (D&C 45:23-30.)

We have seen Joseph begin to reach out to his brother. We have watched Orson Hyde, George A. Smith and others pray for the return of the Jews. They have begun to return, but they cannot fully return to the true God until the time of the Gentiles is full, for God has declared that the first shall be last and the last shall be first. Let us examine this divine decree through the window of inspiration.

Brigham Young Defined the Term Gentile

I want, now, to say a few words with regard to a term that is frequently used in our midst. I refer to the term "Gentile." I have explained this a great many times to the Elders both in public and in private, and I was surprised at the use made of the term this afternoon. "Gentile," or "gentilism," applies only to those who reject the gospel, and will not submit to and receive the plan of salvation. Will you remember this? It does not apply to any only those who are opposed to God and His Kingdom. When the Jews, as a nation, were in their glory, they called the nations around them Gentiles. Why? Because they were opposed to the laws and precepts that the Lord, through Abraham, Isaac, Jacob and Moses, had revealed for the guidance of Israel. But it does not apply to this or any other nation, simply because they are not of our faith; and in fact, in these days, on account of their conduct, the term could be more properly applied to the Jews than to any other people; but it does not apply to them for they are of the chosen seed. Among the nations of the earth there is a great mixture, but there are many millions that we shall yet gather into this Church.

The Use of the Term "Gentile" is clarified

Remember this, O, ye Elders of Israel, and do not apply the term "Gentile" to a man because he is not baptized. There are some of pure gentile blood who will come into this Church. There are a few already, but very few. When a person of real gentile blood, through honesty of heart, submits to the gospel and is baptized and receives the laying on of hands from a man duly authorized, you might naturally suppose, from the contortions of the muscles, that such a person had a fit, for the power of the Holy Ghost falls upon and renovates that rebellious blood and stirs it up, and perhaps the person thus administered to falls prostrate on the floor. I have seen this, and it is in consequence of the power of the Holy Ghost operating upon the power of the enemy within the individual. Whoever has been in our Councils would never make the application of "Gentile" to a man or woman, simply because he or she was not baptized, for that has nothing to do with it either one way or the other. I want the brethren to learn this, and everything that is useful. (Brigham Young, *JD* 12:270-271, August 16, 1868.)

The Gospel was Restored to the Gentiles Because of Their Faithfulness

...The gospel is now restored to us Gentiles for we are all Gentiles in a national capacity, and it will continue with us if we are faithful, until the law is bound, and the testimony is sealed and the times of the Gentiles are fulfilled, when it will again revert to the Jews. (Wilford Woodruff, *JD* 18:220, August 13, 1876.)

When the Gentiles reject the gospel, it will be taken from them and go to the House of Israel.... They will rebuild Jerusalem.... They are held now from this work only because the fulness of the Gentiles has not yet come in. (Wilford Woodruff, *JD* 2:200, February 25, 1855.)

How many times have I seen them [the Jews],...their faces to the east, calling on the great Eloheim to open the door for them to go back to Jerusalem, the land of their fathers, and to send their Shiloh, their king of deliverance. When I have seen this, my soul has been filled with a desire to proclaim unto them the word of God unto eternal life, but I knew I could not do this, the time had not come, I could not preach to them. (Wilford Woodruff, *JD* 4:232, February 22, 1857.)

An army of Elders will be sent to the four corners of the earth to seek out the righteous and warn the wicked of what is coming.... The judgment of God will be poured out upon the wicked to the extent that our elders will be taken from the Gentiles and later on carried to the Jews. (Heber C. Kimball, *Deseret Weekly,* May 23, 1851.)

Fulfilling of the Times of the Gentiles

We believe,...that before the times of the Gentiles can possibly be fulfilled, a proclamation must come from heaven and be sounded in their ears—namely, that an angel must come from heaven and bring the everlasting Gospel, not for the Jews, the descendants of Israel, alone, but for every nation, kindred, tongue, and people. Gentiles and Jews, all must hear it, for the prediction is that when the angel comes forth with that message from heaven, it is to be preached to all nations, kindreds, tongues, and people. This, of course, includes Gentiles as well as Jews. We cannot, therefore, suppose that the times of the Gentiles will be fulfilled until after that event takes place. When the angel comes, when the servants of God are sent forth by Divine authority with a proclamation and have fulfilled that prediction by declaring the everlasting Gospel to all the nations and kingdoms of the Gentiles, then their times will be fulfilled, and not before.

How many more years will pass over our heads that we will have the privilege of declaring the fullness of the everlasting Gospel among the nations of the Gentiles is not revealed. All that we know on the subject is what the Lord told us some forty years ago, that the times of the Gentiles would be fulfilled in the generation in which he established his Church, that is, that before the generation living forty years ago have all passed away the times of the Gentiles will be fulfilled. And what then? The prediction of Isaiah, in another place, will be literally fulfilled—the "Law will be bound up and the testimony sealed" so far as sending the Gospel to the Gentile nations is concerned. (Orson Pratt, *JD* 14:61-62, March 26, 1871.)

The Tame and Wild Olive Tree Allegory

This fulfillment of the times of the Gentiles is something to which I wish to call special attention.... In what matter will the Lord fulfill this work among the Gentiles, that the fullness of their times may come in? We have a little information on this subject, recorded in the eleventh chapter of Romans, which makes the subject very plain in regard to the two great classes of people—the Jews and the Gentiles. They are spoken of in that chapter under the figure of two olive trees, one—the House of Israel—being represented by a tame olive tree, and the other—the Gentiles—by a wild olive tree. Paul, in speaking of the branches of Israel, says—"If some of the branches be broken off and thou (the Gentiles), being a wild olive tree, were grafted in among them, and with them partakest of the root and fatness of the olive tree, boast not against the branches. But if thou boast thou bearest not the root, but the root thee. Thou (that is the Gentiles) wilt say then, the branches were broken off that I might be grafted in. Well, because of unbelief they were broken off, and thou standest by faith. Be not high-minded but fear, for if God spared not the natural branches, take heed lest he also spare not thee. Behold therefore the goodness and severity of God on them (meaning Israel) which feel severity; but towards thee (the Gentiles) goodness if thou continue in his goodness, otherwise thou also shalt be cut off. And they also (the House of Israel) if they abide not in unbelief shall be grafted in again, for God is able to graft them in again. For if thou (the Gentiles) were cut out of the olive tree which is wild by nature and were grafted contrary to nature into a good olive tree, how much more shall these, which be the natural branches, be grafted into their own olive tree? For I would not, brethren, that ye should be ignorant of this mystery, lest ye should be wise in your own conceits, that blindness in part is happened to Israel, until the fullness of the Gentiles be come in. And so all Israel shall be saved. As it is written, "There shall come out of Zion the Deliverer, and shall turn away ungodliness from Jacob. For this is my covenant unto them, when I shall take away their sins. As concerning the Gospel, they are enemies for your sakes; but as touching the election they are beloved for the fathers' sake." Again he says in the 30th and 31st verses—"For as ye in times past have not believed God, yet have now obtained mercy through their unbelief, even so have these now not believed, that through your mercy they also may obtain mercy."

Gentiles Were Grafted Into a Spiritual Kingdom

We can see from the instructions that Paul has given,...that the Gentiles were grafted in instead of the House of Israel; in other words, the Jews were broken off, as our Savior predicted to them. Said he—"Therefore say I unto you that the kingdom of God shall be taken from you, and shall be given to a nation bringing forth the fruits thereof." That is, it should be taken from the Israelites, and delivered over into the hands of the Gentiles. The kingdom that was thus rent from the Jews and transferred to the Gentiles may be called a spiritual kingdom, inasmuch as the Saints, to whom the kingdom was given in that day, did not form any particular constituent portion of the nations of the earth, but here was a branch, and there was a branch, one in one place another in another; having received the blessings of the fullness of the Gospel, the blessings of that spiritual kingdom which was built up in their midst, they partook of the fatness of the olive tree, though they were wild branches. But by and by we find the Gentiles following after the same example of unbelief; they to whom the kingdom had been transferred from Israel got into darkness, unbelief and apostacy, the same as the Jews had done before them. Paul further warns them...not to boast.

Why Were the Jews Broken Off?

...Like the ancient Jews, the Christians of the second and following centuries had apostatized, and were entirely destitute of the Spirit of God. The Jews had apostatized before Jesus came among them to that degree, that there were sects and parties among them, just as we find in the Christian world...and these Jewish sects were destitute of the spirit of prophecy which their ancient fathers had; they were destitute of the ministration of angels, and scarcely one feature existed which was among their fathers in the days of their righteousness. It was because of this that the Jews were broken off, and the Gentiles were grafted in, and were made partakers of the riches, blessings, and glories formerly enjoyed by the ancient Jews. (Orson Pratt, *JD* 16:341-345, January 25, 1874.)

Why Take the Gospel to Asia?

...In the fifth chapter of the Book of Jacob...is a parable. No greater parable was ever recorded. It is a parable of the scattering of Israel. The Lord revealed to Jacob that he would scatter Israel, and in this figure, Israel is a tame olive tree. It is an olive tree that begins to decay. The branches that are dying are cut off. But the gardener takes certain of those branches off that seem to be decaying and plants them in all parts of the Lord's vineyard. And the Lord says, "I will take these branches and plant them in the distant parts of my vineyard. Have my servants attend to them. The old tree seems to be dying and we shall see if we can't take these several branches and raise fruit."

Not only that, but they took some of the branches and grafted them in to all the wild olive trees. Who were the wild olive trees? The Gentiles. And so the Lord sent his servants to all parts of his vineyard, which is the world, and planted these branches of the tree. As they grew, they bore fruit. In the course of time, some of these branches began to wither and decay. And the Lord nurtured them. He had his servants dig around them, cultivate them, care for them the best they knew how, and yet some of them practically died. Others bore fruit. Then comes the times of the harvest. The Lord says, "I will cultivate my field for the last time. These branches that I have taken to various parts of the world are dying. I'll gather the fruit and do the best I can with them."

Now that in substance is the revelation given to Jacob. There is not a greater parable in the Bible or anywhere else, and yet we read it through and fail to grasp the meaning of it.

Now in that parable the olive tree is the House of Israel, as I have said. In its native land it began to die. So the Lord took branches like the Nephites, like the lost tribes, and like others that the Lord led off that we do not know anything about to other parts of the earth. He planted them all over his vineyard, which is the world. No doubt he sent some of these branches into Japan, into Korea, into China. No question about it, because he sent them to all parts of the world. (Joseph Fielding Smith, *Answers to Gospel Questions,* 4:203-205.)

Times of the Gentiles Not Fulfilled Until an Angel Brings the Gospel to all Nations, Kindreds, Tongues, and People

...The belief of the Latter-day Saints in regard to the fulfilling of the times of the Gentiles...is...that before the times of the Gentiles can possibly be fulfilled, a proclamation must come from heaven and be sounded in their ears—namely, that an angel must come from heaven and bring the everlasting Gospel, not for the Jews, the descendants of Israel, alone, but for every nation, kindred, tongue and people. Gentiles and Jews, all must hear it, for the prediction is that when the angel comes forth with that message from heaven, it is to be preached to all nations, kindreds, tongues, and people. This, of course, includes Gentiles as well as Jews. We cannot, therefore, suppose that the times of the Gentiles will be fulfilled until after that event takes place. When the angel comes, when the servants of God are sent forth by Divine authority with a proclamation, and have fulfilled that prediction by declaring the everlasting Gospel to all the nations and kingdoms of the Gentiles, then their times will be fulfilled, and not before.

Gospel to be Preached to the Gentiles and the Jews

What would be the use of sending the Gospel to the Gentiles if their times were fulfilled and there was no hope or chance for them to receive salvation? The very declaration—that an angel shall come forth with the Gospel in the latter days before the destruction of the wicked, and that that Gospel is to be preached to Gentiles as well as Jews, is proof and evidence to every reflecting mind that believes the Bible that the Gentiles will have an opportunity, until that message is delivered and the prediction concerning it fulfilled. When that is done the law is bound, the testimony is sealed, so far as they are concerned. (Orson Pratt, *JD* 14:61-62, March 26, 1871.)

Gospel Preached to Gentiles Until Every One is Warned and Testimony Sealed

The Lord has brought to light these ancient records, containing the fullness of the Gospel, which he has commanded to be preached and published to every nation and in every tongue upon the face of the earth, that all of his numerous children may have the opportunity to hear, and, through obedience to its requirements, may receive the Holy Ghost, the Comforter, which should reveal to them the mind and will of God concerning them, and lead them in the path of truth. This command strictly specifies that this Gospel is to be preached to all the world, but first to the Gentile nations, and when they are fully warned, and their times are fulfilled, then the Lord will declare the law and the testimony sealed, so far as preaching any more to them is concerned; and he will once more commission his servants to go to the Jews, the House of Israel, whom the Lord will prepare, through his own power and wisdom, to receive the message, and not reject it as they anciently did. Scores of thousands, among the different nations, have already received the ministry of the Gospel, revealed by the angel, and they have been filled with the Holy Ghost, according to the promise made to every soul who will believe and repent of his sins; and they have measurably become revelators and prophets. This, therefore, is the beginning of the great latter-day work, which will never end, until all flesh, that will not be destroyed from the face of the earth by the judgments spoken of, will be made partakers of this same Spirit, and it will have the same effect promised. (Orson Pratt, *JD* 19:170, December 2, 1877.)

The Time of the Gentiles Predicted by Jesus

...Jesus predicted, in the 21st chapter of Luke, that Jerusalem should be trodden down by the Gentiles until the times of the Gentiles should be fulfilled, and from the day of the dispersion of the Jew, seventy years after Christ,...that land has been trodden down by the Gentiles, and the house of Israel have not enjoyed their former location, their beautiful city nor their land of promise, and they cannot enjoy it—God will not permit them until the times of the Gentiles are fulfilled.

The Testimony of Two Nations Growing Into One

The question is, How will he [Jesus] bring about the fulfillment of the times of the Gentiles? I answer, by sending forth to them the stick of Joseph, written upon for Joseph, in connection with the Bible, by his servants who go forth to the nations of the earth. They will proclaim to all people, nations and tongues, to the Gentiles first, the fullness of the Gospel of the Son of God, contained in these two records. The testimony of two nations running together and growing into one is stronger than the testimony of one nation; and when the Lord makes the ancient continent of America bear record to the same great truths; when he unites the Bible of the Western hemisphere, with the Bible of the East, and sends it forth to the nations of the earth, it will be a witness, an evidence and a testimony sufficient to bring about what is termed the fullness of the Gentiles, or to fulfill their times.

That Which God Spake to the House of Israel by the Mouths of Their Ancient Prophets is Being Fulfilled

This is the reason why,...God has restricted us to the Gentile nations, and would not suffer us to go with the Book of Mormon to the house of Israel until the times of the Gentiles were fulfilled. How much longer the Lord will bear with the Gentile nations I know not; but I do know that when they count themselves unworthy of eternal life, when the servants of God have thoroughly warned them by preaching to them the fullness of the Gospel of his Son, then the commandment will go forth from the Almighty to his servants—"Turn from the Gentile nations and go to the dispersed of Israel. Go, ye fishers and ye hunters, and fulfill that which I spake by the mouth of mine ancient Prophets, that Jacob may no longer be made ashamed, that his face may no longer wax pale. Go and say to the house of Israel in the four quarters of the earth that the God of Jacob has again spoken. Go and tell them that that which he spake by the mouths of their ancient Prophets is being fulfilled." And they will go, and their proclamation will be to Israel the same as to the Gentiles, with the exception of gathering the Jews to old Jerusalem, instead of to the land of Zion.

...The work is before the nations, and they can examine it. It has received its foundation and start, and there is no power beneath the heavens that can stay the hand of the Almighty. His work will roll forth, whatever the conduct of the unfaithful may be. The work of the Almighty is onward, and will progress in its majesty and power until every prophecy is fulfilled that has been spoken by the mouth of his ancient servants. It will come to pass, and the people will be gathered, for the powers of the earth can not stay the hand of the Almighty. (Orson Pratt, *JD* 15:189-191, September 22, 1872.)

Jerusalem Shall be Trodden Down of the Gentiles, Until the Times of the Gentiles be Fulfilled

"For there shall be great distress in the land, and wrath upon this people." That is, in the land of Judea, upon the Jews, and in that city.

"And they shall fall by the edge of the sword, and they shall be led away captive among all nations, and Jerusalem"—what will become of it finally?—"shall be trodden down of the gentile, *until*"—that is a big word, and means much in the position it occupies here—"UNTIL"—on that word is suspended that nation's fate, and the fate of all the neighboring nations—"Jerusalem shall be trodden down of the Gentiles, until the times of the Gentiles be fulfilled."

...There is meaning in these words, contained in that single line. O ye nations of the earth, if I had the voice of an angel's trump, that I could be heard to earth's remotest bounds, by kings, rulers, captains, generals, armies, and nations, I would wish to read that one line in their ears, and tell them the things that are summed up in it.

"Jerusalem shall be trodden down of the gentiles *until* the times of the gentiles be fulfilled." What is meant by it? One thing we know certain, we have no need to conjecture, that is, that all these things happened literally. The Roman army on the outside, and the three factions on the inside of the city of Jerusalem, and the famine, and the pestilence helping it on, performed their work until finally it came to an end by the city being taken by the Romans, the temple set on fire, and burned, and the whole city desolated, and brought under Gentile rule, namely, Roman rule. And it is said, in the history written by Josephus, that one million and a half of Jews perished in that siege, that is, in that one city, in putting an end to a national polity; a national corrupted form of government, a national priesthood, a national house of worship.

Judah Scattered Among All Nations

...They fell by the edge of the sword, by pestilence, and by famine, and the remnants of the Jews were carried captive among all nations. To remain how long? ...We know this prophecy has been literally fulfilled, for we see them scattered among all nations to this day.

I have seen them in San Francisco, in Chili, in Scotland, in England, and in every part of the United States, and Canada; and wherever my brethren, the Elders of this Church, have been; I can assure them of one thing, if they have looked about them they have seen a Jew or Jews. Wherever there is a nation to be found, or a people of commerce, ships, camels, or any other means of conveyance, there will be found Jews; that we know.

Gentiles Ploughed the Temple Site in Search of Treasure

But about one stone of the temple at Jerusalem not being left one upon another—the fire itself would not do this—but history has informed us that the Jews concealed their treasures under the stones of the temple, and the Roman army went to work and tumbled them about, and did not leave one stone upon another, and finally they were removed.

In fulfillment of another scripture, they took a plough and ploughed the temple site—so completely was the scripture fulfilled. (Parley P. Pratt, *JD* 3:134, October 7, 1855.)

When the Gentiles Shall Sin Against the Gospel, It Will be Taken From Them

And thus commandeth the Father that I should say unto you: At that day when the Gentiles shall sin against my gospel, and shall be lifted up in the pride of their hearts above all nations, and above all the people of the whole earth, and shall be filled with all manner of lyings, and of deceits, and of mischiefs, and all manner of hypocrisy, and murders, and priestcrafts, and whoredoms, and of secret abominations; and if they shall do all these things, and shall reject the fulness of my gospel, behold, saith the Father, I will bring the fulness of my gospel from among them.

And then will I remember my covenant which I have made unto my people, O house of Israel, and I will bring my gospel unto them. (3 Nephi 16:10-11.)

Wherefore, I must bring forth the fulness of my gospel from the Gentiles unto the house of Israel. (D&C 14:10.)

And again, I command thee that thou shalt not covet thine own property, but impart it freely to the printing of the Book of Mormon, which contains the truth and the word of God—

Which is my word to the Gentiles, that soon it may go to the Jew, of whom the Lamanites are a remnant, that they may believe the gospel, and look not for a Messiah to come who has already come. (D&C 19:26-27.)

The Fulness of the Gentiles Has Not Yet Come

When the Gentiles reject the Gospel, it will be taken from them, and go to the house of Israel, to that long suffering people that are now scattered abroad through all the nations upon the earth, and they will be gathered home by thousands, and by hundreds of thousands, and they will re-build Jerusalem their ancient city, and make it more glorious than at the beginning and they will have a leader in Israel with them, a man that is full of the power of God and the gift of the Holy Ghost; but they are held now from this work, only because the fulness of the Gentiles has not yet come in. Tens of thousands among the Gentile nations will receive the Gospel, but the majority of them will reject it, and then the Jews will receive it; and it will go to them with all the gifts, blessings, and powers it possessed when it was taken from them. (Wilford Woodruff, *JD* 2:200, February 25, 1855)

Chapter

7

The Gathering, Object of all Prophecy

Wherefore, the Jews shall be scattered among all nations; yea, and also Babylon shall be destroyed; wherefore, the Jews shall be scattered by other nations.

And after they have been scattered, and the Lord God hath scourged them by other nations for the space of many generations, yea, even down from generation to generation until they shall be persuaded to believe in Christ, the Son of God, and the atonement, which is infinite for all mankind and when that day shall come that they shall believe in Christ, and worship the Father in his name, with pure hearts and clean hands, and look not forward any more for another Messiah, then, at that time, the day will come that it must needs be expedient that they should believe these things.

And the Lord will set his hand again the second time to restore his people from their lost and fallen state. Wherefore, he will proceed to do a marvelous work and a wonder among the children of men.

Wherefore, he shall bring forth his words unto them, which words shall judge them at the last day, for they shall be given them for the purpose of convincing them of the true Messiah, who was rejected by them; and unto the convincing of them that they need not look forward any more for a Messiah to come, for there should not any come save it should be a false Messiah which should deceive the people; for there is save one Messiah spoken of by the prophets, and that Messiah is he who should be rejected of the Jews. (2 Ne. 25:15-18)

And as I spake concerning the convincing of the Jews, that Jesus is the very Christ, it must needs be that the Gentiles be convinced also that Jesus is the Christ the Eternal God; (2 Ne 26:12)

And now behold, my beloved brethren, I would speak unto you; for I Nephi, would not suffer that ye should suppose that ye are more righteous than the Gentiles should be. For behold, except ye shall keep the commandments of God ye shall all likewise perish; and because of the words which have been spoken ye need not suppose that the Gentiles are utterly destroyed.

For behold, I say unto you that as many of the Gentiles as will repent are the covenant people of the Lord; and as many of the Jews as will not repent shall be cast off; for the Lord covenanteth with none save it be with them that repent and believe in his Son, who is the Holy One of Israel.

And now, I would prophesy somewhat more concerning the Jews and the Gentiles. For after the book of which I have spoken shall come forth, and be written unto the Gentiles, and sealed up again unto the Lord, there shall be many which shall believe the words which are written; and they shall carry them forth unto the remnant of our seed. (2 Ne. 30:1-3.)

And it shall come to pass that the Jews which are scattered also shall begin to believe in Christ; and they shall begin to gather in upon the face of the land; and as many as shall believe in Christ shall also become a delightsome people.

And it shall come to pass that the Lord God shall commence his work among all nations, kindreds, tongues, and people, to bring about the restoration of his people upon the earth. (2 Ne. 30:7-8.)

And then shall the Jews look upon me and say: What are these wounds in thine hands and in thy feet? (D&C 45:51.)

Q. What is to be understood by the two witnesses, in the eleventh chapter of Revelation?

A. They are two prophets that are to be raised up to the Jewish nation in the last days, at the time of the restoration, and to prophesy to the Jews after they are gathered and have built the city of Jerusalem in the land of their fathers. (D&C 77:15.)

And again, the hearts of the Jews unto the prophets, and the prophets unto the Jews; lest I come and smite the whole earth with a curse, and all flesh be consumed before me. (D&C 98:17.)

We therefore ask thee to have mercy upon the children of Jacob, that Jerusalem, from this hour, may begin to be redeemed;

And the yoke of bondage may begin to be broken off from the house of David;

And the children of Judah may begin to return to the lands which thou didst give to Abraham, their father. (D&C 109:62-64.)

And I will remember the covenant which I have made with my people; and I have covenanted with them that I would gather them together in mine own due time, that I would give unto them again the land of their fathers for their inheritance, which is the land of Jerusalem, which is the promised land unto them forever, saith the Father.

And it shall come to pass that the time cometh, when the fulness of my gospel shall be preached unto them;

And they shall believe in me, that I am Jesus Christ, the Son of God, and shall pray unto the Father in my name.

Then shall their watchmen lift up their voice, and with the voice together shall they sing; for they shall see eye to eye.

Then will the Father gather them together again, and give unto them Jerusalem for the land of their inheritance. (3 Ne. 20:29-33.)

All the prophecies have aimed at the gathering of the people and saving them in the last days. (George A. Smith, *HC* 6:18.)

We have watched the great Jewish saga unfold before us. We have seen the procession which began with Abraham's rise to glory only to be cut off and scattered to the nations of the world. We have watched Jehovah restore his gospel to Joseph and we have seen this brother offer help to Judah. Now, finally, we will watch the Jewish procession pull together again as prophesied since the beginning. God will move the nations to fulfill their roles in this great work and Palestine will be offered again to a nation long in need of a home, for thus has God decreed.

Gathering Began When Columbus Discovered the New World

When Columbus sailed out upon the ocean and turned his face toward this land, it was a preparatory move towards its redemption, that it might be opened up again to civilization. The people who had occupied it—the Jaredites, the Nephites, the people of Mulek—had reverted to idolatry. They had turned away from the Lord, and no people in the history of the world that have turned from God our Father and renounced their faith in Him, have ever been perpetuated. But...the Lord had said that he would gather scattered Israel together again, and that gathering, or the preparatory work for it, really began in our dispensation when Columbus was led to discover a new world. The same applies to the Pilgrim fathers. (Anthony W. Ivins, *Utah Genealogical Magazine,* 23:3, January 1932.)

Gathering: A Part of the Restoration of the Gospel

When the Lord restored the gospel, the spirit of gathering came with it. The Lord commanded the people to gather together, and that they should not only be organized as a Church, but that they should be organized under the laws of the land, so that they might not be helpless and dependent and without influence or power; but that by means of united effort and faith they should become a power for the accomplishment of righteousness in the earth. (Joseph F. Smith, *CR,* p. 47, April 8, 1900.)

Jews Commanded to Prepare to Return to Jerusalem

And we further testify that the Jews among all nations are hereby commanded, in the name of the Messiah, to prepare to return to Jerusalem in Palestine, and to rebuild that city and temple unto the Lord.

And also to organize and establish their own political government, under their own rulers, judges and governors, in that country. (Proclamation of the Twelve Apostles, *Millenial Star,* 6:136, October 15, 1845.)

On April 6, 1845, the Twelve Apostles of The Church of Jesus Christ of Latter-day Saints issued the following proclamation to the rulers and people of all nations:

> For be it known unto them that we now hold the keys of the priesthood and kingdom which are soon to be restored unto them.
>
> Therefore let them also repent, and prepare to obey the ordinances of God.
>
> A great, a glorious and a mighty work is yet to be achieved, in spreading the truth and kingdom among the Gentiles—in restoring, organizing, instructing, and establishing the Jews in gathering, instructing, relieving, civilizing, educating, and administering salvation to the remnant of Israel on this continent—in building Jerusalem, and the cities, stakes, temples, and sanctuaries of Zion in America; and in gathering—the Gentiles into the same covenant and organization—instructing them in all things for their sanctification and preparation, that the whole Church of the Saints, both Gentile, Jew and Israel, may be prepared as a bride for the coming of the Lord.

All Men Will Find it Necessary to Choose Sides

There is also another consideration of vast importance to all the rulers and people of the world in regard to this matter. It is this: as this work progresses in its onward course, and becomes more and more an object of political and religious interest and excitement, no king, ruler, or subject—no community or individual will stand neutral: all will at length be influenced by one spirit or the other and will take sides either for or against the kingdom of God, and the fulfillment of the prophets in the great restoration and return of his long-dispersed covenant people.

Some will act the part of the venerable Jethro, the father-in-law of Moses, or the noble Cyrus, and will aid and bless the people of God; or, like Ruth, the Moabitess, will forsake their people, and their kindred, and country, and will say to the Saints, or to Israel—*"This people shall be my people, and their God my God,"* while others will walk in the footsteps of a Pharoah or a Balaam, and will harden their hearts and fight against God, and seek to destroy his people. These will commune with priests and prophets who love the wages of unrighteousness, and who, like Balaam, will seek to curse, or to find enchantments against Israel.

You cannot, therefore, stand as idle and disinterested spectators of the scenes and events which are calculated, in their very nature, to reduce all nations and creeds to *one* political and religious *standard,* and thus put an end to Babel forms and names, and to strife and war. You will, therefore, either be led by the good Spirit to cast in your lot, and to take lively interest with the Saints of the Most High, and the covenant people of the Lord; or, on the other hand, you will become their inveterate enemy, and oppose them by every means in your power.

Nations of the World Will Use Military Force Against the Jews

To such an extreme will this great division finally extend, that the nations of the old world will combine to oppose these things by military force. They will send a great army to Palestine against the Jews, and they will besiege their city, and will reduce the inhabitants of Jerusalem to the greatest extreme of distress and misery.

Then will commence a struggle in which the fate of nations and empires will be suspended on a single battle. In this battle the governors and people of Judah distinguish themselves for their bravery and warlike achievements. The weak among them will be like God, or like the angel of the Lord.

In that day the Lord will pour upon the inhabitants of Jerusalem the spirit of grace and supplication, and they shall look upon the Messiah whom they have pierced.

Messiah Will Stand Upon the Mount of Olives

For lo! he will descend from heaven as the defender of the Jews, and to complete their victory. His feet will stand in that day upon the Mount of Olives, which shall cleave in sunder at his presence, and remove one half to the north, and the other to the south, thus forming a great valley where the mountains now stand.

The earth will quake around him, while storm and tempest, hail and plague, are mingled with the clash of arms, the roar of artillery, the shouts of victory, and the groans of the wounded and dying.

In that day, all who are in the siege, both against Judea and against Jerusalem, shall be cut in pieces, though all the people of the earth should be gathered together against it.

This signal victory on the part of the Jews, so unlooked for by the nations, and attended with the personal advent of the Messiah and the accompanying events, will change the whole order of things in Europe and Asia, in regard to political and religious organization and government.

Jews to Establish a Holy Nation

The Jews as a nation become holy from that day forward, and their city and sanctuary become holy. There also the Messiah establishes his throne and seat of government.

Jerusalem then becomes the seat of empire, and the great center and capital of the old world.

The Families Will Worship the King, the Lord of Hosts, or Suffer the Consequences

All the families of the land shall then go up to Jerusalem once a year, to worship the King, the Lord of Hosts, and to keep the feast of tabernacles.

Those who refuse to go up, shall have no rain, but shall be smitten with dearth and famine; and if the family of Egypt go not up (as it never rains there), they shall be smitten with the plague. And thus all things shall be fulfilled according to the words of the holy prophets of old, and the word of the Lord which is now revealed, to confirm and fulfill them.

In short the kings, rulers, priests, and people of Europe, and of the old world, shall know this once that there is a God in Israel, who, as in days of old, can utter his voice, and it shall be obeyed.

The courts of Rome, London, Paris, Constantinople, Petersburgh, and all others, will then have to yield the point and do homage, and all pay tribute to one great center, and to one mighty sovereign, or *thrones will be cast down, and kingdoms will cease to be.*

Priests, bishops, and clergy, whether Catholic, Protestant, or Mohammedan, will then have to yield their pretended claims to the priesthood, together with titles, honours, creeds, and names, and reverence and obey the true and royal priesthood of the order of Melchizedek, and of Aaron; restored to the rightful heirs—the nobility of Israel; or, the dearth and famine will consume them, and the plague sweep them quickly down to the pit, as in the case of Korah, Dathan, and Abiram, who pretended to the priesthood, and rebelled against God's chosen priests and prophets in the days of Moses.

A Commandment to Bear Witness

He has commanded *us* to bear witness of it, first to the gentiles, and then to the remnants of Israel, and the Jews—*And we know it.*

He has said, that the time is at hand for the Jews to be gathered to Jerusalem—*And we know it.*

He has said, that the ten tribes of Israel should also be revealed in the north country, together with their oracles and records, preparatory to their return, and to their union with Judah, no more to be separated—*And we know it.*

He has said, that when these preparations were made, both in this country and in Jerusalem, and the gospel in all its fulness preached to all nations for a witness and testimony. He will come, and all the Saints with Him, to reign on the earth one thousand years—*And we know it.* (Proclamation of the Twelve Apostles of The Church of Jesus Christ of Latter-day Saints, No. 7, Spruce Street, New York, pp. 3, 4, 6, 7, 8, 13, April 6, 1845.)

The Return of the Jews to Jerusalem

No people on earth, with the exception of the Jews themselves have more cause for rejoicing and see more clearly the hand of the Lord in the redemption of Jerusalem from the oppression of the Gentile Turk, than do the Latter-day Saints. Our own promises, prophecies and glorious future would be impossible of fulfillment without the redemption of Jerusalem and the return of the Jews to that land. How the Prophet Joseph Smith and Apostle Orson Hyde must rejoice in the heavens over the present condition in Jerusalem!

The heart thrills as we read in the daily press accounts of crowding, Jewish battalions, led by Jewish officers, going out from

England and the United States in the armies of the Allies, to Judea and Mesopotamia; of Jewish gold shed in countless showers over this war of restoration; of companies of Jewish agriculturists and engineers following in the soldiers' wake; of Jewish hopes to rebuild their age-long expected temple once again on Mount Zion!

All this belongs of right to Judah and to them, and through them to us, as we are of Ephraim. That great and glorious day of promise sung of by our Jewish convert, Alexander Neibaur, has come at last, and the Prince of Peace will soon reign over Israel and all the tribes of the earth. God speed the happy day! (Susa young Gates, *Relief Society Magazine,* 5:469-470, August 1918.)

Gathering Essential to This Dispensation

The gathering of this people is as necessary to be observed by believers as faith, repentance, baptism, or any other ordinance. It is an essential part of the gospel in this dispensation, as much so as the necessity of building an ark by Noah, for his deliverance, was a part of the gospel of his dispensation. (Joseph F. Smith, *JD* 19:192, September 30, 1877.)

The Spirit of Gathering Followed Conversion to the Gospel

The Prophet Moses of old, who held the keys of the gathering of Israel, appeared unto them (Joseph Smith and Oliver Cowdery) and conferred this authority upon them, that they might have that privilege or that power in this dispensation of the gospel. Up to this time the gospel had only been preached in a few of the eastern states and in parts of Canada, but within a year of that time, missionaries were sent out in the various states of this nation and across the water into Europe, into Great Britain and the Scandinavian countries, and a most wonderful harvest followed the labors of those men; the spirit of gathering followed conversion to the gospel. Many souls were made members of the Church through the testimonies of these brethren who came to them; they accepted the gospel and the spirit of gathering followed it. Many souls were gathered into the fold of Christ; many joined hands with the Saints in this part of the land. And in addition to this, in part-fulfillment of that prophecy, Orson Hyde and John E. Page were set apart for a mission to Palestine. Their mission was to dedicate that land as a gathering place for the house of Israel.... Mr. Page fell by the wayside: Orson Hyde continued that wonderful journey through privations and hardships, and after a year-and-a-half's labor and work and worry, reached that part of the country;...on the Mount of Olives, with his face turned toward the city of Jerusalem, he alone offered that dedicatory prayer that he was sent there to offer.... We,...have wondered and have looked with astonishment as to how that condition might come about. But we saw in the great World War a condition brought about indicating that those people may be gathered back to their home country. And that prophecy will be fulfilled. (J. A. Beckstrand, *CR,* p. 124, April 6, 1924.)

Future Fulfillment of Prophecy Foretold in the Scriptures

The Scriptures are replete with the promises of the gathering of Israel. The prophecy of Moses is upheld by the other prophets: Nehemiah says: "Remember, I beseech thee, the word that thou commandest thy servant Moses, saying, If ye transgress I will scatter you abroad among the nations: but if ye turn unto me, and keep my commandments, and do them; though there were of you cast out unto the uttermost part of heaven, yet will I gather them from thence, and will bring thee unto the place that I have chosen to set my name there." The prophet Jeremiah says: "And I will gather the remnant of my flock out of all countries whither I have driven them, and will bring them again to their folds; and they shall be fruitful and increase;" and further, "Behold, I will gather them out of all countries, whither I have driven them in my anger, and in my fury, and in great wrath; and I will bring them again unto this place, and I will cause them to dwell in safety: and they shall be my people, and I will be their God." Isaiah and Ezekiel foretell of the greatness of this gathering. The former says: "And it shall come to pass in that day, that the Lord shall set His hand again the second time to recover the remnant of His people, which shall be left, from Assyria, and from Egypt, and from Pathros, and from Cush, and from Elam, and from Shinar, and from Hamth, and from the islands of the sea. And he shall set up an ensign for the nations, and shall assemble the outcasts of Israel, and gather together the dispersed of Judah from the four corners of the earth." The latter adds his testimony as follows: "And I will bring you out from the people, and will gather you out of the countries wherein ye are scattered, with a mighty hand, and with a stretched out arm, and with fury poured out. And I will bring you into the wilderness of the people, and there will I plead with you face to face, like as I pleaded with your fathers in the wilderness of the land of Egypt, so will I plead with you. saith the Lord God."

These and many other prophecies foretell the gathering of the Jews and the ten lost tribes at some future time. It has not yet taken place, consequently these prophecies are yet to be fulfilled and they are as likely to be fulfilled in our day as in that of coming generations. (J. V. Bluth, *MS* 56:361, June 4, 1894.)

Some Jews to Gather to Their Promised Land in Belief of Christ

...Not only shall "the Jews which are scattered begin to believe in Christ," but "they shall begin to gather in upon the face of the land;" that is, begin to gather to their promised land, to Palestine.

...The British Consular reports of 1856 said that less than fifteen thousand Jews were in all Palestine. Twenty years later this number had increased to sixty-five thousand. Then came the Zionite movement, under the leadership of Dr. Theodor Herzl, supplemented later by the influence of Israel Zangwell, a Jewish writer of some note, and what is known as the "Zionite Movement" received an impetus, and began to grow in the minds of the Jews until there began what we may now call the modern gathering together of the Jews in Palestine. The gathering is continuing. Millions of dollars have been subscribed by that people to establish their exiled brethren in the land of their fathers, and the ambition is to resume the national history of the Jewish people. That movement has grown until it has attained large proportions, and very wide interest in the world. This prophecy, then, is in course of fulfillment—"The Jews that are scattered are beginning to gather in upon the land of their forefathers, to the land of Palestine and to Jerusalem!"

Orson Hyde Prediction Fulfilled—England Exercised Political Influence and Befriended Judah

We may pause here to ask what is the motive power, what is behind all this movement—this change in the mental attitude of that people towards Christ;—this gathering together of the Jews in Palestine? This is the explanation of it: In the Kirtland Temple, in 1836, Israel's great prophet, Moses, appeared to Joseph and Oliver Cowdery and delivered to them the keys of the gathering of Israel and the restoration of the Ten Tribes from the land of the North.... Orson Hyde, returning from his mission [to Palestine] when in Alexandria,...wrote to the *Millennial Star* of the then current date and there made a rather wonderful prediction. He said in substance that it was by political power that Judah had been broken and scattered abroad, and that it would be by the exercise of political power that Judah would be restored: and furthermore he declared that England would be the leading national power that would befriend Judah, and aid him in the re-establishment of his people in the land of Palestine. This was published in the *Millennial Star* of 1842....

...The predictions of Orson Hyde,...in behalf of Judah, are... wonderfully fulfilled. The defeat of the Turks in the World War was by British forces under the English General Sir Edmund Allenby. The official entrance of General Allenby into Jerusalem on the 11th of December, 1917, and the subsequent course of England in respect of Palestine; the fact that Great Britain [once controlled]... the administration of the affairs of that land under the appointment of the League of Nations—this fills out the story of Elder Orson Hyde's mission and prophecy. The policy of England in respect to its administration of the affairs of Palestine as foreshadowed in the declaration by Lord Balfour when, on the 2nd of November, 1919, he said officially, and with the approval of France, Italy and President Wilson of the United States:

> His Majesty's government view with favor the establishment in Palestine of a National home for the Jewish people, and will use their best endeavors to facilitate the achievement of this object. (Quoted as in text. For a full discussion of the Balfour declaration, see chapter 10.)

England has ever since consistently pursued that policy....

God is Underlying Source of Jewish Movement

...God is moving underneath all these facts—this changing of the mental attitude of Jews towards Jesus—this latter-day gathering of the Jews to the land and this city of their fathers. (Brigham H. Roberts, *CR,* pp. 33-38, April 3, 1927.)

The Prophet Ezekiel Was Commanded To Prophesy of the Gathering

And say unto them, thus saith the Lord, Behold, I will take the children of Israel from among the heathen, whither they be gone, and will bring them into their own land;

And I will make them one nation in the land upon the mountains of Israel; and one king shall be king to all, and they shall no more be two nations, neither shall they be divided into two kingdoms any more at all:

Neither shall they defile themselves any more with their idols, nor with any of their transgressions: but I will save them out of their dwelling places, wherein they have sinned, and will cleanse them: so shall they be my people, and I will be their God. (Ezekiel 37:21-23.)

The Lord Promised Israel Would be Gathered and "They Shall All Know Me"

Jeremiah speaking of the gathering of Israel, and the Millennium says: "Behold the days come, saith the Lord, that I will make a new covenant with the House of Israel, and with the House of Judah; not according to the covenant that I made with their fathers, in the day that I took them by the hand, to bring them out of the land of Egypt; which my covenant they brake although I was an husband unto them, saith the Lord; but this shall be the covenant that I will make with the House of Israel; after those days, saith the Lord, I will put my law in their inward parts, and write it in their hearts; and will be their God, and they shall be my people. And they shall teach no more every man his neighbor, and every man his brother, saying, know the Lord: for they shall all know me, from the least of them unto the greatest of them, saith the Lord: for I will forgive their iniquity, and I will remember their sins no more." (Jer. 31:31-34.) This covenant has not yet taken effect: for when it does all shall know the Lord from the least unto the greatest. When the Lord brought the House of Israel out of Egypt, he covenanted with them that they, and their posterity should possess the land of Canaan throughout all their generations, on condition of faithfulness to all his statues; but they were driven from their land; but when the Lord brings them back again, he will make a new covenant with them, that they shall no more be driven out, and he will also imprint his law on their hearts, and all shall know him from the least to the greatest. (Anonymous, *TS* 3:687, February 15, 1842.)

The People of Israel Will Go Again Dry Shod Across the Nile as They Did Anciently

We are told, in the prophecies of Isaiah; that when the house of Israel shall return to their own country, he will strike the river Nile, in the seven great channels, by which it enters into the

Mediterranean Sea. Instead of taking them above these seven different channels, he will make a road through the seven channels of the river Nile; and the people of Israel will go again dry shod, as they did anciently. In the eleventh chapter of Isaiah, and the 15th verse, we read that "the Lord shall utterly destroy the tongue of the Egyptian Sea," not the main body of the sea. Those who are acquainted with the north portion of the Red Sea know there are two prongs, one is called the tongue of the Egyptian Sea; and the children of Israel shall go through dry shod, and through the seven channels of the river Nile, as did Israel in the day that they came up out of the land of Egypt.

Jews Worship that God that Divided the Waters

Here will be a miracle wrought greater than that of speaking in tongues or the healing of the sick—more convincing in its nature. When this is done together with many other things, the children of Israel will no longer feel themselves under the necessity of referring to the day when the Lord wrought wonders as they came up out of the land of Egypt. You know it has been a saying with the Jews some thousands of years, that the God of Israel lives. "We do not worship the kind of God which you heathens worship. We worship that God that divided the waters, that came down on Mount Sinai." They always refer back to miracles four thousand years old, that their God is a God of miracles. This ancient proverb is to be done away, in modern Israel. Instead of referring back to ancient miracles, it will be said, "The Lord liveth that brought the children of Israel from the land of the north, and from the countries he has driven them to the land of their fathers." That will be the time when Israel will be willing. All Israel will be willing to acknowledge the power and glory of that God whom they serve. It seems that the Lord is going to enact over again, a thing that he did after they came through the Red Sea. After they came through the Red Sea, the Lord brought the children of Israel into the wilderness, and kept them there forty years, so that all the people perished except Joshua and Caleb. When the Lord brings the people of the House of Israel, in the latter-days, instead of taking them direct to the land of Palestine, he brings them forth into the wilderness again, which you will find recorded in the 20th chapter of Ezekiel. "I will bring you into the wilderness, and plead with you face to face." Now if the Lord did plead with them face to face in the wilderness of the land of Egypt, and gave them revelations there; if his presence, at first was with them, and was not taken from them at the first, so will he do again—he will plead with them face to face.

I do not think, however, that they will, in the latter days, so far transgress, as to bring upon themselves the curse that came on their fathers, in ancient times; for then he took from them the glories of the covenant of the Gospel, and introduced another covenant, the covenant of the law. (Orson Pratt, *JD* 16:151-152, August 16, 1873.)

The Three Nephites Will Labor Among the Gentiles and Jews

...The three Nephites...have been upon this land,...among the Gentiles and among the Jews.... I doubt not that they are laboring today in the great cause on the earth. There are agencies laboring for the accomplishment of the purposes of God and for the fulfillment of the predictions of the holy Prophets, of which we have but little conception at the present time. (George Q. Cannon, *JD* 16:120, June 29, 1873.)

God Will Lead the Way in This Gathering and Make Bare His Arm to the Nations

The servants of the Lord will also be sent to the Jews, some of whom are here in London. Some are mingled with the various nations of Europe. Many hundreds of thousands of them are in Asia and among the nations. These Jews must be warned, when we get through with the Gentiles; and they will begin to believe in Christ, according to the prophecies, that are contained in the Stick of Joseph. They will begin to believe in the true Messiah and gather unto their land, the land of Palestine; and there will be many of the people of Israel, that are scattered upon the Isles of the sea—on the Pacific Isles—who will receive the work; and the Lord will perform in their midst, miracles, and signs, and wonders, and make bare his arm, just as is prophesied by Isaiah in bringing about his covenants to the House of Israel. And he will make bare his arm very differently from what he has done among the Gentiles; for among the Gentiles, he has, it is true, healed the sick; he has opened the eyes of the blind; he has caused the tongue of the dumb in some instances, to sing; and he has healed them of various diseases; and there has been a certain degree of the power and gifts of the ancient Gospel, manifested as in ancient times, among the ancient Gentile Churches. But I do not call this the making bare of the arm of the Almighty in so great fulness as it is predicted in the Jewish record, the Bible. It is making bare his arm in some small degree. And we have great reason to be thankful, when he does show forth his power as in ancient times, in these spiritual gifts and blessings, which belong especially to the Gospel of his Son. But when I speak of the Lord making bare his arm in the eyes of all the nations, I have reference to that which is predicted in this book, called the Bible, when the waters will again be divided, and Israel will go through dryshod, as they did in ancient times. When the great deep will have a highway cast up through the midst of it and Israel will pass through it dryshod. When I mention about the Lord making bare his arm in the eyes of all the nation, I have reference to that tremendous power, that is specified by the Ancient prophets, which will be made manifest before all people, all governments, nations and countries upon the face of the whole earth. Israel will return with power. Will God be with them when they return? He will. He will go as literally before their camp, as they go out from among the nations, as he did in ancient times when he brought them out from that one single nation of the Egyptians. (Orson Pratt, *JD,* 20:147, March 9, 1879.)

A New Gospel Dispensation Was Opened

...The Lord commenced the work which is destined to result in the establishment of Ephraim, and other descendants of Joseph upon this continent, where the Zion of our God is to be established, and the restoration of the Jews to Palestine, the land of their fathers.

With the organization of the Church the Lord made plain the duty of its members. Men holding the restored priesthood, with its keys of authority, were sent into every country where they were permitted to go, proclaiming the opening of a new gospel dispensation, calling the people to repentance, and bearing witness that the mountain of the Lord's House was to be established in the tops of the mountains, and to be exalted above the hills, where we are today and that people from all nations should flow unto it, in order that they might be taught the way of the Lord, and learn to walk in his paths.

British Protectorate Over the Holy Land Through the Treaty of Versailles

Then came the great world war, and final peace at Versailles when Great Britain was given the responsibility of establishing and maintaining a protectorate over the Holy Land. The British armies, it is true, had already occupied Jerusalem, but it was with the signing of the treaty of Versailles that the first definite step was taken looking to the fulfillment of the words of the prophets, who had declared the redemption of Israel, and the restoration of Judah to the lands of their fathers, thousands of years ago.

Interest of the Jews in the Restoration Has Few Parallels in History

The interest manifested by the Jewish people in the restoration of Palestine has few parallels in the history of the world. One is reminded of the zeal which their fathers showed as they returned from Babylon to Jerusalem to rebuild their city and temple, when women as well as men worked, and gave lavishly of their most cherished possessions that the task might be accomplished.

Jewish societies have been organized in various parts of the world, having for their purpose the creation of a publicly recognized, legally acquired home in Palestine, and the building up of the Jewish homeland in the Canaan of their fathers. Many millions of dollars have been subscribed by Jews throughout the world, to be used in the purchase of land, and the development of the dormant resources of the country.

May the Jews Recognize Shiloh When He Stands on the Mount of Olives

God bless the Jews in this important work. May the eyes of their understanding be opened, and the time soon come when Shiloh, to whose coming they have so long looked forward, shall stand upon the Mount of Olives, and they recognize in him, Jesus of Nazareth, the Redeemer of the world, whom their fathers rejected. And may we, Latter-day Saints, we people who are of Ephraim, appreciate the part we are playing in this great latter-day drama, the like of which was never played before, and never will be again.... (Anthony W. Ivins, *CR,* pp. 49-52, April 5, 1925.)

Jews to Return Because It Is God's Plan

...Our souls are thrilled to see our half brothers, the Jews, turning toward the land of promise: and for the first time since their long dispersion one of their own people, an orthodox Jew, is the ruler of the land of Palestine. The Jews will go there. God knows how to bring them. He did it in our case [Mormons], and he knows how to bring them. They may say they will not go, but they will. The Lord will hedge up the way behind them, and he will open up the way before them, and unto his appointed place they shall go, in preparation for their conversion at the hands of the Master. (Melvin J. Ballard, *CR,* p. 82, 1921.)

The Jews Have Gathered to Jerusalem

God's promise that he would gather [the] Jews to Jerusalem, and I think...now we may well say they *have gathered.* The ultimate returns will come later as they develop this land and are joined by others.

...Recently this statement was made: "About two million Jews have returned to restore land which has lain desolate for centuries. In little more than ten years fetid swamps have been transformed into fertile valleys. Orchards now blossom on stony hillsides. Farms have sprouted the desert and towns and cities have been built on the site of ancient settlements." (George Q. Morris, *CR,* p. 101, April 1960.)

Gathering of the Jews a Sign of the Times

To the Latter-day Saints, those of them especially who are fully awake to the importance of the work the Lord is performing, the movement among and in relation to the Jews and Palestine is of peculiar interest. It is one of the signs of the times, for which the disciples of the Savior are commanded to watch and, on beholding which, they can "lift up their heads and rejoice: in the assurance that their redemption draweth nigh. (W. Budge *MS,* 41:186, March 24, 1879.)

Gathering to the Lands of the Jews Inheritance a Great Epoch in World History

The signs of the time point strikingly to one great epoch in world history which prophets of the Lord, from Abraham to Christ, sung, wrote, and prophesied of as a time when the remnants of Israel, dispersed throughout the nations, would be gathered to the lands of their inheritance, the realization of which was to be one of the outstanding signs of the Second Advent of the Messiah and the

Millennial reign. (Octave Ursenbach, *Liahona* 19:427, April 25, 1922.)

House of Israel and Judah Restored to the Favour of God

The first important consideration which presents itself while examining the prophets on this subject, is, that God will set his hand the second time to restore the house of Israel and the house of Judah to their national rights, to the favour of God, and to their own land. They will gather out from every nation under heaven, with their silver and gold, &c., employing the ships, steam-boats, railroad carriages, canal-boats, litters, horses, mules, camels, and swift beasts, and every kind of conveyance which the nations can furnish. This gathering will be by a mighty hand, with a stretched out arm, and with fury poured out; and in short, Jehovah's arm will be made bare in the eyes of all the nations, in signs, in wonders, in miracles, in revelations, in judgments, and in mercies. (Anonymous, "The Millennium," *MS* 1:5-6, May 1840.)

The Land Prepared for the Jews Gathering

I see manifest signs and tokens that the Holy Land is preparing for the people, and that the people are preparing for the Holy Land. If I turn to Palestine, I perceive indications the most distinct that God is returning to water its desolate places, and clothe its mountains once more with beauty and fragrance. The clouds are again dropping fatness upon its desert places, and many of its wildernesses are beginning to blossom in promise that they shall bloom in due time like the rose. I know not whether you are aware of the fact, but it is one that is fully authenticated, that the "latter rain" returned last year to Mount Zion—a rain that had been withheld, so far as our information goes, ever since the dispersion of the people. And He who has brought back the latter rain in its season, will also give the "former rain" in its season; and these returning showers of earthy blessings are the harbingers of returning showers of spiritual benediction from on high.

The Valley of Jehoshaphat was Made to Bloom as the Garden of the Lord

There is another fact which, though small in itself, is not a less striking one—the well of En-rogel, or Job's well, supplies the little stream that waters the once blooming valley of Jehoshaphat. That well, in Israel's palmy days of plenty and of peace, used to overflow every year, and its overflow fed the streams that, diverted into various channels and gathered into reservoirs prepared for the purpose, provided a supply of water for each season, and so the valley was made to bloom as the garden of the Lord. But on account of the wickedness of the people, the supply of water from that well was long diminished. For centuries the well of En-rogel has, it is supposed, overflowed but once in the four of five years; but during the last four years, since Christianity has been shedding its light on Mount Zion, and the first-fruits of Israel have been gathered in, the well has overflowed year by year again. The little stream has tricked along its course annually, with its sweet silvery music: the various reservoirs and tanks have been replenished; and the valley of Jehoshaphat is beginning again to blush with the vine and to wave with the cedar. There are other incidents of an equally intersting character in connection with the preparation of the land for the people. (Hugh Stowell, *MS* 15:788-789, December 3, 1853.)

Great Numbers of Jews Returning to Palestine Today

The door is wide open for all Jews who are able to return to Israel, and fifty thousand returned [in 1971]. They came from many nations and for many reasons. Most of them expected a better life and most of them found it.

Hundreds of thousands of Jews are waiting to return to Israel. Since May 14, 1948, more than 1,350,000 newcomers have arrived.

Many Jews feel that one of the miracles of their history is that those Jews who were restrained for 50 years or more still want to return to their native land and their children who have never known a homeland feel the necessity of returning. (J. M. Heslop, *DNCS,* December 4, 1971.)

Chapter 8

Zionism, Prophecy Fulfilled

And it shall come to pass in the last days, that the mountain of the Lord's house shall be established in the top of the mountains, and shall be exalted above the hills; and all nations shall flow unto it.

And many people shall go and say, Come ye, and let us go up to the mountain of the Lord, to the house of the God of Jacob; and he will teach us of his ways, and we will walk in his paths: for out of Zion shall go forth the law, and the word of the Lord from Jerusalem. (Isaiah 2:2-3.)

And it shall come to pass, that he that is left in Zion, and he that remaineth in Jerusalem, shall be called holy, even every one that is written among the living in Jerusalem. (Isaiah 4:3.)

O Zion, that bringest good tidings, get thee up into the high mountain; O Jerusalem, that bringest good tidings, lift up thy voice with strength; lift it up, be not afraid; say unto the cities of Judah, Behold your God! (Isaiah 40:9.)

Awake, awake; put on thy strength, O Zion; put on thy beautiful garments, O Jerusalem, the holy city; for henceforth there shall no more come into thee the uncircumcised and the unclean. (Isaiah 52:1.)

And it shall come to pass, that whosoever shall call on the name of the Lord shall be delivered: for in mount Zion and in Jerusalem shall be deliverance, as the Lord hath said, and in the remnant whom the Lord shall call. (Joel 2:32.)

The Lord also shall roar out of Zion, and utter his voice from Jerusalem; and the heavens and the earth shall shake: but the Lord will be the hope of his people, and the strength of the children of Israel.

So shall ye know that I am the Lord your God dwelling in Zion, my holy mountain: then shall Jerusalem be holy, and there shall no strangers pass through her any more. (Joel 3:16-17.)

Cry yet, saying, Thus saith the Lord of hosts; My cities through prosperity shall be spread abroad; and the Lord shall yet comfort Zion, and shall yet choose Jerusalem. (Zechariah 1:17.)

> Deliver thyself, O Zion, that dwellest with the daughter of Babylon.
>
> For thus saith the Lord of hosts; After the glory hath he sent me unto the nations which spoiled you: for he that toucheth you toucheth the apple of his eye.
>
> For, behold, I will shake mine hand upon them, and they shall be a spoil to their servants: and ye shall know that the Lord of hosts hath sent me.
>
> Sing and rejoice, O daughter of Zion: for, lo, I come, and I will dwell in the midst of thee, saith the Lord.
>
> And many nations shall be joined to the Lord in that day, and shall be my people: and I will dwell in the midst of thee, and thou shalt know that the Lord of hosts hath sent me unto thee.
>
> And the Lord shall inherit Judah his portion in the holy land, and shall choose Jerusalem again. (Zechariah 2:7-12)

As the Jews begin to see, as we have seen, the power of God moving upon the nations to free Palestine for their use, they are quick to lay hold of the wheel and to guide their own ship home. "Zionism" is the cry ringing in Jewish hearts and ears which pushes them to give up their money and their home, to leave all security for the promise of a modern Israel. Aware or not, they are fulfilling the prophecies themselves. The window of inspiration opens for us a new vision of this worldwide movement.

The Zionist Movement Was a Great International Question

Ever since its first dedication by Elder Hyde, and...since its second dedication by President Smith and party, the land of Palestine has been taking on more and more favorable conditions. The Jewish population of Jerusalem has been increasing steadily and rapidly. The Zionist movement, which had its rise not many years after the second dedication, has spread with amazing rapidity and has come to be one of the greatest international questions of the day. It promises the early fulfillment, upon a gigantic scale, of these dedicatory prayers, and of the predictions of Joseph Smith and the Book of Mormom relative to the future of the Jews, predictions which are in perfect harmony with those of the ancient Jewish prophets and seers, who foretold the final redemption and glorification of their race. (Anonymous, "Future of the Jews," *Liahona,* 6:233-236, August 22, 1908.)

Zion In the Land of America and Judah Will Return to Jerusalem

...the tribe of Judah will return to old Jerusalem. The city of Zion spoken of by David, in the one hundred and second Psalm, will be built upon the land of America, "And the ransomed of the Lord shall return, and come to Zion with songs and everlasting joy upon their heads" (Isaiah 35: 10); and then they will be delivered from the overflowing scourge that shall pass through the land. But Judah shall obtain deliverance at Jerusalem. See Joel 2:32; Isaiah 26:20-21; Jeremiah 31:12; Psalm 1:5; Ezekiel 34:11-13. These are testimonies that the Good Shepherd will put forth His own sheep, and lead them out from all nations where they have been scattered in a cloudy and dark day, to Zion, and to Jerusalem; besides many more testimonies which might be brought. (Joseph Smith *HC* 1:315)

Zionism—As Viewed by the Jews

From the standpoint of a Jew there is a sublimity in the conception of Zionism that the Gentile world is unable to comprehend. To him it is the solution of a gigantic race problem. On this point Mr. DeHaas says:

There is a land thousands of miles from here in a state of devastation, only partly fruitful, broken, dimly recognized as living soil, and yet filled with many ancient and cherished memories. To reach that land, to make it flow once more with milk and honey, to restore it as a country amongst the countries of the world—that is Zionism.

There is a people, not as old as the land, but as old as its most important history, which was a great and glorious people, self-possessed, self-ruling, now a people scattered over the face of the earth, the servants of the races amongst whom they dwell, a people disunited, disassociated, persecuted. To raise that people, the Jews, to organize centralized life, to give them a standing among the nations, to free them from persecutions, to let them live a noble and distinguished life once more—that, too, is Zionism.

There is a religion, and it is the Jewish religion, which was once great among the people. To restore that religion to power—that, too, is Zionism.

At the beginning of the nineteenth century, when English, French and Arabian were making a battle-ground of the barren country that lies eastward from the Mediterranean, the colonization of Palestine by the Jews seemed as far from accomplishment as it did at the beginning of the ninth century—a period during which Syria first felt the baneful effect of the early Turkish conquest. Even the Jews themselves dared not openly express the longings of their hearts, if any such yet existed. No Scripture prophecy seemed less probable of fulfillment than that pertaining to the descendants of Abraham. Outside of Palestine, the Jew was still under a ban that, in spite of wealth and intellectual power, kept him in both political and social bondage. In his homeland he was beaten by the Moslem, spat upon by the Christian, a misery to himself and of no use to the world at large.

Zionist Movement—From Obscurity to World-shaping Force

(When)...Elder Orson Hyde visited Palestine on a special mission, the time was ripe for the gathering of the dispersed and despised people. The world saw no procession with banners; heard no blare of trumpet. The Lord does not herald His great enterprises in any such manner. It is a far cry from Commerce to Jerusalem, and few there were who recognized the Apostle in the plain garb of the missionary; fewer still who sensed the vast import of the work with which he was commissioned. With authority directly from the Prophet, and inspired by the Holy Spirit, Elder Hyde dedicated the Holy Land that it might once more become the home of its right-ful owners; that Judah might gather from all quarters of the earth unto his inheritance, and that the land might be blessed for his sake. So far as the Latter-day Saints are concerned that act of dedication is the one important event in their history that connects them with Palestine. The missionary efforts in that country have been intermittent, and have not yet been crowned with success. Whether the hand of God has been made manifest since that time to prove that Elder Hyde was obeying a divine command when he made a journey that to the world would have seemed the very acme of folly, let...history...demonstrate.

There are great movements, spontaneous, world-wide, changing the whole tide of human events, of which no adequate explanation can be given. At rare intervals the same is true in nature. An epidemic, like Asiatic cholera, may break out simultaneously in Bombay, London, New York, and on vessels crossing the ocean, when, apparently, there has been no contagion, nor any extraordinary conditions to produce such a dreadful scourge. In the same way the world is often rudely awakened from a dream of peace to find every zone, each horizon blackened by clouds of war. Not different was the beginning of the Zionist movement. One day unknown; the next a living force in every civilized nation of the world and in some countries upon which the light of civilization had scarcely begun to dawn.

Zionism Became an Entity

Almost half a century ago, by one common impulse, the Jews commenced to turn their faces homeward, with full purpose of heart to sacrifice all, that they might die under the shadow of Mount Moriah, or by the blue waters of Galilee. At first they came in very small companies from the far east, where isolated communities had existed for centuries, even as far as the borders of Tibet, and the northern Caspian region. Russia, Germany, England, America, all felt the impelling force. Zionism became an entity. Yet, in its inception, the movement seemed doomed to speedy failure. The elements entering into it were heterogeneous, leaderless. In many respects it reminds one of the first crusade. But gradually men of note, men of world-wide influence and power, came to the assistance of their struggling and ignorant co-religionists. They gave more than financial aid to the cause, though their donations were liberal. They gave freely of time, talents and the masterful ability that had made them great among even their enemies. Such were Sir Moses Montefiore, Baron Hirch and Baron Rothschild. Their efforts seemed at first to be concentrated on the emigration of the poorer classes of Jews from the countries in which they were the most oppressed, in order that they might obtain greater personal and political freedom, and become practically independent. They hoped to develop in old Judea a noble spirit of religious nationalism. They wanted to re-invest the throne of David with its ancient dignity, although that throne could not yet be set up in any literal sense. They also desired to have their race elevate itself, and work out its own salvation in solving the problems which new and improved conditions present. But the people, as a whole, were incapable of rising to the occasion. Two thousand years of serfdom had imprinted characteristics and habits, had formed a life that a single generation could, at best, only slightly modify. They were as helpless as is one born blind when he first beholds the light of day. Inured to lives of toil, they now gave way to a spirit of indifference and absolute indolence. Their time, instead of being devoted to redeeming the land from the curse of barrenness, was spent in frivolous dissipation. Their minds, that for ages had grappled only with the question of self-preservation, now that preservation was assured, became blanks. Palestine reached, ambition, personal interest, race pride, knew no additional incentive to growth or exertion. So the master minds came once more to the rescue. The Jews must be fitted for the great work of colonization and development before Zionism could be the grand success of which its promoters dreamed.

Economic Aspects of Zionism

The economic side of Zionism now became prominent. The Jew in the Gentile world had never been a successful agriculturist. On his native heath he must learn to cultivate the vine and olive, to plough, to sow, to reap; to change conditions so as to create a demand, and then to be able to supply that for which the demand exists. In time, business enterprises would arise in which the Jew might legitimately be expected to excel. He would control the capital of Syria even as he had controlled the capital of the great cities of the world, but with this change for the better, instead of having all the wealth in the hands of the few, it would be distributed among the many, each being a sharer, and having a personal interest in the welfare of the whole. To meet the requirements of the times, schools must be founded and factories established. They are essential, for southeastern Asia has herself experienced an awakening. The camel train has been superseded by the steam-engine. The possibilities of Asia Minor are just beginning to be grasped. Why should not each new enterprise and industry be controlled by Jews? Why should not the success in finance that they have achieved in the new world be repeated in the most ancient part of the old? This dream of the Zionists is visibly approaching its realization from day to day.

Jews Must be Prepared to Assume New Responsibilities and Duties

Nor is this all. If the Jew can be fitted for the new duties and responsibilities which devolve upon him before he returns to the land of his fathers, so much the better. He must be removed from the ghettos, the slums, of London and New York, and given a more favorable environment, better suited to his individual requirements. In nations like Russia efforts must be made to ameliorate conditions that are a relic of barbarous ages. Above all he must be given higher ideals than ever he has dreamed of before. In all these vast plans organization is essential, and that work is going on with wonderful rapidity. Within the past...years more than two thousand societies have been established by the Zionists....

The Zionist Movement is an Essential Feature of the Dispensation of the Fulness of Time

The world does not accept the fact which the Latter-day Saints know to be true, that this movement is one essential feature of the dispensation of the fulness of time; that it had to be properly inaugurated, as has every other great work of these latter days, by one holding the proper authority and keys; that the authority and keys for this work were delivered by the Prophet Joseph Smith to Elder Orson Hyde, and that his work made not only possible, but practicable, the Zionism of to-day. The Jew does not yet believe that he is being gathered to the Holy Land to await the second coming of the once rejected Messiah, whose feet shall once more stand upon the Mount of Olives; that, in the very place where Jesus of Nazareth was crucified, they will again have the opportunity of accepting him, and of becoming again, in very deed, the children of the covenant. Even as Ephraim is gathering in the valleys of the mountains to build up a new Zion, so is Judah gathering, where once the temple towered in divine splendor, to build again the waste places of Jerusalem. For "the time of restitution of all things, which were spoken of by the prophets since the world began," is at hand, even at our door. (Walter M. Wolfe, *MS* 65:539-543, August 20, 1903.)

Zionism's Progress and Its Meaning

The Zionist movement is undoubtedly preparing the way for the fulfillment of the purposes of the Lord concerning His people in the land of Palestine... From the *Morning Leader* (London), of April 5th, 1912, the following article,...appeared under the heading "Zionism's Progress and Its Meaning":

"From Berlin, the central office of the Zionist movement, comes an interesting document that tells of the hopes, fears, and accomplishments of Zionism during the...years it has engaged the attention of the world's Jewries."

"Zionism, according to Mr. I. Cohen,...is still misunderstood and misrepresented, and suffers from a lack of appreciation in Jewish circles."

"Throughout the years Zionism has worked hard in the cause of Jewish regeneration. 'It represents the first organized endeavor of the Jewish people since its banishment from Palestine nearly two thousand years ago to put an end to its alternating lot of oppression, tolerance, or fatal drift by securing the status and dignity of a nation in the land in which its national life first came into being.

Exiled Jews Working for the Restoration of Zion

"Zionism represents in modern form the traditional love of Zion which animated the Jew throughout the centuries, the hope in the gathering of Israel in the Holy Land which soothed the sufferings of exile.' In years gone by the Jew prayed for the restoration of Zion; today he is working for it, and although the attainment of the goal may seem far off and political upheavals may upset cherished dreams, Zionists are still working wholeheartedly. No apology, it is urged, is needed for a movement that will ultimately solve what has long been known as 'the eternal Jewish problem.' For the suffering Jews of Eastern Europe Zionism offers 'the hope of a land where they will be able to till the soil of their forefathers in peace, where they will be able to live 'every man under his vine and under his fig tree.'

"In Roumania Jews are treated as foreigners, 'although they have an uninterrupted history of 1,500 years in the country. Emigration, then, is the only remedy for the social and economic ills from which the Jew in Eastern Europe suffers. Even this loophole to liberty is partially closed by the increasing severity of anti-immigration laws. The creation of a legally secured home in Palestine will render these restrictions of no account.

Some Evidence of the Progressive Accomplishments and Successes of the Zionist Movement

"To the Jews of the West, Zionism offers its call to the hope of a land 'where they will be able to live naturally and normally, free from any social hostility or hindrance, where they will be able to devote their gifts and energies to the service of their own people.'

"Zionism has done something more than disseminate propaganda. Its colonization work in the old home of the Hebrew nation is sufficient proof of 'the practical measures which it has in contemplation for the near future. Far from pursuing aims detrimental to the interests of the Ottoman Empire, it has rendered, and will continue to render, splendid services to a rejuvenated Turkey. It has established banks in the Holy Land, conferring a boon on all classes of society and all grades of industry. It has promoted the formation of co-operative loan societies among artisans, small traders, and agricultural workers, a movement that is now represented by about thirty societies.

"In the Bezalel School of Arts and Crafts in Jerusalem it has brought into being a world-known institution, which in addition to solving the ever present problem of poverty in the Holy City, is doing much to reawaken interest in a Jewish national art. The Bezalel has departments for carpet-weaving, lace manufacture, filigree work, carpentry, metal work, and basket-making. Bezalel products may be found in Jewish homes throughout the world.

"Large tracts of land have been acquired in Palestine, and divided into small holdings for farmers of moderate means, while 17,000 has been raised for reafforestation. An agricultural experimental station at Haifa is to investigate the agricultural resources of the country. Improved housing, the spread of hygiene, and the establishment of a Hebrew gymnasium at Jaffa, where two hundred pupils can be prepared for university courses, are evidences of what Zionism has done. So the movement proceeds, quietly, hopefully. 'The fate of the Jewish people,' says the author, 'lies in its own hands.' "

Enmity Among Judah, Israel and Ephraim Shall Depart

Not only Judah, but the whole house of Israel, are to be gathered and restored, as we learn from the Old Testament prophets. The enmity between Judah and Israel shall pass away, and they shall become again a united people. "The enmity also of Ephraim shall depart, and the adversaries of Judah shall be cut off: Ephraim shall not envy Judah, and Judah shall not vex Ephraim. (Isaiah 11:13.) Ephraim and the ten tribes will gather to the land of Zion—in fact, they have been gathering there for many years—while Judah will return to Jerusalem, the land of their inheritance. Before all this takes place, however, the Jews will come to a knowledge of the true Messiah, their Lord and their Redeemer. Then shall they be fully restored to their own land, and be privileged to possess and enjoy it in peace for ever. (H. Ireland, *MS* 74:264-266, April 25, 1912.)

The Zionite Movement is the Hope and Desire of the Jew and the Christian

"May we celebrate the next Passover in Jerusalem."—Jews.

"Thy kingdom come, Thy will be done on earth as it is in heaven."—Christians.

...These two sayings...represent the hope of the Jews, and...the desire of the Christians. ...The first has become a perfunctory remark of the master of the house at every Passover feast since the destruction of Jerusalem by the Romans, and the second, since the apostasy from Christianity, a perfunctory part of a prayer offered by the Christians. ...The time will soon come, when the hope of the Jew and the ostensible desire of the Christian—however meaningless and merely formal the two expressions may have become to ordinary Jew and to ordinary Christian—will be realized. Jerusalem, and all Palestine, in fact, will be again restored to the house of Israel, as their inheritance; the kingdom of God will come, and His will be done on earth as in heaven. The word of God assures us of that.

Here and now, however, we have to do with those facts which relate to the first idea—the restoration of the Jews to the land of their inheritance—to the "Zionite Movement" as it is called. And a strange movement it is, at least to the Gentile world. "The wind bloweth where is listeth" said the Savior of the Spirit, "and you hear the sound thereof, but cannot tell whence it cometh and whither it goeth;" and this is as true when it operates upon an individual. ...The Jew, especially the Jew of Russia, or Roumania, of France, of Germany...was the most helpless, friendless of men. If spat upon, he endured it; if mocked, he reviled not again; if spurned by a Christian foot, he resisted not, for now as in former times, "sufferance" was still the badge of all his race.

Jews Admonished to Strike Back at Their Adversaries

"Why are they persecuted," recently asked a great Jew of our own country," in referring to the Jews of the parts of Europe above named—"Why? Because they are Jews. What matters it that they suffer; they are Jews. Behind them stand no guns, nor armored ships. They are Jews. They have suffered eighteen centuries; let them suffer more." But even after giving expression to this bitterness the great, and admirable Rabbi, gave evidence of the change of spirit coming over the Jews, by saying: "Let the Jew learn to strike back when he is struck, and they will learn to leave him alone. His condition will be bettered if he will keep the rest in wholesome fear of a Jewish fist and a Jewish kick." Moreover, we hear of Jewish aspirations for national existence; for the perpetuation of Jewish customs and Jewish ideals. After saying so long "may we celebrate the next Passover in Jerusalem," the brilliant thought seems to have occurred to some Jewish minds that if that expressed wish is ever realized, some particular steps must be taken looking to the actual achievement of that possibility—hence the "Zionite Movement."

"Palestine Needs a People, Israel Needs a Country"

The keynotes of that movement are heard in the following utterances of some of the Jewish leaders in explanation of it: "We want to resume the broken thread of our national existence; we want to show to the world the moral strength, the intellectual power of the Jewish people. We want a place where the race can be centralized."—(Leon Zoltokoff). "It is for these Jews (of Russia, Roumania and Galacia) that the name of their country (Palestine) spells 'Hope.' I should not be a man if I did not realize that for these persecuted Jews, Jerusalem spells reason, justice, manhood and liberty"—(Rabbi Emil G. Hirsch). "Jewish nationalism on a modern basis in Palestine, the old home of the people"—(Max Nordau). "Palestine needs a people, Israel needs a country. Give the country without a people to the people without a country"—(Israel Zangwill). In a word, it is the purpose of "Zionism" to redeem Palestine, and give it back to Jewish control,—create, in fact, a Jewish state in the land promised to their fathers.

...for hundreds of years there has been talk of the Jews returning to Jerusalem, and from time to time societies have been formed to keep alive that hope, and keep the Jew's face turned to the chief city and the land of his forefathers; but little was achieved by them except to foster the hope of Israel's return in the heart of a widely dispersed, persecuted and disheartened race, who have waited long for the realization of the promises made to the fathers:

> And I will bring again the captivity of my people of Israel, and they shall build the waste cities, and inhabit them.—(Amos. 9:14).
>
> The house of Jacob shall possess their possessions.—(Obadiah 17).
>
> For thou art an holy people unto the Lord thy God; the Lord thy God hath chosen thee to be a special people unto Himself, above all people that are upon the face of the earth.—(Deut. 7:6).
>
> The Lord shall inherit Judah his portion in the holy land, and shall choose Jerusalem again. (Zechariah 2:12).

> For the Lord will have mercy on Jacob and will yet choose Israel, and set them in their own land.—(Isaiah 14:1).
>
> Thus saith the Lord God: Behold I will take the children of Israel from among the heathen, whither they be gone, and will gather them on every side, and bring them into their own land; and I will make them one nation in the land upon the mountains of Israel; and one king shall be king to them all: and they shall be no more two nations, neither shall they be divided into two kingdoms any more at all:****and David my servant shall be king over them; and they shall have one shepherd: they shall also walk in my judgments, and observe my statues, and do them.****Moreover I will make a covenant of peace with them; it shall be an everlasting covenant with them: and I will place them and multiply them, and will set my sanctuary in the midst of them for evermore. My tabernacle also shall be with them: yea, I will be their God, and they shall be my people—(Ezekiel 37:21-27).

..."little" was accomplished by the various Jewish societies existing before the Zionite movement began beyond fostering the hope of Israel based on the prophecies here quoted; but that "little" was much. It was nourishing in secret and through ages of darkness that spark of fire which when touched by the breath of God should burst forth into a flame that not all the world could stay. They made possible this larger movement, now attracting the attention of the world, and known as the "Zionite Movement;" which, in reality, is but the federation of all Jewish societies which have had for their purpose the realization of the hopes of scattered Israel.

Annual Zionist Conferences Since 1896 Have Resulted In One of the World's Greatest Movements

"Zionism may be said to have grown out of the persecution of the Jews...in such European countries as Russia, France, Germany and Roumania. It held its first general conference in August, 1896, in Basle, Switzerland; and since then has continued to hold annual conferences that have steadily increased both in interest and the number of delegates representing various Jewish societies until now it takes on the appearance of one of the world's great movements. It is not so much a religious movement as a racial one; for prominent Jews of all shades of both political and religious opinions have participated in it under the statesmanlike leadership of Doctor Herzl of Austria.

...years ago negotiations were entered into with the Sultan of Turkey, whithin whose political dominions Palestine is included, for the purchase of the Holy Land for the Jews, and some announcements in the press by Dr. Herzl, just previous to the assembling of the Zion conference in 1902, for a time justified the high hopes that were entertained of securing the promised land by purchase. These hopes, however, were doomed to disappointment by reason of a sudden change coming over the ruler of Turkey with reference to the matter. It is more than likely that his advisors persuaded him that the establishment of a Jewish state under his suzerainty would be adding one more perplexing feature in the administration of that heterogeneous collection of such states which already constitute the loose-jointed empire over which Abul Hamid presides, by the sufferance of the European powers. The matter of the Sultan's present refusal to grant, or sell Palestine to the Jews is not a serious difficulty in the progress of such a wide spread movement as Zionism, however, if God indeed be with it; for ere now the Lord has changed the hearts of rulers in order to bring to pass his great purposes, and may do so again. So *Israel Zangwill*, one of the most enthusiatic leaders in the movement, views that subject; and also in like spirit he views the difficulty of obtaining the necessary millions to purchase the land. On this subject he says: "It matters little that the Zionists could not pay the millions, if suddenly called upon. They have collected not two and a half million dollars. But there are millionaires enough to come to the rescue once the charter was dangled before the Zionists. It is not likely that the Rothschilds would see themselves ousted from their familiar headship in authority and well-doing. Nor would the millions left by Baron Hirsch be altogether withheld. The Sultan's present refusal is equally unimportant, because a national policy is independent of transcient moods and transcient rulers. The only aspect that really matters is whether Israel's face be or be not set steadily Zionward—for decdes, and even for centuries."

The Prophet Joseph Smith Declared the Time Had Come for the Fulfillment of the Prophecies Which Decreed Israel's Return to Their Own Lands

...there need be no fear as to Israel's face being set Zionward, which means Jerusalem-ward, for the set time to favor Israel has come; the time for the fulfillment of the old promise that Jerusalem should be inhabited as a city without walls, when the laughter of children shall again be heard in her streets, draws near; and while troubles and perplexities and national and international complications may vex and at times may seem to hinder the progress of God's people toward the realization of the promises made to their fathers, still God will not leave them; and the spirit that gave rise to the Zionite movement will never cease to burn in the hearts of that people until they inherit the land of their fathers and make the needed preparation for the glorious coming of their Messiah. This, of course, I speak not of myself, nor out of any wisdom that is mine, I simply am assured of it because God through his great servant and prophet of these last days, Joseph Smith, even near the commencement of his prophetic career (1827) declared that the time had come for the fulfillment of the prophecies which decreed Israel's return to their own lands; and later (1836) Moses appeared to him in the Kirtland temple and conferred upon him the keys of the gathering of Israel and their restoration to the lands of their fathers. Under that divine authority Joseph Smith sent an Apostle of the Lord Jesus Christ to the land of Palestine to bless it and dedicate it once more to the Lord for the return of his people. This Apostle was Orson Hyde, and he performed his mission in 1840-1842. Since then, acting under the same divine authority and power, other apostolic delegations have been to that land and from the summit of Mount Olivet with upraised hands have blessed the land, and again, dedicated it for the return of the Jewish people. It is not strange, therefore, to those who look upon such a movement as Zionism in connection with faith in God's great latter-day work, to see this mysterious spirit moving upon the minds of the Jewish people. It is but the fulfillment in part of one of the many prophecies found on that wonderfully prophetic page of the Book of Mormon...."It shall come to pass that the Lord God shall commence his work among all nations, kindreds, tongues, and people to bring about the restoration of his people upon the earth." It is in view of these things that God has made known in our day through his prophets that I confidently assert the permanent presence of his Spirit upon the Jewish people, until they are returned to their promised land. (B. H. Roberts, *Young Woman's Journal* 15:51-54, February 1904)

A Proposed Jewish Colony in Uganda, British East Africa

...The British foreign minister, Lord Lansdowne, on behalf of the British government, (offered) a tract of fertile territory in Uganda, British East Africa for the establishment of the Jewish colony. It is an elevated tract of country extending some two hundred miles along the Uganda railway, between Mau and Nairobi. It is said to be well watered, fertile, cool, covered with noble forests, almost uninhabited and as healthful for Europeans as Great Britain. This tender on the part of the British government was a cause of some confusion in the Basle conference, and...a cause of great anxiety to the Zionists. It is a Jewish state in Palestine, not a colony in East Africa that the great body of Zionists are looking forward to; and when it was moved in the conference that a commission of nine be appointed to look into details and decide upon the advisability of sending an expedition to investigate the proposed site of the colony, even this preliminary step was so opposed by the Russian delegates that they arose en masse and left the conference hall, in protest against such a movement. The commission, however, was appointed and the investigation (approved). Since the close of the Basle conference many of those interested in the proposition have been searching their scriptures and some claim to have found prophetic warrant for such a movement and come to regard the settlement in Africa as a preliminary to the final movement into Palestine. The prophecies supposed to justify this view are to be found in the following from Isaiah:

Jerusalem Restored

The Gentile fulness now comes in,
And Israel's blessings are at hand;
Lo! Judah's remnant, cleansed from sin.
Shall in their promised Canaan stand.

Judah to Return to His Homeland!

Not in all the centuries of the Christian era until now has there been such a thrill of certainty of that coming event, close at hand, as awakens the Jewish heart in every land and clime. Not only with the Jew, but with the professed, and even nonprofessed, Christian in every civilized nation not fully dominated by the present German dynasties there rests the conviction of this soon-to-be-accomplished event; how the sentiment is in Germany and Austria may not be definitely ascertainable in existing circumstances, but from pre-war conditions there it may be inferred that on this one feature the Jewish heart beats in unison the world over.

Gentile Turk Forced From Judean Capital

It is a wonderful change in the aspect of affairs, dating from December 9, 1917, when was flashed to the continents of Europe and

America news that the Gentile Turk had been forced from the Judean capital.

Before then, "Zionism" was a term covering notable efforts of leading Jewish philanthropists to gather many of their race into Palestine, in hope of improving the condition largely of those who were suffering persecution and ostracism in certain nations; but despite the strength of wealth and diplomacy enlisted in that movement, results were so meagre as to be classed only as defeats. In such nations of Europe and America as the Jews were prosperous, not only was there little desire for, but there really was an aversion to Palestine as a homeland for Judah.

This is all changed; even the Jew who has no desire personally to remove from his present scene of prosperity, or who has forgotten for the time the promises and predictions of the ancient seers of his race, now is giving of his wealth and energy to make of "Zionism" a term synonymous with national Judaism in the land of his fathers. So noticeably emphatic and unanimous is the present trend in this direction, in contrast with conditions of only a year ago, that it seems almost as if a Judean nation had been "born in a day" as to this sentiment.

Great Britain Occupied Jerusalem

When, at the close of December, 1917, the German chancellor made his much-heralded Christmas "peace offer," there was in it a clause that "Turkey must remain intact," which is that Jerusalem was to go back to where it had been for four centuries—to the Gentile Turk. The instant response, coming to the world with the light of the next morning after the statement of the German chancellor, was from the premier of Great Britain, whose troops had occupied Jerusalem but twenty days before: "Whatever may be agreed upon at the close of this war, Palestine never will be relinquished to Turkey!" And all the entente allies have set their teeth on that as a now undebatable issue.

Hence, it is Palestine for Judah's homeland, although it may take months or even years to clear the way; the predictions of Jehovah's inspired servants are in due process of fulfillment. (James H. Anderson, *Relief Society Magazine,* 5:425-426, August 1918)

Epochs of Zionism

Yet,...remember that the gathering of all Israel is one great achievement for the latter days, although there may be therein several epochs; the prophetic word is that God "shall assemble the outcasts of Israel" as well as "gather together the dispersed of Judah"—Ephraim "and the house of Israel his companions." Both are to be gathered in this dispensation.

Jerusalem Redeemed Through the Law of Tithing

One of the most interesting developments in the efforts (being made) by the Zionist organization to redeem the ancient land of Jerusalem and Palestine is that they shall adopt the law of Tithing or as they term it "Maaser." Contribution to the Zionist fund both in Europe and America has been necessarily spasmodic and very uncertain for any business proposition or financial enterprise. The Zionists are trying to conduct Hebrew schools. They have instituted a hospital, a medical unit; they are building houses and financing the poor and ragged emigrants who pour into that land by the thousands every month. Modern machinery for agriculture and associated trades costs a great sum of money. Irrigation is necessary and the Zionist authorities find themselves seriously handicapped by the uncertainty of their contributions from generous-minded patrons. In consequence of this, they have prepared a little book.

Israel Will Not Be Redeemed Except Through the Power of Maaser

This little book will serve as a record of your devotion to the Jewish people in the greatest moment of its history. Preserve it in your family to show your children and your children's children that you have helped in the rebuilding of Palestine as the Jewish Homeland.

These simple but touching words greet the recipient of the neat little Maaser book which is being issued by the Keren Hayesod Bureau for America to Maaser payers. In its formal or mechanical aspect the little book serves as a record of Maaser payments. In its emotional and historic aspect it represents one of the noblest and most ancient institutions revived and dedicated to the rebuilding of the Jewish Homeland in Palestine."

What is Maaser?

Time was when the word Maaser was as familiar to every Jew as the Ten Commandments or the "Shema." The Keren Hayesod is again making Maaser a familiar thing, a Jewish institution.

Maaser is the ancient Jewish tithe or ten per cent tax on income. It is as old as the Jewish people.

Its purpose, in the past, was to provide the means with which to maintain the Jewish national institutions and the Jewish Kehillahs (communities); in the present its purpose is to provide the means with which to rebuild the Jewish National Home in Palestine.

Its method, in the past, was the levying of a ten percent tax by the Jewish state of Kehillah upon the income of every individual; in the present, it is a tax self-imposed by each individual on his or her income.

The task which the Jewish people must accomplish in rebuilding Palestine is so immense that without Maaser it cannot be accomplished. With Maaser, Palestine is sure to be rebuilt to the credit and glory of all Israel.

The Maaser "Scale"

In November 1921, there came together in New York City some 400 delegates representing Keren Hayesod workers in the United States. One of the things the conference did, the most important, perhaps, was to interpret the principle of Maaser and embody it in definite rules and formulas. A minimum Maaser scale was formally adopted. It enables every individual to figure out what his Maaser should be. The scale is as follows:

Maaser of incomes $2,000 or less	$ 25.00
Maaser of incomes between $2,000 and $3,000	50.00
Maaser of incomes between $3,000 and $4,000	100.00
Maaser of incomes between $4,000 and $5,000	150.00

Persons whose income is in excess of $5,000 are required to pay Maaser, 10 per cent, upon that amount which is subject to the United States Income Tax.

The figures, of course, are minimum figures, the least a man or woman must pay to be enrolled as a Maaser payer and receive the Maaser Book.

In answer to a question, Mr. Peter J. Schweitzer, who heads the growing list of Maaser payers in the United States, replied:

"Yes, it is a difficult thing to make people Maaser payers. That is quite true. Rebuilding the Jewish Homeland is a difficult undertaking. Not so many years ago the whole thing looked like a dream. It was a very difficult thing to get people to subscribe to the idea. Today, how many Jews are there who will not subscribe to it?

"And Jews will become Maaser payers. They will pay because they must, because their honor and their future are pledged to the rebuilding of the Jewish Homeland."

The little Maaser Book resembles a great deal the ordinary bank pass book. Maaser payments are entered as they are made. It is issued only to those who have paid in the minimum sum of $25.00 to the Keren Hayesod. It contains part of Dr. Weizmann's first manifesto to the Jews of America in behalf of the Keren Hayesod. Its keynote is the quotation from the Talmud: "Israel will not be redeemed except through the power of Maaser." (Susie Young Gates, *Relief Society Magazine,* 9:202-205, April 1, 1922.)

Zionism Offered the Jew Liberty, National Pride, and Intellectual Development

The idea, therefore, of a return to the Holy Land has its historic justification. It has found its gradual development in the movements of the past [few decades]. It is also an economic one, for it offers great inducements for the future. And there is still another reason for this idea which is now taking growth in the Zionist movement. During the last century there has been a gradual development of liberty for the Jews throughout all Europe—Russia and even in Russia there has been a growth of power, and in Europe there has been among the Jews an intellectual development that has created feelings of national pride. The Jew begins to feel his power, and in Europe there has been among the Jews an intellectual development that has created feelings of national pride. The Jew begins to feel his power, his place, and his influence in the world as he has not felt them for more than two centuries. He is an important factor in politics as well as in commerce. The Jewish school, within the last [few] years, have turned out some of the most brilliant and promising scholars of the world; and with the feeling of this power comes the thought of its exercise. I speak chiefly of the orthodox Jew who has no idea that his race can ever become assimilated with other races, or that his habits and religion will ever so change that he can take on the characteristics of other races. The Jews have never so united as to become a partisan factor in national politics. In America there is no Jewish vote. They do not consolidate in Europe to achieve any race advantages or national purpose. They are constantly overshadowed by the fear of anti-semistism. They prefer to surrender their privileges or forego their political rights rather than to venture upon a career which they feel sure must result in the strongest race prejudice, prejudice that may be as direful to the Jew as it has been calamitous in the past. They have the power, they feel it; how and where shall it be exercised? Not in a Jewish faction in other countries; that is really impossible. It must be exercised where the Jew himself constitutes the great majority, where the Jewish idea is the prevailing one; and there is no country in the world, which the Jew can look upon, that affords as excellent an opportunity for working out the manifest destiny of his race, as he now sees it, as Palestine.

So that within the last [few] years new ambitions, new economic questions, religious rivalry, and race communion, have all conspired to create a feeling in favor of the Holy Land. Dr. Herzl, an eminent journalist of Vienna, was one of the first to fully grasp the situation. He wrote a pamphlet on the subject. However, at first the appeal was little noticed, but it soon created an intense interest among the Jews. In 1897, a conference of those in favor of this movement was called to meet in Basle, Switzerland. It faced strong opposition, especially among the leading Rabbis of England and America. The commercial classes, as a rule, did not support it, but still it appealed strongly to the racial side of Jewish life. Zionism had its economic aspect, and Jewish economists were attracted by that. It had its religious aspect, and the orthodox Jews were attracted by that. It had its national aspect, and the young scholars from the universities were attracted by that. It offered an asylum for those of Roumania and Russia, who still feel the heavy hand of their oppressors, and they were attracted by that.

Herzl's Folly

Thus we see how it appeals to every phase of Jewish character and nationality. In the beginning, the movement was radically opposed. It was called Herzl's folly. By some it was looked upon as something more serious than folly. It was thought that it would arouse old antagonisms, that the Turkish government would oppress the Jew, there being more than 60,000 of them already in Palestine. It was believed that Russia, which has so much interest in some of the sacred places of Palestine, would strongly oppose any concerted movement, and that by these oppositions new dangers would come to the unfortunate race.

A Spirit of Conciliation Among the Orthodox Jews

However, the Zionists were not daunted. Another conference met in 1898. It manifested greater life, and showed that there was a spirit of conciliation among the orthodox Jews of every land. The German Jew, the Spanish Jew, the Arabic Jew were there from both hemispheres, and in the synagogue at Basle offered a prayer in the Hebrew tongue with an unanimity which betokened an enthusiasm that the critics of this movement felt was entirely wanting. While the movement may have had its origin largely in a religious feeling, economic questions soon began to develop, and the third conference which was held in Basle,...developed political aspects. The Christian powers were to be sounded; the Sultan of Turkey was to be approached; a colonial trust company was to be formed, and altogether the movement has now so grown as to give assurance of permanent life. A corporation has been organized in London under English law. A trust company is now to be established carrying a capital of ten million dollars. Since June last, more than a million of this sum has been contributed, not by the wealthy Jews but by the proletariat of America and Europe. Thousands and tens of thousands of Jews are taking stock in this company, which has a final object in the purchase of land in Palestine and the aid of those who are already there, and it will further undertake the establishment of factories as well as the development of the soil. The leaders assert their intention to acknowledge the suzerainty of the Sultan. They want autonomy for local government. They will ask for commercial freedom, but are willing to pay a royalty to the Sultan of Turkey.

New Jewish Enthusiasm, Ideas and Accomplishments

So imbued have these Jews become with the idea of national life that they have already selected a national flag. It is to be the six-pointed shield of David, in blue, on a ground of white. The new societies aiding the Zionist movement have increased tenfold within the last [few] years, and whatever may be said about the universality of this movement, it is certain that it has already received strength sufficient to make itself felt and to direct its activities along lines of practical value. The number of Jews in Palestine at [that] time is estimated all the way from sixty to eighty thousand. It is said also that in that country there are 600,000 inhabitants, but it may be doubted whether there is so large a number. A railroad has already been built from Jaffa to Jerusalem, and one must sooner or later be built from Haifa to the interior, and beyond the Jordan. Technical schools are established, and at the present time there is an energy and enthusiasm manifested among the Jewish race that have never been felt since its dispersion. There is behind all this movement, likewise, a moral force. The idea prevails among the Jews that they can promote the advancement of learning and morality by adherence to their ancient religion; that their sacred records have been the inspiration of Christians, and that a rejuvenated life and a return to those fundamental principles which made them great as a nation, will produce the same blessings and advantages to the future that the written word has furnished for the past. (J. M. Tanner, *Improvement Era* 3:4-7, November 1899.)

Chapter

9

The Miracle of Judah's Identity

> And yet for all that, when they be in the land of their enemies, I will not cast them away, neither will I abhor them, to destroy them utterly, and to break my covenant with them: for I am the Lord their God." (Leviticus 26:44.)

This great procession, this stream of Jewish history has wound its way to the present. And now, as it rushes past us toward a glowing future, we pause to reflect upon a true miracle. Though perhaps a hundred empires have risen and fallen since Abraham left his home in Ur, though the most powerful nations and peoples have passed quietly or violently into oblivion, the Jewish nation, the Jewish race has never been utterly destroyed. Read how modern prophets explain the divine preservation of Judah.

Jewish Identity Remarkable

The Jews are the most remarkable people on the face of the globe. Scattered as they are among all the nations of the earth, they still preserve their identity as a race, and retain their physiognomic peculiarities, their religious observances, and their ancient traditions. They are a standing and worldwide evidence of the truth of ancient prophecy. (Franklin D. Richards, *MS* 30:121, February 22, 1868.)

God Has Not Forgotten the Promise Made to the Forefathers

In some respects the Jews are the most remarkable race that the world has ever produced. Although their [the Jewish] nationality had been destroyed for upwards of two thousand years, yet are they separate and distinct to-day as much as any people who have not been in contact with others. When the Normans conquered Great Britain, a deadly hatred was engendered between the victors and the vanquished, as deep seated apparently as that which formerly existed between the Jews and the Samaritans; when Rome was overthrown by the barbarian hosts, there seemed no likelihood that the warring factions would ever unite together; yet at the time of these events the Jews had been scattered for several centuries, some of them here and a few there: to-day the Saxon and the Norman are indistinguishable in England: the Roman as such is no longer known among men, while the children of Judah are as distinct as they were in the days of Christ.

The history of these remarkable people is indeed wonderful. Choosing as they did to reject Him who came to save them if they would follow Him, and vehemently crying "His blood be on us, and on our children," the result has been most disastrous. The woes pronounced upon Jerusalem and her inhabitants have all been realized in every particular. The path of the Hebrews since the armies of Rome overcame them has been a thorny one. Yet in all the dispersions, persecutions, and oppressions, it is apparent that God has not forgotten the promises He had made to the forefathers of the race, nor suffered it to lose its identity among surrounding tribes.

Efforts have been made at different times, by nearly all the nations among whom the Jews have dwelt, to drive them forth to destruction, or end their existence by ruthless massacre. The recollection of Russia's latest attempt to banish the hated race is still fresh in the mind. What other people could have endured the buffetings and scourgings that have been administered with such unrelenting fury to the Jews? (A. L. Booth, *MS* 58:264-265, April 23, 1896.)

Jews Dwelt Among the Nations as a Broken and Dispersed People

"And the Lord shall scatter thee among all people from the one end of the earth unto the other," was one of the curses pronounced by Moses, the prophet of God, against Israel, if they should be disobedient. The fulfillment has been marvellously correct. From the pole to the equator—amid the frozen glaciers of the North and burning deserts of the South, thronging the populous marts and cities of the temperate zones, and wandering lonely and desolate over the steppes and arid plains of Asia and Africa, are seen the descendants of God's peculiar people—the children of him whom God honored with his friendship. Mingling with all nations, born under the same government, breathing the same atmosphere, speaking the same language, subject to the same mutations, they are still distinct! While other nations, organized and bound together by the strongest ties known to men, among whom the Jews dwelt as a broken and dispersed people, without a prophet, king or lawgiver, have passed away and lost their identity—*they* still exist, still maintain their peculiar customs, still preserve the language of their fathers and still cherish, with undeviating and unflinching faith, the promise that "He that scattered Israel will gather him, and keep him as a shepherd doth his flock." (George Q. Cannon, Writing from the Western Standard, *WFWS,* p. 215, October 5, 1856, published in 1864.)

Jews Maintained Their Ancient Moral Code

Aside from the fact that the Jews, in spite of the vast magnitude of their trials, adhere with great tenacity to their ancient moral code, and maintain principles of benevolence and charity which many professedly enlightened Christians would do well to imitate, the existence of that people as a nation and a distinct people, after having been for so many years expelled from their own country, and dispersed over the face of the earth, is so unparalleled by any instance in the history of other nations as to be considered a miracle equal, perhaps, to any recorded in the sacred writings. (W.B. Dougal, Jr., *MS* 55:165, March 6, 1893.)

Despite Persecution, Jewish Race Preserved Its Identity

Among the many glorious events that are to transpire in this last and crowning dispensation is the gathering of the Jews to the land of Palestine. The eventful history of this remarkable people is full of interest and instruction. While Israel as a people has been scattered over the whole earth, yet one branch alone—the Jewish race—has preserved its identity through all the centuries that have intervened since the dispersion. As has been truly said: "It is a fact which is the miracle of history, and the wonder of the world, that the ties which unite this people seem to be indissoluble. While other nations have risen and reigned and fallen; while the ties which unite them have been sundered, and their fragments lost amid earth's teeming population, the stock of Abraham endures, like an incorruptible monument of gold, undestroyed by the attrition of the waves of time, which have dashed in pieces and washed away other nations whose origin was but yesterday, compared with this ancient and wonderful people." This is all the more remarkable when we consider how the Jewish race has been derided and persecuted by all nations and peoples. (H. Ireland, *MS* 74:264, April 25, 1912.)

The Jews are a Living Echo of Heaven's Holy Tones

The Jews—The present physical, moral, and social condition of the Jews must be a miracle. We can come to no other conclusion. Had they continued, from the commencement of the Christian era down to the present hour, in some such national state in which we find the Chinese walled off from the rest of the human family, and by their selfishness on a national scale, and repulsion of alien elements, resisting every assault from without in the shape of hostile invasion, and from an overpowering national pride forbidding the introduction of new and foreign customs, we should not see much mystery interwoven with their existence. But this is not their state—far from it. They are neither a united and independent nation nor a parasitic province—They are peeled; scattered; and crumbled into fragments; but like broken globules of quicksilver, instinct with a cohesive power, ever claiming affinity, and ever ready to amalgamate. Geography, arms, genius, politics, and foreign help do not explain their existence; time and climate and customs equally fail to unravel it—None of these are or can be the springs of their perpetuity. They have been spread over every part of the habitable globe; they have lived under the *regime* of every dynasty; they have shared the protection of just laws, the proscription of cruel ones, and witnessed the rise and progress of both; they have used every tongue, and have lived in every latitude. The snows of Lapland have chilled, and the suns of Africa have scorched them. They have drunk of the Tiber, the Thames, the Jordan, the Mississippi—In every century, and every degree of latitude and longitude, we find a Jew. It is not so with any other race. Empires the most illustrious have fallen, and buried the men that constructed them; but the Jew has lived among the ruins, a living monument of indestructibility. Persecution has unsheathed the sword and lighted the fagot. Papal superstition and Moslem barbarism have smote them with unsparing ferocity, penal rescripts and deep prejudice have visited on them most unrighteous chastisement, and notwithstanding all, they survive. Robert Montgomery, in his Messsiah (sic), thus expresses the relative position of the Jews:

> "Empires have sunk and kingdoms past away.
> But still, apart, sublime in misery stands
> The wreck of Israel. Christ hath come and bled.
> And miracles around the cross
> A holy splendour of undying truth
> Preserve: but yet their pining spirit looks
> For that unrisen sun which prophets hail'd.
> And when I viewed him in the garb of wo;
> A wandering outcast by the world disowned,
> The haggard, lost, and long oppressed Jew,
> *'his blood be on us'* through my spirit rolls
> In fearful echo from a nation's lips.
> Remembered Zion! still for thee awaits
> A future teaming (sic) with triumphal sounds
> And shape of glory."

Like their own bush on Mount Horeb, Israel has continued in the flames, but unconsumed. They are the aristocracy of Scripture, reft of their coronets—princes in degradation. A Babylonian, a Theban, a Spartan, an Athenian, a Roman, are names known in History alone; their shadows alone haunt the world, and flicker on its tablets. A Jew walks every street, dwells in every capital, traverses every exchange, and relieves the monotony of the nations of the earth. The race has inherited the heir-loom of immortality, incapable of extinction or amalgamation. Like streamlets from a common head, and composed of waters of a peculiar nature, they have flowed along every stream, without blending with it, or receiving its color or its flavor, and traversed the surface of the globe, and the lapse of many centuries, peculiar, distinct, alone. The Jewish race, at this day, is perhaps the most striking seal of the truth of the Sacred Oracles. There is no possibility of accounting for their perpetual isolation, their depressed but distinct being, on any grounds save those revealed in the records of truth. Their aggregate and individual character is as remarkable as their circumstances. Meanness the most abject, and pride the most overbearing—the degradation of helots, and yet a conscious and a manifest sense of the dignity of a royal priesthood—crouching, cozening, squeezing, grasping, on the exchange in the shop, [and] in the world.... Notwithstanding, in the synagogue, looking back along many thousand years to an ancestry, beside which that of our peers and princes is but of yesterday, regarding justly, Abraham, Isaac, and Jacob, as their great progenitors, and pressing forward, on the wings of faith and hope and promise, to a long expected day when they, now kings and princes in disguise, shall become so indeed, by a manifestation the most glorious, and a dispensation the most sublime. The people are a perpetual miracle—a living echo of Heaven's holy tones, prolonged from generation to generation. (*Fraser's Magazine* 22:253, quoted in *TS* 2:461-462, July 1, 1841.)

The Hand of the Lord Manifest in the Preservation of the Jews

The Hebrew people have suffered during the past centuries as no other people have ever suffered, so far as my study and observation entitle me to judge. They have been scattered among strangers, where they have been denied the right of citizenship, and participation in the commercial and industrial activities of the people. They have been ruthlessly robbed of that which they have honestly acquired by the labor of their own hands. Worse than all, pogrom have been declared against them, when the protection of the law has been officially declared to be inoperative, and permission given to wicked men and women to despoil them of their goods, and even deprive them of life itself.

The wonder is that they have survived and maintained their nationality during all these centuries of affliction, and now that they are undertaking to establish a home in the land of their fathers, where they may live in peace,...they certainly must elicit the praise and sympathy of all right thinking people.

From a human point of view it is a movement of great interest... the one outstanding feature is the manifest hand-dealing of the Lord...in it, and which they themselves do not fully realize. (Anthony W. Ivins, *CR,* p. 51, April 5, 1925.)

Preservation of the Jewish Race, a Fulfillment of God's Word

The preservation of the identity of the Jewish race through all the generations that have succeeded each other in the history of that remarkable people, forms an object-lesson to those who have eyes to see, in the dealings of God with the human family, and the fulfillment of His word concerning them. A great portion of the tribes of Israel has been mingled with other nations, and the same marks that distinguish the House of Judah may not be as observable in the seed of Israel, but the identity of each of those tribes will be found to have continued even in their mixture with the Gentiles, and every promise concerning the entire family of Jacob and the seed of Abraham will be fulfilled to the very letter. (Charles W. Penrose, *MS* 72:184-185, March 24, 1910.)

Be Familiar with the Father's Plan of Human Redemption

"To properly comprehend the great plan of human redemption, designed by the Father for the blessing of his children, it is necessary that we be familiar with his hand-dealings with the people of the world, from the beginning of time, as we count it, until the present. It is not sufficient that we familiarize ourselves alone with the dispensation in which we live, important though that may be. We must know something of the past, as history has written it, the present as we see and understand it, and the future as the prophets have declared it. Without this grouping of the past, the present and the future, our vision will be restricted, and incomplete." (Anthony W. Ivins, *CR,* p. 43, April, 1925.)

Saints Should Study the History of Israel

Among the various nations which have flourished on the stage of life, there is none whose history is more interesting, or which ought to occupy the saints more, than that of the house of Israel. Descended from an ancient and honorable stock, and chosen by divine command, to be a peculiar people, distinct and separate from all others on the face of the earth, that they might keep the statutes and judgments of the Most High, and be a light and an example to all surrounding nations.

Whether we trace their history while surrounded with the blessings and privileges enjoyed in the land of Canaan, or while in captivity, and under circumstances of humiliation and wretchedness, there is something peculiar—something striking in their character and procedure, both individually and nationally....

To the saints of the last days, especially, who through obedience to the gospel, claim a relationship with their father Abraham, the events, which have transpired from the time they became a people to the present, must be doubly interesting. (Editors D. C. Smith and R. B. Thompson, *TS* 2:407, May 15, 1841.)

The Lord's Covenant with Abraham

To properly comprehend the occurrences of the past century one must be familiar with the covenant entered into by the Lord with Abraham and the history of the Israelitish people from that time until the present. The Lord declared that covenant to be eternal, everlasting, which means that it would not end until the promises made had been realized. In part, the covenant declared that through Abraham and his seed all nations of the world should be blessed.

It is through the descendants of Abraham that the Holy Bible has come down to us, the book which has done more to civilize and stabilize the world than all others which have been published. It has given to us the fundamentals of our system of government and the laws under which its affairs are administered. From the family of Abraham the Lord has raised up his ancient and modern prophets, and most important of all, Jesus Christ, his Only Begotten Son, through whom redemption from death and salvation in the kingdom of our Father is made possible to mankind. What have we that is of indispensable value to humanity which has not come to us through the Israelitish race? (Anthony W. Ivins, *CR,* p. 15, April 1930.)

Section 3

A Modern Day Miracle and Judah's Prophetic Future

Chapter
10

Advent of Modern Israel

"Thou, O Lord, did once move upon the heart of Cyrus to show favor unto Jerusalem and her children. Do Thou now also be pleased to inspire the hearts of kings and the powers of the earth to look with a friendly eye towards this place, and with a desire to see Thy righteous purposes executed in relation thereto. Let them know that it is Thy good pleasure to restore the kingdom unto Israel—raise up Jerusalem as its capital, and constitute her people a distinct nation and government, with David Thy servant, even a descendant from the loins of ancient David to be their king." (*HC* 4:457, November 22, 1842.)

Israel a Reality

The prophecies and prayers of millenia have been fulfilled and answered, Israel is a reality. But what is this reality of which we speak? To provide an adequate answer to this question we must examine present-day Israel from several angles. We must look at the historical perspective, her internal developments, and, if we can, into the very souls of her people to begin to appreciate what forces are at work within this state called Israel. Perhaps by so doing we can better trace the hand of divine guidance reaching forward from the past and onward into the future.

Historical Glimpse of Israel

The history of the State of Israel is regarded with great interest by most of those religionists interested in prophecy and indeed by people from throughout the world, as the fate of Jerusalem-of-Israel is truly a pivotal point of the events surrounding the winding-up scene, and in a purely secular sense the fate of Israel is without doubt of critical importance in world affairs. Israel's history can provide some answers for us, but not all, for while the Zionists say "We have done all this by the strength of our arm," referring to the bloodshed, labor and hardships endured, the Prophet Brigham Young provided the following reminder of the hand of God in all things: "His providences are constantly ruling and overruling, to a greater or less degree, in the affairs of the children of men." (*JD* 7:237.)

Early Settlements

To trace the history of the modern state of Israel we must go back to a desire, back through the long years of persecution and of scattering and feel the longing in the hearts of the people for the return to the lands of their fathers. Expressed in folk-songs and in hymns, it was best expressed in the words so often included in the daily prayers—"next year in Jerusalem." We must realize that a certain remnant of Judah has lived continuously in the land of Palestine. Thanks to a measure of tolerance on the part of the various Moslem rulers, Jews returned to Palestine, sometimes in massive messianic movements, most often in small groups. Most settled in the four holy cities of Jerusalem, Hebron, Safad, and Tiberias. It is in the second half of the nineteenth century that such immigration begins to increase dramatically, in direct fulfillment of Orson Hyde's prayer.

Initial Hardships

This first period of immigration, known as the First Aliya, was one of extreme hardship. The Land was a neglected corner of the Turkish empire, often swampy and producing frequent cases of malaria, with fatalities striking three or four members of a family a not uncommon occurrence. With persistence and ingenuity, the swamps were drained. Obtaining adequate water was a problem in some areas. One pioneer family recalls leaving their Liverpool, England home with servants and luxuries, for primitive little houses with only enough water for drinking and the most minimal of other uses. Philanthropic assistance for the Jewish community in Palestine began to come in from throughout the world. Wealthy Jews contributed money for the construction of schools, hospitals, printing presses were set up and more villages were founded.

Zionism

In the last decade of the nineteenth century a significant event occurred that was to have a lasting effect upon the history of Israel. Having been exposed to the anti-Semitism exhibited during the Dreyfuss incident in France, Theodor Herzl formulated an idea that soon took the name—Zionism. As outlined in his treatise, *Der Judenstaat,* Herzl's idea was to solve the problems of minority persecution of the Jews by political means—the establishment of a national homeland for the Jews. Published in 1896, *Der Judenstaat* provided the spark needed to rekindle Jewish hopes for a return. In 1897 the 1st World Zionist Congress was held in Basel, Switzerland with the end result that Herzl's idea was adopted as a goal for Jews everywhere. So profound was the hope that in his journal Herzl made this famous and even prophetic statement, "At Basel I created the Jewish State." Spurred by this new hope, immigration was increased. In the last few years of the nineteenth century, the Jewish population doubled, from 24,000 to 50,000.

The Second Aliya

This new surge of immigration, specifically the years 1904 to 1914, is known today as the Second Aliya. Instilled by the Zionist fervor, Jewish youth, who regarded their labors as the way to rebuild the Land, threw themselves heart and soul into working the Land itself. One of the results of this attitude was the *kibbutz,* a communal or collective cooperative settlement, which works according to the principle—from each according to his ability, to each according to his need. The first kibbutz, Deganyz, was founded in old Arab huts on a mud flat 200 meters below sea level. This Second Aliya, with its attendant formulation of Jewish priorities in Palestine, brought the population level to 85,000 Jews in Palestine by 1914.

Restoration of Hebrew

One of the most pressing problems of absorbing the new immigrants was language; Jews arrived from Spain speaking a dialect of Spanish, from North Africa speaking Arabic, from the Caucasus speaking Georgian, from Europe, speaking Yiddish. Palestine was described as sounding like a tower of Babel. When the leaders met together, they spoke Hebrew, which had never really become a forgotten language, although it was used more by the scholarly elite than by the common folk. It could be compared to Greek or Latin. However, Eliezer Ben Yehuda, the father of modern Hebrew, devoted his whole life to the vision of modern Hebrew. To make Hebrew the language of everyday life required a fanatic missionary zeal, for the orthodox argued that it was blasphemous to vulgarize the sacred words of scripture for everyday purposes, and even the non-religious Zionists admitted a feeling of discomfort as they read soap advertisements in the language of Isaiah.

Eliezer Ben Yehuda and his wife took a vow on shipboard on the way to Palestine never to speak any other words than Hebrew, and he worked for thirty years to accomplish the same for the Jews in Palestine. His worst opponents were the practical people who thought children should be taught some more "useful" language. But poverty-stricken, terribly ill, ridiculed, Ben Yehuda worked to complete a Hebrew dictionary. He tracked every word down to its roots, and created new words for modern needs. When Hebrew became the language of the schools, even in the new technical college near Tel Aviv, the nationalization of Hebrew was assured. And without that, Palestine might never have been able to so rapidly assimilate the influx of new immigrants.

The Balfour Declaration

World War I brought new changes to the land of Palestine. In an effort to secure the aid of the inhabitants of Palestine in the battle against the Central Powers, which included Turkey, Britain held discussions with various leaders in the area. The result of one such discussion was the now famous "Balfour Declaration." In 1917, Britain's Foreign Secretary, Arthur James Balfour, sent to Lord Rothschild, a significant landholder in Palestine as well a scion of one of the richest and most influencial Jewish families in the world, the following letter:

"Foreign Office
November 2, 1917

"Dear Lord Rothschild,

"I have much pleasure in conveying to you, on behalf of His Majesty's government, the following declaration of sympathy with Jewish Zionist aspirations which has been submitted to, and approved by, the Cabinet.

"His Majesty's Government view with favour the establishment in Palestine of a national home for the Jewish people, and will use their best endeavors to facilitate the achievement of this object, it being clearly understood that nothing shall be done which may prejudice the civil and religious rights of existing non-Jewish communities in Palestine, or the rights and political status enjoyed by Jews in any other country.

"I should be grateful if you would bring this declaration to the knowledge of the Zionist Federation.

Yours sincerely,
James Balfour"

The Declaration had been carefully worded in an attempt to solicit Jewish support without endangering the support promised by the Arabs in the area. While the Declaration appears on first glance to give blanket support to the Zionist cause, the significance both in 1917 and today of the second clause of the Declaration is of critical importance. Britain pledges to support the Zionists, "it being clearly understood" that the rights of the Arabs are also respected. Herein lies the root of the problems that began after the war and the root of many of the problems that remain with us today.

Palestine Under British Mandate

At the end of World War I, Palestine was placed under the tutelage of Britain in the form of a mandate. In the years following 1919, the population rose rapidly. By 1931 it had reached 175,000, the result of the Third Aliya. During these years of increasing immigration, the Jewish settlers, called the *Yishuv,* evolved their own political institutions and parties; established a democratically elected Representative Assembly and a National Council; organized defense formations; educational systems; and bodies dealing with economic and social affairs. These preparations facilitated the transition later on to an independent state.

Arab Reaction

At the outset the leaders of the Arab countries generally accepted the Jewish claims to Palestine as endorsed in the Balfour Declaration (King Hussein of the Hejaz wrote that "the country was for its original sons, for all their differences, a sacred and beloved homeland," *Al Qibla,* Mecca, No. 183, 23 March 1918).

When Jewish industry began to transform Palestine, Arab landowners, who were violently opposed to letting their laborers, who were paid barely enough to subsist, see the happy lot of Jewish laborers, for it began to foment riots among Arab villagers. This was a separate sentiment from the valid Arab nationalist spirit which rose in young Arabs at the end of the First World War. In fact, the official representative of the Arab leaders during the post-war settlements, Emir Feisal, wrote: "We Arabs look with the deepest sympathy on the Zionist movement. We will wish the Jews a most hearty welcome home." And the Jewish leaders sought to reach mutual agreement with the Arab community.

The efforts of the British, beginning with the careful wording of the Balfour Declaration, to placate both Arabs and Jews began to fail. Militant Arabs objected to the increased Jewish immigration and took it as a threat to their "civil and religious rights." *"The* underlying cause," said a Jewish spokesman discussing the problem," is that we *exist."*

In order to appease the rising tensions, which revealed themselves in every-increasing terrorist attacks against people and property on both sides, a Royal Commission was set up in 1936 to examine the problem and to propose solutions. The Peel Report, while paying tribute to the Jews for having turned the generally poor land they had bought into very productive land (a refutation of the Arab charge that the Jews had taken a disproportionate amount of good land and therefore was in violation of their rights), acknowledged that the situation was untenable as it stood. The solution, it proposed, was a partitioning of Palestine into two unequal parts, with a Jewish state in the smaller part (in the north and west) and an Arab state combined with the Transjordan in the south and east.

White Paper Decisions

Although the debates were vigorous in the British Parliament, the government announced, in a White Paper, that the British government agreed with the conclusions of the Commission. Even though the partition was a bitter disappointment in view of the promises of the Balfour Declaration as they interpreted it, the leaders of the Jewish community in Palestine accepted it in principle; the Palestine Arab leadership rejected it. The leader of the Palestine Arab community at the time was the Grand Mufti, Haj Amin al-Husseini of Jerusalem, who was responsible for most of the terrorist bloodshed during the years before the Second World

War. (During that war he joined the Nazis and spent the war years in Berlin with Hitler.)

Illegal Immigration

With the failure of the partition proposal, the British government decided that the only solution was to restrict immigration. During the four years preceding World War II, over 86,000 immigrants reached the Land, many of them illegally, as the British attempted to placate the Arabs. But any limit on immigration was either too high for the Arabs or too low for the Jews, and the British were either witness to or the victim of terrorist activities perpetrated by both sides. Finally, just before the war, the British published a new White Paper on Palestine. It stated that no further Jewish immigration would be allowed and that in 10 years Jews would be allowed to acquire land in only 5 percent of the country's area under an Arab State. This document was a complete reversal of the British government's former promises. To this the Zionists replied that the Jews would not allow their bond to the land to be broken, and continued illegal immigration.

Jewish Participation in the War

When World War II broke out, David Ben-Gurion, then the leader of the Yishuv, declared, "We shall fight side by side with Britain in our war against Hitler as if there were no White Paper, and we shall fight the White Paper as if there were no war." In September 1939, 130,000 Jewish men and women registered to fight in the British army. The British government at first refused to accept Jewish volunteers until an equal number of Arabs came forward. However, few Arabs volunteered, and most of their leaders in Palestine and in neighboring countries supported Hitler. Finally, Jewish volunteers were accepted and took part in the decisive battles of the war.

The Holocaust

Ironically, during this time of Jewish military assistance, all throughout Europe the Nazis were dragging the Jewish people through the most tragic experiences of their long history. The distance of time and perhaps our callousness to violence created by the vividness of the mass media may have numbed us and caused us to forget the horror of the Nazi crimes upon the Jewish people.

The Holocaust was organized mainly by the German Nazis, however, they were assisted in some European countries by local elements, who helped to round up the Jews for shipment to the death camps. Some commentators have casually concluded that the genocide was God's punishment on the Jewish people for killing Christ; however, the enormity of the massacre defies any attempt at reason.

This book will not examine the atrocities committed, as there are many books which chronicle the Holocaust. Let the reader imagine the extent of a number such as six million, many times the population of a city such as Salt Lake, and compare the enormity of that loss to the soul-searching anguish we feel when a cold-blooded killer is made to suffer the needs of justice. In a few instances, the Jews were able to resist and even escape the Nazis, but on the whole propaganda, in the form of forged mail and films, and a vastly superior force allowed the mass murder of nearly six million Jews in Europe. We shall examine the effect this horror has today on Israel later in this chapter. It is important to note, however, that the tragedy even further galvanized the desire for a separate national state—where Jews could determine their own destiny.

Displaced Persons' Camps

When the war ended, the Allied armies found about 30,000 Jews still alive in the concentration camps. They were broken and disheartened, unwilling to return to the tragic sites of their homelands, left with the memories of the fate of their families. The military authorities set up Displaced Persons' Camps to provide temporary food and shelter and status for the victims of Nazism. These camps soon became oppressively full, with people registering not only from the concentration camps but from countries that still suffered from the vestiges of war. By 1947 there were 177,000 Jews in the camps when the American authorities who administered the camps closed off registration. Many of these people, hopeful at first, remained in the camps until after the War of Independence and the formation of the new State of Israel, a very long time after their sufferings. Their entry into Israel became one of the State's first priorities and problems of absorption.

Israel is Born

In 1948, the British, weary of trying to satisfy both sides, relinquished the mandate they had held for over 30 years, and at the same time the United Nations, after strenuous debates, approved the founding of a partitioned Palestine with a Jewish State and an Arab State. The Jews accepted the proposal, but the Arabs rejected it. When the British withdrew, the Jews raised the flag of Israel and proclaimed the new State of Israel, issuing the following Declaration of Independence:

The Proclamation of Independence

In the land of Israel the Jewish people came into being. In this land was shaped their spiritual, religious and national character. Here they lived in sovereign independence. Here they created a culture of national and universal import, and gave to the world the eternal Book of Books.

Exiled by force, still the Jewish people kept faith with their land in all the countries of their dispersion, steadfast in their prayer and hope to return and here revive their political freedom.

Fired by this attachment of history and tradition, the Jews in every generation strove to renew their roots in the ancient homeland, and in recent generations they came home in multitudes. Veteran pioneers and defenders, they made the wilderness bloom, revived their Hebrew tongue, and built villages and towns. They founded a thriving society, master of its own economy and culture, pursuing peace but able to defend itself, bringing the blessing of progress to all the inhabitants of the Land, dedicated to the attainment of sovereign independence.

In 1897 the First Zionist Congress met at the call of Theodor Herzl, seer of the vision of the Jewish State, and gave public voice to the right of the Jewish people to national restoration in their land.

This right was acknowledged in the Balfour Declaration of 2 November 1917, and confirmed in the Mandate of the League of Nations, which accorded international validity to the historical connection between the Jewish people and the Land of Israel, and to their right to re-establish their National Home.

The holocaust that in our time destroyed millions of Jews in Europe again proved beyond doubt the compelling need to solve the problem of Jewish homelessness and dependence by the renewal of the Jewish State in the Land of Israel, which would open wide the gates of the homeland to every Jew and endow the Jewish people with the status of a nation with equality of rights within the family of nations.

Despite every hardship, hindrance and peril, the remnant that survived the grim Nazi slaughter in Europe, together with Jews from other countries, pressed on with their exodus to the Land of Israel and continued to assert their right to a life of dignity, freedom and honest toil in the homeland of their people.

In the Second World War, the Jewish community in the Land of Israel played its full part in the struggle of the nations championing freedom and peace against the Nazi forces of evil. Its war effort and the lives of its soldiers won it the right to be numbered among the founding peoples of the United Nations.

On November 29, 1947, the General Assembly of the United Nations adopted a resolution calling for the establishment of a Jewish State in the Land of Israel, and required the inhabitants themselves to take all measures necessary on their part to carry out the resolution. This recognition by the United Nations of the right of the Jewish people to establish their own State is irrevocable.

It is the natural right of the Jewish people, like any other people, to control their own destiny in their sovereign state.

Accordingly, we, the members of the National Council, representing the Jewish people in the Land of Israel and the Zionist Movement, have assembled on the day of termination of the British Mandate for Palestine, and, by virtue of our natural and historic right and of the resolution of the General Assembly of the United Nations, do hereby proclaim the establishment of a Jewish State in the Land of Israel—the State of Israel.

We resolve that, from the moment the Mandate ends, at midnight on the Sabbath, the sixth day of Iyar, 5708, the fifteenth day of May, 1948, until the establishment of the duly elected authorities of the State in accordance with a Constitution to be adopted by the Elected Constituent Assembly not later than 1 October, 1948, the National Council shall act as the Provisional Council of State, and its executive arm, the National Administration, shall constitute the Provisional Government of the Jewish State, and the name of that State shall be Israel.

The state of Israel will be open to Jewish immigration and the ingathering of the exiles. It will devote itself to developing the land for the good of all its inhabitants. It will rest upon the foundations of liberty, justice and peace as envisioned by the Prophets of Israel. It will maintain complete equality of social and political rights for all its citizens, without distinction of creed, race, or sex. It will guarantee freedom of religion and conscience, of language, education and culture. It will safeguard the Holy Places of all religions. It will be loyal to the principles of the United Nations Charter.

The state of Israel will be prepared to cooperate with the organs and representatives of the United Nations in carrying out the General Assembly resolution of 29 November, 1947, and will work for the establishment of the economic union of the whole Land of Israel.

We appeal to the United Nations to assist the Jewish people in the building of their State, and to admit the State of Israel into the family of nations.

Even amidst the violent attacks launched against us for months past, we call upon the sons of the Arab people dwelling in Israel to keep the peace and to play their part in building the State on the basis of full and equal citizenship and due representation in all its institutions, provisional and permanent.

We extend the hand of peace and good-neighbourliness to all the States around us and to their peoples, and we call upon them to cooperate in mutual helpfulness with the independent Jewish nation in its land. The State of Israel is prepared to make its contribution in a concerted effort for the advancement of the entire Middle East.

We call upon the Jewish people throughout the Diaspora to join forces with us in immigration and construction, and to be at our right hand in the great endeavour to fulfil the age-old longing for the redemption of Israel.

With trust in the rock of Israel, we set our hands in witness to this Proclamation, at this session of the Provisional council of State, on the soil of the homeland, in the city of Tel Aviv, this Sabbath Eve, the fifth day of Iyar, 5708, the fourteenth day of May, 1948. (Keter Publishing House, Ltd. *Facts About Israel,* 1971, The Israel Program for Scientific Translations, Ltd. Keter Books, Jerusalem, 1971, pp. 8-10.)

Immediately Israel was attacked on all sides by Arab forces, these supported by British military equipment, and, in the case of Transjordan, military leadership.

Everyone expected that the vastly superior forces of the combined Arab armies would quickly defeat the tiny country of Israel. At first, the Arabs achieved stunning victories, including the city of Jerusalem (which was to have been under international control under the partition agreement) and the Negev Desert which had been given Israel according to the U.N. agreement. However, the Israelis rallied, and because of their fierce spirit and the realization that this was a last-stop effort, not only drove the Arabs from the territory they had captured (with the exception of Old Jerusalem), but actually took more territory. Indeed, the United Nations forced truces during the critical points in the fighting; one in particular when the Jews had beaten back the Egyptians so far they could even have marched on Cairo! During this war, convinced by Arab leaders' promises that they should soon recover their homes, nearly 500,000 Arabs fled their homes in Palestine and took what they thought was temporary refuge in neighboring Arab countries. These people became the inhabitants of the Arab refugee camps still in existence today, although many Arabs remained in their homes and villages and still enjoy autonomy and local Arab leadership and representation in the Israeli parliament.

When the new government was organized and elections took place, immigration increased in a way that was unprecedented by any other country. In a little over a year, nearly a quarter of a million newcomers entered Israel. The sheer numbers caused terrific problems, especially of housing, culture, and of language. The infant government accepted them all, however, and in a few years rallied with an expanding economy.

The Sinai War

Coping with the burdens of creating a new State, absorbing an incredible number of immigrants, and developing a vigorous economy, however, were manageable compared to the ever-present threat of invasion by neighboring countries. In 1956, Egypt's Nasser nationalized the Suez Canal, blockading Israeli trade. Attacks by Arab raiders were increasing rapidly, and in October, with support from the British government, Israel attacked Egypt. Her victories brought U.N. assurance of separation by U.N. forces of Israel and Egypt and use of the Suez Canal among other promises. These, however, were not recognized by the Egyptians.

The Six-Day War

During the next ten years, Arab countries strengthened their arsenals, and Israel strengthened its military as well. Various statements of Arab policy are typified by this one from Nasser and President Aref of Iraq: "The Arab national aim is the elimination of Israel." The Arab forces concentrated in Sinai, demanded the withdrawal of the U.N. security force, formed a war pact among Arab nations, and on 5 June 1967, war broke out.

During that war, which was highlighted by a brilliantly coordinated destruction of Arab planes on the ground at a number of Egyptian military bases, Israel established new cease-fire lines and reunified Jerusalem; it was a time of intense rejoicing among Jews who had longed for the City for centuries. Soldiers, some of them still with their guns, worshipped and wept at the Wailing Wall, which had not been in Jewish hands since 70 A.D. Not long after, thousands of Jews flocked to the Wall, as it is a sacred place of worship.

After the 1967 war, Israel sought to negotiate with the Arab Governments to establish a true peace, to establish secure borders and develop a productive inter-relationship. However, in 1967, the Arab leaders met in a Summit Conference in Khartoum and laid down four principles: "No peace with Israel; no negotiations with Israel; no recognition of Israel; and insistence on the rights of 'the Palestinian people in their own country.' " Recent negotiations in 1977-78 with Egypt have given hope for a change in these principles, although in the years following the Six-Day War (1968-70) there followed what is called a War of Attrition along all the cease-fire lines, especially along the Suez Canal and the Jordan River. This war became more difficult for the Israelis as the Soviet Union assembled and manned a growing number of ground-to-air missile sites. The United Nations called a cease-fire and attempted to defuse the situation and open talks, but even so in the years following, Israel had to vigilantly repulse terrorist attacks along the cease-fire lines.

The Yom Kippur War

In 1973, an Egyptian-Syrian attack against Israel on Yom Kippur, the Day of Atonement, caught the Israelis unaware. Masses of Egyptian and Syrian armor attacked simultaneously across the Suez Canal and across the cease-fire lines in the Golan Heights. The small regular forces of Israel put up a heroic fight and inflicted heavy losses on the enemy but could not prevent a penetration of the cease-fire lines. The superior forces, amounting to 12:1, resulted in significant military achievements, but Israel rapidly mobilized and drove the Syrians back over the cease-fire lines, and even came within shelling distance of the suburbs of Damascus! On the southern front, Israel came within 101 km. (about 75 miles) of Cairo. However, Israel suffered proportionately heavy losses, the most since the war in 1948. After the war the U.N. again attempted to establish peace agreements between the countries, in which

Egypt, Syria and Israel agreed to stabilize the cease-fire. And, although there seems to be a continual problem with terrorist activity along the borders, full-scale war has been avoided until present (1978).

Peace Initiatives

After the hostilities were halted, efforts were made to try and stabilize the situation. Through the U.N. both sides agreed to respect the cease-fire but the continual problem of terrorist attacks kept the situation tense. In the years since the war ended various efforts at a negotiated peace were attempted. It was not, however, until 1977 that prospects began to brighten. Since those initial overtures were carried out by both Egypt and Israel, some progress has been made. At the writing of this book, however, no firm lasting peace has been achieved, although the efforts continue. One can only hope for the best.

Achievements of the State of Israel

(See tables at end of chapter for more information.)

It is one thing to bring a nation into being; it is perhaps an even greater task to keep it alive. Israel today is an active and productive member of the world's community of nations. We could therefore fill a volume in an attempt to catalog her many achievements. Instead, the following selected list of Israeli achievements is intended to paint in general terms the reality that is Israel.

Agriculture

As has been already noted, the first settlements in Palestine were agricultural in nature. From these often very humble beginnings, Israel has expanded phenomenally. Soon after the establishment of the State of Israel, a concerted project for the irrigation of the vast amount of arable but as yet arid land began. Projects, such as the Yarkon-Negev water pipeline, brought water from the Sea of Galilee to the kibbutzim and moshavim cooperative settlements which form the backbone of the country's agriculture.

With a climate varying from the cooler climes of the north to the warmer ones of the south, now watered by the pipelines, Israel is able to produce a wide variety of products ranging from apples to bananas, from strawberries to grapefruit. So successful have the

Israelis been in producing citrus fruits, for example, that their export made up 24% of the $886 million exported in 1976 to the European Common Market alone.

In addition to fruits and vegetables, Israel has made tremendous strides in other food oriented production. The country boasts the highest milk-producing cow in the world and is about third in per-cow production.

The overall effect of these strides in agriculture is that Israel is able to a great degree to feed herself and also to export certain products. The contrast to the days prior to Jewish settlement when the area was thought to be unproductive is striking.

Reforestation

An interesting sidelight to the increased emphasis on agriculture has been a concerted effort to turn those lands otherwise not suited to regular agriculture to forest lands. Trees have been planted where none have grown for millenia. The goal is not only for possible economic benefit, but also for the overall beauty of the country. One part of this reforestation drive is the construction of the Jerusalem Gardens National Park, a circular belt of green around the entire city of Jerusalem.

Industry

In the modern world it seems that in order to "succeed" as a nation, a successful industrial capacity is essential. Despite a scarcity of raw materials, which makes heavy importation a necessity, sometimes over great distances, industrial exports reached nearly $2 million in 1976.[2] Israel exports electric and electronic equipment (since they produce such items they are less dependent on imports during times of war), textiles and clothing, manufactured from locally grown cotton, and diamonds.

Although the raw materials must be imported, diamond cutting is such a large industry that Israel has a virtual monopoly in the type of stone in which it specializes—industrial diamonds, and the

---

1. Ben-Moshe, A., "Processed Foods Exports," *The Israel Year Book, 1978* (Tel Aviv: Israel Year Book Publications, Ltd., 1978), p. 169.

2. "Israel's Industrial Development Objectives, 1975-1985," *The Israel Year Book, 1978* (Tel Aviv: Israel Year Book Publications, Ltd., 1978), p. 244.

EXTERNAL TRADE (million U.S. $)

	1969	1970	1971	1972	1973	1974	1975	1976
Imports	1,304.4	1,433.5	1,811.6	1,961.4	2,968.6	4,176.5	4,108.7	4,068.6
Exports	688.7	733.6	915.1	1,099.8	1,391.8	1,737.4	1,834.6	2,306.6
						(U.S. $'000)		
Diamonds, worked					617,109	641,131	640,744	799,726
Edible fruits					127,854	137,528	200,797	203,922
Fruit and vegetable products					73,399	88,654	77,905	99,079
Inorganic chemicals					16,315	36,473	45,428	33,930
Electrical machinery					27,082	42,704	78,112	93,467

(*The Europa Year Book, 1978, A World Survey,* Vol. II, London: Europa Publications Limited, 1978), p. 594.)

diamonds are almost exclusively marketed abroad. This export makes up a very significant portion of the nation's export trade.

In addition to manufactured products, Israel is able to produce commercial quantities of copper from the Timna mines near Eliat, phosphates from the Oron deposits, and potash extracted from the Dead Sea.

STATISTICAL SURVEY

AREA AND POPULATION

Area	Population December 31st, 1977	Birth Rate (per '000) 1976	Marriage Rate (per '000) 1976	Death Rate (per '000) 1976
20,325 sq. km.*	3,650,000	27.6†	8.4†	7.1†

* 7,848 square miles.

†These figures include the population of the Old City of Jerusalem and the surrounding areas (area 70 sq. km.), which Israel annexed in 1967.

ADMINISTERED TERRITORIES*
(1976)

	Area (sq. km.)	Population (1976)
Golan	1,150	n.a.
Judea and Samaria	5,879	689,700
Gaza Strip (incl. El-Arish)	378	444,400
Sinai	61,181	
Total	68,588	n.a.

*The area and population of the Administered Territories have changed as a result of the October 1973 war.

The area figures in this table refer to October 1st, 1973. No later figures are available.

POPULATION OF CHIEF TOWNS*
(January 1977)

Town	Population	Town	Population
Jerusalem (capital)	366,000	Holon	117,600
Tele-Aviv—Jaffa	348,600	Petach-Tikva	109,600
Haifa	228,100	Beersheba	98,900
Ramat Gan	121,800	Bene Beraq	84,600

* Provisional.

GROWTH OF POPULATION AND JEWISH IMMIGRATION, 1962-1976

End of Year	Permanent Population	Jews	Others	Immigration
1964	2,525,600	2,239,000	286,400	54,716
1965	2,598,400	2,299,100	299,300	30,736
1966	2,657,400	2,344,900	312,500	15,730
1967 *	2,773,900	2,383,600	390,300	14,327
1968 *	2,841,100	2,434,800	406,300	20,544
1969 *	2,929,500	2,506,800	422,700	23,510
1970 *	3,022,000	2,582,000	440,100	20,624
1971 *	3,120,500	2,662,000	458,700	41,930
1972 *	3,225,000	2,752,700	472,300	55,888
1973 *	3,338,200	2,845,000	493,200	54,886
1974 *	3,421,600	2,906,900	514,700	31,979
1975 *	3,493,400	2,959,400	533,800	20,028
1976 *	3,570,900	3,017,500	553,400	19,754
1977 *	3,650,000	3,076,000	574,000	n.a.

* These figures exclude the population of the areas administered by Israel since June 1967 (*see* above), but include the population of the Old City of Jerusalem and the surrounding areas.

EMPLOYMENT
('000)

	1973	1974	1975	1976
Agriculture, Forestry and Fishing	82.5	71.5	71.1	72.1
Mining, Quarrying and Manufacturing	273.4	278.4	274.4	273.8
Electricity, Gas and Water	10.3	10.4	11.1	11.5
Construction	95.8	88.5	90.2	86.3
Trade, Restaurants and Hotels	138.5	131.2	136.2	139.6
Transport, Storage & Communications	79.1	83.3	80.3	78.6
Financing, Insurance & Business Services	66.8	68.4	73.8	76.3
Community, Social & Personal Services	344.7	357.8	369.2	381.6
Others	3.4	7.1	6.2	7.1
Total	1,094.4	1,096.7	1,112.6	1,126.9

AGRICULTURE
Agricultural Land Usage
('000 dunums or '00 hectares)

	1970-71	1971-72	1972-73	1973-74	1974-74 *	1975-76 *
Field Crops.......	2,660	2,650	2,672	2,739	2,790	2,795
Fruit, incl. citrus...	835	845	861	870	880	890
Vegetables, potatoes, etc........	370	396	354	376	368	370
Nurseries, flowers, fish ponds, etc..	275	274	283	285	282	285
Total Cultivated Area............	4,140	4,165	4,170	4,270	4,320	4,340

* Provisional

PRODUCTION
(metric tons)

	1970-72	1971-72	1972-73	1973-74	1974-75	1975-76
Wheat............	199,500	301,400	241,500	274,000	243,300	205,500
Barley............	17,600	32,800	17,900	30,200	20,600	18,200
Sorghum.........	20,600	40,400	29,700	34,200	32,200	12,600
Hay..............	141,200	132,500	126,800	138,000	148,400	140,100
Groundnuts.......	21,200	19,800	14,600	18,000	18,800	23,500
Cotton lint........	36,700	40,300	37,400	49,800	48,800	53,650
Cottonseed.......	69,000	67,400	63,400	84,000	82,000	87,000
Sugar beet........	258,600	248,500	217,300	116,700	259,000	323,600
Melons & pumpkins	132,900	161,700	127,000	124,000	134,800	134,800
Vegetables.......	490,400	502,000	532,700	496,200	609,200	581,100
Potatoes..........	142,000	143,100	165,100	152,400	163,000	174,700
Citrus fruit........	1,513,500	1,552,800	1,688,600	1,698,000	1,506,000	1,513,350
Grapefruit........	361,300	334,300	390,800	395,500	416,800	456,450
Lemons...........	46,400	39,900	45,400	36,500	37,700	37,350
Oranges: Shamouti	746,500	842,200	817,000	834,400	679,800	648,100
Lates....	298,100	273,500	362,600	358,500	299,700	298,250
Other varieties....	61,200	62,900	72,800	73,100	72,000	73,200
Other fruit........	307,700	359,800	297,000	332,600	347,950	376,950
Milk (kl.) (incl. sheep and goat milk)...........	497,500	519,200	565,900	590,900	627,700	704,250

FISHING
(tons)

1972-73	1973-74	1974-75	1975-76
26,500	22,700	22,200	24,350

LIVESTOCK
('000)

	1974	1975	1976
Cattle	300	323	345
Poultry *	12,000	12,500	14,000
Sheep	197	202	218
Goats	138	140	142

* Except broilers

MINING

		1973	1974	1975	1976
Crude petroleum	million litres	44	45	40	41
Natural gas	million cu. m.	54	66	60	58
Copper ore	'000 metric tons	10.5	9.5	8.0	n.a.
Phosphate rock	'000 metric tons	780	1,026	882	639

INDUSTRY
Selected Products

		1973	1974	1975	1976
Wheat flour	'000 metric tons	420	401	452	443
Refined sugar	'000 metric tons	23.6	11.5	28.4	35.6
Margarine	'000 metric tons	34.2	34.8	33.1	31.2
Wine	'000 hectolitres	401.6	403.0	n.a.	n.a.
Beer	'000 hectolitres	355.1	340.9	355.1	350.9
Cigarettes	metric tons	4,938	5,243	5,553	5,488
Cotton yarn	metric tons	20,950	20,241	21,533	21,244
Woven cotton fabrics*	metric tons	10,650	12,098	11,100	n.a.
Newsprint	metric tons	8,958	7,095	7,472	12,689
Writing and printing paper	metric tons	41,416	45,405	45,742	39,498
Other paper	metric tons	26,450	27,494	26,232	30,593
Rubber tyres	'000	1,688	1,650	1,466	1,680
Sulphuric acid	'000 metric tons	193	187	194	208
Caustic soda	metric tons	18,797	20,458	24,156	24,009
Cement	'000 metric tons	1,258	1,796	2,189	2,042
Passenger cars	number	4,014	2,936	2,382	3,934
Commercial vehicles	number	4,262	5,388	3,922	3,097
Electricity	million kWh.	8,722	9,153	9,712	10,354

* After undergoing finishing processes.
†Israel Electric Corporation only (8,837 million kWh. in 1974).

FINANCE

100 agorot (singular, agora) = 1 Israeli pound (I£).
Coins: 1, 5, 10, 25 and 50 agorot; 1 pound.
Notes: 50 agorot; 1, 5, 10, 50 and 100 pounds.
Exchange rates (December 1977): £1 sterling = I£28.02;
U.S. $1 = I£15.30; I£100 = £3.57 sterling = $6.54.

Note: The Israeli pound was introduced in August 1948, replacing (at par) the Palestine pound, equal to the pound sterling, then worth U.S. $4.03. In September 1949 the Israeli pound was devalued (in line with sterling) to $2.80 and this valuation remained in effect until February 1952. Multiple exchange rates were in operation between February 1952 and mid-1955. From July 1955 to February 1962 the official exchange rate was U.S. $1 = I£1.80. Between February 1962 and November 1967 the exchange rate was $1 = I£3.00. From November 1967 to August 1971 the rate was $1 = I£3.50 (I£1 = 28.57 U.S. cents). It was $1. = I£4.20 (I£1 = 23.81 U.S. cents) from August 1971 to November 1974; $1 = I£6.00 (I£1 = 16.67 U.S. cents) from November 1974 to June 1975. Since June 1975 the currency has been frequently devalued. In July 1976 the Israeli pound was linked to a "basket" of five currencies of the country's main trading partners, instead of being linked to the U.S. dollar alone. The average market rate (£I per U.S.$) was 4.50 in 1974; 6.39 in 1975, 7.98 in 1976. The exchange rate was £1 sterling = I£8.40 from February 1962 to August 1971; and £1 sterling = I£10.944 from December 1971 to June 1972.

CENTRAL GOVERNMENT BUDGET
(I£ million, twelve months ending March 31st)

Revenue	1974/75	1975/76	1976/77 *	1977/78 *
Ordinary Budget	25,500.1	35,364.3	70,100	95,000
Income Tax and Property Tax	7,566.7	13,164.5	19,704	29,015
Customs and Excise	7,552.2	9,056.8	11,320	13,420
Purchase Tax	2,924.2	4,721.2	5,825	7,600
Employers' Tax	—	865.0	1,015	1,750
Value Added Tax	—	—	4,720	9,480
Other Taxes	1,070.5	1,534.2	1,918	2,372
Interest	993.1	1,417.1	1,687	2,073
Loans	3,085.7	1,135.9	1,370	1,505
Other Receipts	2,307.7	3,470.6	2,643	3,511
Transfer from Development Budget	—	—	19,898	24,274
Development Budget	15,317.7	27,406.0	17,500	27,500
Foreign Loans	8,646.2	14,865.2	23,080	28,850
Internal Loans	5,791.9	5,762.9	10,345	16,400
Other Receipts	879.6	6,777.9	3,973	6,524
Transfer to Ordinary Budget	—	—	-19,898	-24,274
Total	40,817.8	62,770.3	87,600	122,500

* Estimates

Expenditure	1974/75	1975/76	1976/77 *	1977/78 *
Ordinary Budget	32,412.5	49,719.1	70,100.0	95,000.0
Ministry of Finance	252.8	320.6	407.9	603.6
Ministry of Defence	16,481.7	25,623.3	34,685.0	41,625.0
Ministry of Health	1,037.4	1,320.1	1,059.3	1,660.0
Ministry of Foreign Affairs	309.8	305.0	335.7	487.0
Ministry of Education and Culture	2,522.7	3,681.5	3,966.0	6,931.0
Ministry of Police	505.8	753.9	906.2	1,362.5
Ministry of Social Welfare	507.5	547.2	679.6	1,023.0
Other Ministries	1,120.7	1,644.0	2,050.2	3,107.8
Interest	3,808.7	5,209.4	9,000.0	14,750.0
Transfer to National Insurance Institute	589.6	1,849.8	2,190.0	3,701.0
Transfers to Local Authorities	1,198.8	2,333.5	3,008.0	4,127.0
Subsidies	3,251.7	4,928.0	5,525.0	8,840.0
Other Expenditures	921.5	1,202.8	1,350.4	2,064.2
Reserves	3.8	—	4,936.7	4,717.9
Development Budget	8,708.4	13,009.1	17,500.0	27,500.0
Industry and Crafts	416.2	691.4	862.5	1,461.0
Transport	325.3	315.7	326.0	466.0
Communications	473.3	557.0	565.0	495.0
Housing	2,266.7	3,391.0	3,293.0	4,550.0
Public Buildings	816.4	1,169.3	1,335.4	1,468.9
Debt Repayment	3,757.4	5,482.1	9,000.0	15,500.0
Other Expenditures	653.4	1,402.6	2,118.1	3,559.1
Total	41,121.2	62,728.2	87,600.0	122.500.0

* Estimates

GENERAL CONSUMER PRICE INDEX
(1970 = 100)

1972	1973	1974	1975	1976
126.4	151.6	211.9	295.1	387.6

MONEY SUPPLY
(million I£ at year end)

	1972	1973	1974	1975	1976
Currency held by the public	1,974	2,716	3,173	3,970	4,777
Current deposits	3,613	4,677	5,549	6,644	8,709
Total Money Supply	5,587	7,393	8,722	10,614	13,486

EXTERNAL TRADE
(million U.S. $)
Excluding trade with the administered territories.

	1969	**1970**	**1971**	**1972**
Imports c.i.f.	1,304.4	1,433.5	1,811.6	1,961.4
Exports f.o.b.	688.7	733.6	915.1	1,099.8
	1973	**1974**	**1975**	**1976**
Imports c.i.f.	2,968.6	4,176.5	4,108.7	4,068.6
Exports f.o.b.	1,391.8	1,737.4	1,834.6	2,306.6

PRINCIPLE COMMODITIES
(U.S. $'000)

Imports	1973	1974	1975	1976
Diamonds, rough	488,017	442,960	469,126	670,252
Boilers, machinery and parts	279,724	327,955	434,502	403,501
Electrical machinery	158,828	212,141	241,252	182,722
Iron and steel	226,055	428,642	349,153	253,970
Vehicles	196,008	263,651	188,848	194,760
Chemicals	180,800	244,144	301,362	282,515
Crude oil	208,816	583,568	628,319	675,516
Cereals	140,915	226,972	267,650	235,854
Textiles and textile articles	102,368	130,911	106,958	119,690
Ships, boats, aircraft, etc.	204,019	166,462	42,658	53,250

Exports	1973	1974	1975	1976
Diamonds, worked	617,109	641,131	640,744	799,726
Edible fruits	127,854	137,528	200,797	203,922
Textiles and textile articles	142,838	160,234	164,748	209,105
Fruit and vegetable products	73,399	88,654	77,905	99,079
Fertilizers	34,191	67,246	72,263	51,377
Organic chemicals	25,744	59,287	67,904	75,161
Inorganic chemicals	16,315	36,473	45,428	33,930
Iron and steel	33,734	51,685	98,604	169,142
Non-electric machinery	30,293	46,887	54,471	67,387
Electrical machinery	27,082	42,704	78,112	93,467

PRINCIPAL COUNTRIES
('000 U.S. $)

Imports	1974	1975	1976	Exports	1974	1975	1976
Argentina	27,700	29,723	26,230	Australia	18,991	18,991	24,863
Austria	38,200	28,955	25,827	Austria	22,481	17,989	20,443
Belgium/Luxembourg	152,800	159,162	126,609	Belgium/Luxembourg	91,622	79,798	102,079
Brazil	14,300	52,576	13,471	Canada	27,833	29,833	39,125
Canada	41,400	40,479	43,156	France	90,726	112,097	134,737
Denmark	18,500	18,095	16,826	Germany, Fed. Rep.	127,102	151,492	200,587
Finland	38,600	34,211	30,108	Greece	24,612	28,466	25,415
France	168,700	154,969	150,563	Hong Kong	118,423	113,196	139,344
Germany, Fed. Rep.	535,700	457,538	416,632	Iran	54,270	92,402	103,608
Italy	245,400	205,877	171,498	Italy	67,096	56,599	76,856
Japan	133,000	88,768	106,870	Japan	65,033	99,382	79,284
Netherlands	230,900	182,070	241,794	Netherlands	135,924	129,218	163,644
South Africa	45,800	20,242	45,229	Singapore	23,081	23,531	25,643
Spain	20,100	30,929	18,963	South Africa	28,722	34,724	26,786
Sweden	69,300	67,305	62,219	Sweden	19,849	27,859	32,561
Switzerland	123,500	124,361	158,255	Switzerland	104,955	80,994	93,313
United Kingdom	551,800	560,698	633,580	Turkey	9,801	15,890	10,811
U.S.A.	783,900	1,001,511	888,268	United Kingdom	156,940	171,086	185,638
Uruguay	12,800	16,717	7,280	U.S.A.	305,542	307,282	436,513
Yugoslavia	22,400	13,844	18,136	Yugoslavia	14,187	15,307	15,291

RAILWAYS

	1974	1975	1976
Passengers ('000)	3,720	3,579	n.a.
Freight ('000 metric tons)	3,658	3,332	3,467

ROADS 1976
Motor Vehicles ('000)

Private Cars	292.4
Trucks, Trailers	98.0
Buses	6.0
Taxis	4.8
Motorcycles, Motorscooters	27.8
Other Vehicles	3.4
Total	432.4

SHIPPING
('000 tons)

	1974	1975	1976*
Cargo Loaded	3,720	3,486	3,668
Cargo Unloaded	6,250	5,359	5,121

*Estimates.

CIVIL AVIATION (El Al revenue flights only)
('000)

	1973	1974	1975
Kilometres flown	33,077	28,881	27,656
Passenger-km	3,490,500	3,776,900	3,744,800
Cargo ton-km	454,000	n.a.	n.a.
Mail (tons)	738	764	770

TOURISM
Tourist Arrivals

1971	656,756
1972	727,532
1973	661,651
1974	624,727
1975	619,554
1976	796,598

EDUCATION
(1975/76)

	Schools	Pupils		Schools	Pupils
JEWISH:			ARAB:		
Kindergarten	4,528	144,508	Kindergarten	261	17,202
Primary Schools	1,211	376,667	Primary Schools	292	108,369
Secondary Schools	218	56,267	Secondary Schools	79	13,926
Vocational Schools	318	65,677	Vocational Schools	23	1,825
Agricultural Schools	27	5,655	Agricultural Schools	2	690
Teachers' Training	52	11,586	Teachers' Training	2	813
Others (Evening, Handicapped)	495	75,740	Others (Evening, Handicapped)	45	10,455

Source: Central Bureau of Statistics, Jerusalem.

COMMUNICATIONS MEDIA

	1974 (December)	1975 (December)	1976 (December)
Telephones	735,300	796,300	869,042
Daily newspapers	27	27	27

Radio receivers: 485,000 in 1976.

TV receivers (number of households): 520,00 in 1972; 579,000 in 1973; 652,000 in 1974.

The Europa Year Book, 1978, A World Survey, Volume II, British Dependent Territories—Zambia. Europa Publications Limited, 18 Bedford Square, London, WC1B, 3JN.

Orson Hyde Memorial Gardens

As part of the Jerusalem Gardens National Park project, the LDS Church announced in October 1977 plans for the establishment of the Orson Hyde Memorial Gardens on the slopes of the Mount of Olives. Covering a five-acre tract, the Gardens will include a small amphitheater surrounded by wooded walkways and shrubbery. Within the amphitheater will be a grotto on whose walls will be placed a plaque commemorating the dedication of Palestine for the return of the Jews by Orson Hyde in 1841. The plaque will contain excerpts of the dedicatory prayer in Arabic, English and Hebrew. It seems only fitting and proper that such an historic event in the overall history of the people of Judah should at last have its expression in the city of Jerusalem.

Gardens to Blossom in Israel

A five-acre tract of land on the slopes of the Mount of Olives in Jerusalem will be developed as the Orson Hyde Memorial Gardens.

Elder LeGrand Richards of the Council of the Twelve and president of the Orson Hyde Foundation, disclosed plans for the garden at a news conference October 26, along with plans to launch a $1 million fund drive to finance the project.

In 1840 Orson Hyde and John E. Page, both of the Council of the Twelve, were selected for a mission to the Holy Land to dedicate the area for the regathering of the Jews.

They were separated early in their mission (see related story this page) and eventually only Elder Hyde reached Jerusalem. Looking down on the city from the Mount of Olives, October 24, 1841, he offered the dedicatory prayer, writing it down as he spoke.

The Orson Hyde Memorial Gardens will become part of the larger Jerusalem Gardens National Park, a 600-acre development, protecting the historic area around the Old City of Jerusalem.

The national park is the result of efforts by the Jerusalem Foundation to preserve the beauty and heritage of the Old City for future generations.

Biblically significant sites like Mount Zion, the City of David, the valleys of Kidron and Hinnom, Gethsemane and the slopes of the Mount of Olives and Mount Scopus will now be protected from the erection of unsightly structures and haphazard planning.

The national park features archaeological, historical and spiritual gardens financed by benefactors from throughout the world and developed by the National Park Authority of Israel.

A garden honoring the Bicentennial of the United States will be among the developments already under construction. Others include the Beth Shalom Garden located between Dung Gate and Zion Gate; B'nai B'rith Garden and Mitchel Garden on the Jerusalem Brigade Road and others, as yet unnamed, along the Old City walls.

The Orson Hyde Memorial Gardens will occupy five-and-one-quarter acres just east of Jerusalem on the Mount of Olives above the Garden of Gethsemane.

Elder Richards noted that the gardens will feature winding pathways with groves of trees, plants and shrubbery that will lead to a grotto-like area and amphitheater. Within this area, a plaque, inscribed with portions of Orson Hyde's dedicatory prayer in Arabic, English and Hebrew, will be placed.

The amphitheater will provide seating for visitors and permit them to view the old walled city and the surrounding area and landmarks.

Elder Richards said the Orson Hyde Foundation shares Israel's desire to preserve an area of unique historic importance.

He said, "The Lord has made great promises concerning that world center of religious influence. Three great religions have been centered there; Jerusalem is a Holy City to millions of people around the world.

"If you feel as I do about our responsibility to Jerusalem and her people, please join us in raising funds for this monument, park and amphitheater. We extend this invitation to good people everywhere. Join with us and share the joy of doing something positive to beautify the historic Mount of Olives."

Elder Richards noted that the project has the approval and support of the First Presidency and also the support of the National Parks Authority of Israel as well as many religious groups, Christian and non-Christian alike.

Orson Hyde's dedication of the Holy Land was the first of five such dedications over a period of 92 years.

On March 2, 1873, George A. Smith of the First Presidency, rededicated the land from the Mount of Olives. Francis M. Lyman of the Council of the Twelve held dedicatory services on two occasions in 1902 and John A. Widtsoe of the Council of the Twelve rededicated the Holy Land again in 1933.

Contributions to the project should be sent to the Orson Hyde Foundation, Elder LeGrand Richards, President, 47 E. South Temple, Salt Lake City, Utah 84150.

The names of all who contribute to the fund will be inscribed on a scroll. This scroll will be placed in a time capsule in the stone wall of the grotto.

The $1 million will provide for development of the gardens. The government of Israel and municipality of Jerusalem have agreed to provide care and maintenance for the property for 999 years.

Chairman of the board of trustees for the Orson Hyde Foundation is Orson Hyde White of Provo, Utah, with Elder Richards, president and trustee. ("Gardens to Blossom in Israel," Deseret News, *Church News,* October 29, 1977, page 3. Used by permission of Editor).

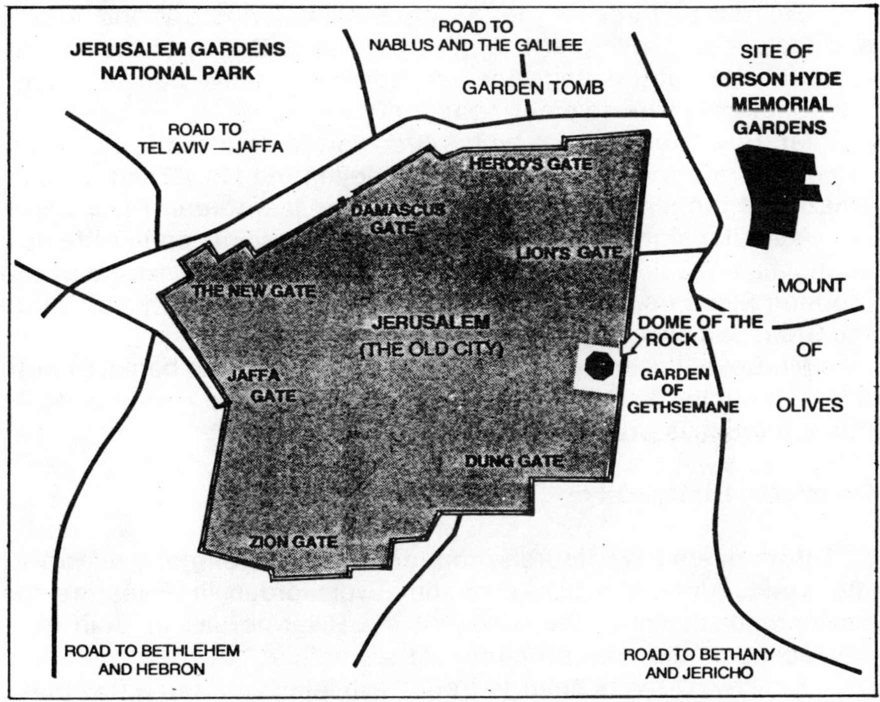

Orson Hyde Memorial Gardens will be located on the Mount of Olives.

Geographical 'Twins': Jordan Rivers Figure in Religious History

With so much of man's history having occurred within her boundaries it is no chance occurrence that tourism is a major industry within Israel. As the home of the world's three great monotheistic religions and as a land of great variety both in people and places, Israel plays host to millions of visitors each year. Of particular interest to some readers may be the following article which appeared in the *Deseret News,* Church News Section, December 20, 1958, which points out the very striking similarities between Palestine and features in Utah.

Travelers Amazed at Similarity in Features of Utah, Palestine Areas

Two short rivers each figuring in religious history yet on opposite sides of the earth, have similar characteristics. They are featured in the December issue of the National Geographic Magazine.

Both are named the Jordan River.

Colored pictures of the "Geographical Twins a World Apart" and the accompanying article are by David S. Boyer, of the foreign editorial staff, of the magazine. Mr. Boyer is a native Salt Laker and spent several years as a newspaper photographer in Salt Lake City.

Mr. Boyer relates that on his first visit to Jerusalem while driving out from the hill to the Jordan Valley in the Holy Land, he was amazed at the sight before him as he saw the Jordan River there.

A similar sight he had beheld many times in his earlier life as a young man in Salt Lake Valley where the Jordan River named by the Mormon Pioneers, flows from Utah Lake in Utah County north into the Great Salt Lake.

Mr. Boyer has collected pictures taken along the banks of both rivers in similar settings, which may require some deciphering to discern which is which.

Prominent Historically

Both rivers have figured prominently in the religious history of the world. Along the banks of the River Jordan in Palestine the Savior walked. Along the banks of the River Jordan in Utah have walked the modern day prophets of the Lord.

The "twin" rivers emerge from fresh lakes, run but a few miles till they reach their destinations—the Dead Sea in Palestine some 1,286 feet below sea level, and the Great Salt Lake in Utah, at an altitude of 4,200 feet.

Bathers in either the Dead Sea or the Great Salt Lake find the briny waters offer such buoyancy that swimmers float like corks.

Caves along both river banks have yielded finds of great archeological value. The Black Rock Cave near the Great Salt Lake, according to Mr. Boyer, has yielded Indian relics estimated to be centuries old. Archeologists believe this cave sheltered man thousands of years ago.

Along the shores of the Dead Sea in Palestine from the caves at Qumran archeologists have unlocked secrets of the Essenes, a pre-Christian Jewish sect. In the most recent years the finding of the Dead Sea Scrolls from this area have brought new additional attention to the Holy Land.

Beauty and scenery in the area of both rivers has an unmistakable sameness.

Parallel Characteristics

Mr. Boyer recalls his first view of the Jordan River in the Holy Land thus:

"What I saw that day was the snakelike Jordan River and the Dead Sea, salty and glistening, against the baking mountains of Moab. Yet this must have been almost the same scene that my Mormon pioneer ancestors saw in 1847 when they came down Emigration Canyon by covered wagon and looked out over a treeless plain stretching away toward Great Salt Lake.

"These religious refugees from Illinois named their winding river after the Jordan of the Bible; this barren land became their Canaan.

"Some 2,000 years before Christ, Abraham came from Mesopotamia to Canaan, the ancient land of the Jordan, and founded the nation of Israel. In those days, archeologists say, thriving farm villages dotted the entire region, even in today's parched Negev.

"Now the Jordan and its tributaries rush unchecked and little used from the moutains of Lebanon and Syria, Israel and the Kingdom of Jordan to waste themselves in the Dead Sea. They wait only the genius of modern engineers—and political peace—to turn this forsaken area once more into good farmland....

"Early dwellers in the Holy Land understood irrigation. And the ruins of vast canal systems in the southwestern United States indicate that prehistoric man in that part of America practiced the art long before the time of Columbus.

Irrigation in Utah

"Hardy necessity required the Mormon pioneers to be the first modern Americans to establish irrigation on extensive scale.

"Today water runs fresh and clean down the gutters of Salt Lake City streets, recalling the days of Brigham Young, who laid out the 'Heavenly City.' "

Today steam shovels are busy on the bank of the Jordan in Israeli digging a canal which will carry 115 billion gallons of Jordan water yearly to the arid plains of southern Israel.

Mr. Boyer relates additional history of the Jordan River in the Holy Land. He relates how the migrating quail saved the Israelites and just as that "bread from heaven" saved the people in the times of Moses so the Lord sent flocks to relieve the Pioneers of the hunger late in September of 1846. The Pioneers had just crossed the Mississippi River. They were sick and without shelter and had subsisted on parched corn for 10 days.

Flocks of Quail

Quoting the History of Brigham Young, Mr. Boyer states the "Lord sent flocks of quail, which lit...upon the ground within their reach, which the saints, and even the sick caught with their hands until they were satisfied."

Explanation by another writer indicates the quail had attempted to cross the wide Mississippi, were unsuccessful, fell back and were scooped up by the Pioneers.

Mr. Boyer said he recalled while standing in the Jordan Valley and watching swarms of locusts devour every blade of grass, that in the Salt Lake Valley a little more than a century ago sea gulls devoured the crickets. The first crops of the pioneers were about to be eaten up by the hordes of crickets. After fasting and praying, flocks of sea gulls came to gobble up the crickets.

"Locusts are not the Holy Land's only plague" writes Mr. Boyer. He states much of its "misery and desolation" can be attributed to the ravages of the common goat. Overgrazing has left the hills of Canaan barren. Top soil gives way easily, and rains bring flood and erosion."

However, he points out that reforestation is aiding Modern Israel to win back land being restored to fertility.

Both Rich in Metals

Both areas, he writes, are rich in metals. Near the Great Salt Lake is located the world's largest open cut copper mine. Copper is also being mined today near the ancient smelters which served the men under Solomon and Moses.

Tourists by the thousands schedule in their vacations, at home or abroad, with visits to the Holy Land and the Great Salt Lake.

Another reminder of his home, writes Mr. Boyer, are " 'Ayn Fashkhah' fresh warm springs which flow into the Dead Sea. After a dip in the briny blue waters the warm springs wash off the accumulated salt. Similar situation is located in Utah. Pioneers found hot springs in the Great Salt Lake Valley.

It was at a meeting on Sunday, Aug. 22, 1847 in the Bowery that President Brigham Young moved that "we call this place the Great Salt Lake City of the Great Basin of North America." Heber C. Kimball moved that we call the river running west of this place "The Western Jordan." "The Western" was later dropped.

The river for a period was used to float logs (ties) for the Central Utah Railroad being built in 1869.

First bridge over the Jordan River in Salt Lake Valley cost $700 and was paid for through a one per cent property tax.

Mr. Boyer concludes his story by stating "it would be hard for a Utahn to visit the Holy Land, look across the Jordan River and the Dead Sea and not seem to hear strangely ringing in his ears the words of Brigham Young, 'This is the Place!' " (Deseret News, *Church News,* December 20, 1958, page 3.)

Israel a World Leader

While the preceding discussion is very limited in scope, it is hoped that the reader is now aware of one fact—Israel is a reality in a modern competitive world. With a highly developed agriculture, efficient land management, and a thriving industrial base, Israel has became a world power to be reckoned with.

Israel—The Formative and Binding Forces

So far we have discussed Israel in an historical sense and from the standpoint of her achievements since independence. But Israel is more than industry, more even than a nation, it is people. What kind of people? What are they made of, what "makes them tick?" Many things could be examined, but the following list will perhaps provide the reader with some insight into the mind and soul of the modern Israeli.

Religion as a Binding Force

If you were to walk the streets of any Israeli town today, you would perhaps be overwhelmed with the diversity you would see.

UTAH
From Utah Lake to Great Salt Lake

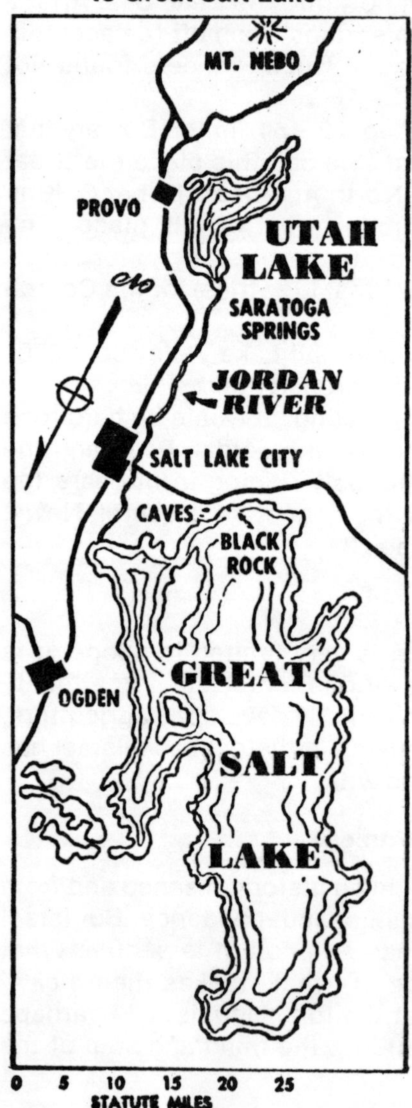

JORDAN RIVER, UTAH—This map of the Jordan River in the Great Salt Lake Valley has been turned upside down to allow for comparison with the Jordan River area of Palestine.

THE HOLY LAND
From Sea of Galilee to Dead Sea

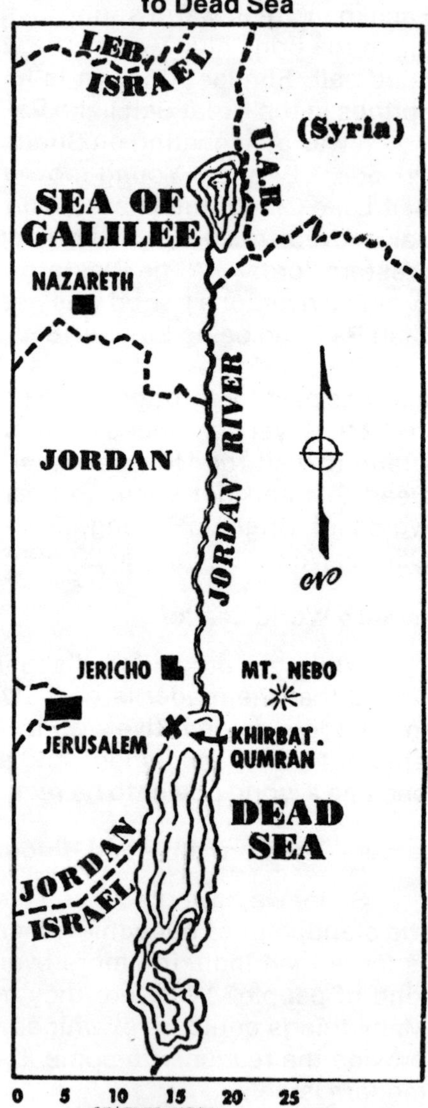

JORDAN RIVER, PALESTINE—Like the Jordan River of Utah the Jordan in the Holy Land begins from a fresh water source and empties into a salty (Dead Sea) lake.

Mixed in with European Jews—both West and East—you would find Jews from Arab lands, Russia, Persia, and other places equally as exotic. This mixing of cultures continues to pose great problems of assimilation for Israel. There is, however, one binding force that contributes significantly to the cohesion of Israel as a people-Judaism. While not all Israelis are practicing Jews in a religious sense, the deep-rooted ties with Judaism that transcend previous national origin remain very strong. The thousands upon thousands of synagogues that dot the Israeli countryside are little different from the synagogues to be found anywhere in the world. It is this millenia-long heritage, tempered by the adversity of time that helps to bind people who would otherwise have little in common.

The Dead Sea Scrolls as a Binding Force

A further strengthening of this bond of religion, something of that event the non-practicing Jew can relate to is the possession of the Dead Sea Scrolls. Beautifully preserved in the Shrine of the Book, the scrolls give powerful witness to the unity of all Jews, to their distinctness. They also serve as a bond that ties the ancient traditions of the Jewish people to the present generation. Since the scrolls were found and preserved in jars, the building housing them was constructed in the shape of the top of one of the jars. It was reported that the scrolls were discovered in a series of caves, one source stated that there were as many as eleven caves close by the Dead Sea in an area now known as Qumran. It isn't the purpose of this manuscript to give a treatise on this monumental discovery nor to elaborate on any of the Dead Sea Scroll's significant contributions to biblical study. What is significant, however, is their effect upon the people of Israel. Such feelings were, perhaps, best expressed by Moshe Raviv, director of the North American Division of Israel's Ministry of Foreign Affairs:

> You must go to the museum and look at the Dead Sea Scrolls and realize that any Israeli school kid can read them; they're written in the same language we use today. Then you will understand something of who we are, our sense of identity and our determination to inhabit this land of our forefathers. (William B. Smart, "Deseret News," page A3, March 21, 1978.)

The Holocaust as a Binding Force

To any Jew who was old enough to remember, the names of Dachau and Auschwitz and a whole host of other names still have meaning. And even to those who were not directly involved, the memory has placed its indelible mark on the souls of a people. So that no one will ever forget, the Yad Vashem Memorial was built as a sign of remembrance. On plaques are memorialized the names of the 21 largest concentration and extermination camps where an estimated six million Jews were killed during World War II.

The memorial contains photographs, sketches and numerous other types and forms of evidence documenting the horror that was the Holocaust. It was from the evidence contained at Yad Vashem that such as Adolf Eichmann were brought to justice for their part in the terrible massacre. A central piece of the memorial is a 70-foot pillar of herosim dedicated to the martyrs, heroes and the resistance fighters.

Yad Vashem is a reminder to those who visit and to those who call Israel home, that the price for freedom is paid in blood.

Masada—Symbol of Resistance

To a nation born out of war and constantly having to defend herself from attack, the "fortress" of Masada has come to symbolize the spirit of resistance that still burns within each Israeli. On a butte overlooking the Dead Sea is a huge gray and black monument about 220 yards wide and one half mile long. It was here in 73 A.D. that Jewish zealots held out for three years against the Romans under the leadership of Flavius Silva. Rather than surrender, some 900 died in a mass "murder-suicide." The heroic stand of these courageous patriots has become a legend about a few against the many who preferred to die rather than lose their struggle for freedom:

> No Israeli child passes through adolescence without making a pilgrimage to Masada, climbing the tortuous trail to the top, and hearing the story of the martyrs. Units of the Israeli army hike 50 miles through the desert, climb up to Masada, and there take their oath of loyalty. (William B. Smart, "Deseret News," page A3, March 21, 1978.)

To an Israeli, Masada is a symbol of courage, a monument to the free and patriotic spirit that must live within each Israeli if they are to survive—for each a solemn vow, "never again."

Summary

Up to this point in this book we have seen the rise of Judah to a nation in ancient times and her subsequent enslavement and the dispersal of her people; only to rise again in our time, in the "latter days." We have heard the words of prophets speaking of Judah, promising both dispersal and gathering, and more. Where are we today?

We have examined in this chapter, the foundation in this century of the modern State of Israel, literal fulfilment of prophecies made both anciently and by modern prophets called forth from the house of Joseph. Israel exists! Israel is an historical reality for the first time in nearly two millenia, and intends to remain free and independent. Whether you choose to give the credit to the divine intervention of God or to the blood of earthly martyrs, the result is much the same. Israel is a world force. The products of what was once thought to be a useless desert now are marketed throughout much of the world. In a very real sense Israel's voice is heard and heeded. And finally, Israel as a people exist. Molded by powerful forces, not always understood, each Israeli senses a belonging and a powerful need to protect that which he now feels is his; something more precious than material wealth, more precious even than life itself—the Land of his Inheritance!

Jerusalem is one of the oldest and most notable religious centers in the world and in a few hours the Israeli can walk through several thousand years of colorful ancient historical sites. In close proximity to each other are many memorable and unforgetable places such as the Mount of Olives, Gethsemane, Garden Tomb, Mount Zion, Dome of the Rock, and Calvary. In addition to its intrinsic beauty, Jerusalem is unique in that it is probably the only city in the world that can claim to be the home of "three of the world's major religions—Christianity, Islam, and Judaism—and here their cherished edifices and symbols are intricately mixed." To many millions of religionists throughout the world, Jerusalem represents the heartbeat and pulse of religious worship and to many it is a sacred city.

But what of the future? Not all of the prophecies have been fulfilled. Where now? And what of that man from out of the past who still calls to his people—what of Jesus Christ of Nazareth?

Immigrants and visitors alike express a unique and special feeling about coming to Israel. When a group of immigrants, in an airport interview, were asked why they came to Israel, some said better jobs, some said better living conditions, others religious freedom, a wholesome life, etc. One young man answered, "I just have a feeling here (with a hand on his heart) to come to Israel." Everyone else in the group nodded in agreement, for that was their real reason too. Israel has a spirit which draws her people home, and compels them once they are there, so that even tourists, as they leave on the plane from Tel Aviv, invariably say to themselves, "I must come back again soon."

The Land of Jesus

Leaving Israel renewed the compelling feeling that here occurred the most important event in the world. No matter how many varied claims of the actual sites were made—of tombs and miracles and so on—I knew that this was the land where Christ performed his ministry, where He died, where He rose. Israel gave an additional dimension to my testimony that He lived and yet lives today. The feeling at the Garden Tomb typifies your general feeling about Israel, the truly Holy Land of Jesus Christ, our Savior and Redeemer.

Chapter 11

Then Shall They Know That I Am the Lord

> And I will remember the covenant which I have made with my people; and I have covenanted with them that I would gather them together in mine own due time, that I would give unto them again the land of their fathers for their inheritance, which is the land of Jerusalem, which is the promised land unto them forever, saith the Father.
>
> And they shall believe in me, that I am Jesus Christ, the Son of God, and shall pray unto the Father in my name.
>
> Then shall their watchmen lift up their voice, and with the voice together shall they sing; for they shall see eye to eye.
>
> Then will the Father gather them together again, and give unto them Jerusalem for the land of their inheritance.
>
> Then shall they break forth into joy—Sing together, ye waste places of Jerusalem; for the Father hath comforted his people, he hath redeemed Jerusalem.
>
> The Father hath made bare his holy arm in the eyes of all the nations; and all the ends of the earth shall see the salvation of the Father; and the Father and I are one. (3 Nephi 20:29-35.)

We gaze, now, through the sparkling window of prophecy into the future. We see the glorious day when, in the hour of his greatest need, when he is near utter destruction, Judah will see the Lord Jesus Christ and know He is the Messiah. Imagine the joy in Jewish hearts as they look upon their King, as they watch Him fight their battles and win their glory. And then imagine the pain in their souls as they realize their forefathers once murdered their Anointed One. The tide is already beginning to turn. Christ is accepted by more and more Jews. The signs of his coming indicate the time is nigh when "every knee shall bow" and Judah's true God shall reign.

Address to the Jews, Prepare for the Coming of the Messiah

To the Jews we would say—Turn from your sins, and seek the God of your fathers. Search the Prophets; for lo, your Messiah cometh speedily, and all the Saints with him. Yea, he will descend upon the Mount of Olives, near your ancient city, disperse your enemies, defend Jerusalem, and establish his kingdom over your nation and city, and over all the earth.

But what will be your astonishment, when gazing at him, and falling at the feet of HIM as your great deliverer, you discover the wounds in his feet, in his hands, and in his side, and inquire, "What are these wounds in your hands and in your feet?"

And he will exclaim, "These are the wounds with which I was wounded in the house of my friends. I am Jesus of Nazareth, whom your fathers crucified. I am the Son of God, your deliverer, and your eternal King."

O who can describe the mingled feelings of joy and gladness, and gratitude, and shame, and remorse, and repentance, and amazement, and wonder, which will then fill your bosoms! How you will repent, and flock to the water, and be baptized in his name for the remission of your sins. With what power the Holy Ghost will fall upon you, when the Apostles shall lay their hands upon your heads in the name of that Jesus who will stand in your presence. Tears of joy will flow forth and stream upon the ground, while many of you will fall upon his neck, or kiss his feet, and bathe them in your tears.

Those Who Accepted Christ by Faith are More Blessed

Blessed is he that has seen him and believed; but more blessed are they who have not seen him and yet believed.

If any of you can so far overcome your prejudices and traditions, as to admit the probability, or even possibility, that Jesus of Nazareth is the Messiah, and that when your Messiah comes to fulfil your national redemption, and to establish his kingdom over all the earth, it will not be the first time that he has appeared among men, or even to your own nation—why, then, search diligently on the subject, and earnestly pray to Jehovah that you may understand this truth of such thrilling and vital importance.

Search, Study and Pray to Obtain a Testimony

After you have carefully reviewed your own Prophets, search the New Testament with the same careful and prayerful attention, and then obtain a copy of the Book of Mormon, and search that with the same degree of candour and earnestness. Your minds will expand, and you will be constrained to acknowledge that Jesus of Nazareth is truly the Christ.

If so, then come to the Standard of the New Dispensation—to the Apostles and Elders of The Church of Jesus Christ of Latter-day Saints; for you will readily see that there is no other system now extant which even resembles, or will compare at all with the system established by him and his former Apostles. Yea, come to them, repenting and turning from your sins, and go down into the waters of baptism, in the name of Jesus Christ, the Messiah. Receive the laying on of hands for the Gift of the Holy Ghost. You will then know the truth, and be prepared for less surprise and a more glorious triumph on the Mount of Olives, in the day of your returning King.

Requirements After Entering the Kingdom are Study, Observance of the Commandments and Contribution of Means

We have now shown you the door of admission into the kingdom of God into which you would do well to enter; and after entering therein, it will be required of you to keep the commandments of Jesus, and to look earnestly and daily for the fulfillment of the Prophets which speak of the restoration of Israel and Judah, the downfall of Gentile rule, and the prevalence of that kingdom which shall be universal, and have no end.

You would also in the meantime do well to contribute liberally of your means to the Elders and Missionaries of the Church, for they are your brethren; they verily believe the Prophets, and they look, and pray, and labour earnestly for their fulfilment. (Parley P. Pratt, *MS* 14:468-469, October 15, 1862.)

The Messiah Will Appear First in the Land of America at His Second Coming

...The decree has gone forth from the Almighty that they [the Jews] cannot have the benefit of the atonement until they gather to Jerusalem, for they said, let his blood be upon us and upon our children, consequently, they cannot believe in him until his second coming. We have a great desire for their welfare, and are looking for the time soon to come when they will gather to Jerusalem, build up the city and the land of Palestine, and prepare for the coming of the Messiah. When he comes again, he will not come as he did when the Jews rejected him; neither will he appear first at Jerusalem when he makes his second appearance on the earth; but he will appear first on the land where he commenced his work in the beginning, and planted the garden of Eden, and that was done in the land of America.

When the Savior visits Jerusalem, and the Jews look upon him, and see the wounds in his hands and in his side and in his feet, they will then know that they have persecuted and put to death the true Messiah, and then they will acknowledge him, but not till then. They have confounded his first and second coming, expecting his first coming to be as a mighty prince instead of as a servant. They will go back by and by to Jerusalem and own their Lord and Master. We have no feelings against them. I wish they...knew precisely how the Lord looks upon them. (Brigham Young, *JD* 11:279, December 23, 1866.)

What Will be the Feelings of the Jews Toward Jesus When They Return to Palestine?

When the Jews gather to Palestine, will they be in a condition of belief or unbelief in Jesus Christ?

There are numerous passages in the Book of Mormon that are positive on the side of belief:

2 Nephi, 10:7. But behold, thus saith the Lord God: When the day cometh that they shall believe in me, that I am Christ, then have I covenanted with their fathers that they shall be restored in the flesh, upon the earth, unto the lands of their inheritance.

2 Nephi 25:15. Wherefore, the Jews shall be scattered among all nations; yea, and also Babylon shall be destroyed; wherefore, the Jews shall be scattered by other nations;

2 Nephi 10:16. And after they have been scattered, and the Lord God hath scourged them by other nations, for the space of many generations, yea, even down from generation to generation, until they shall be persuaded to believe in Christ, the son of God, and the atonement, which is infinite for all mankind; and when that day shall come, that they shall believe in Christ, and worship the Father in His name, with pure hearts and clean hands, and look not forward any more for another Messiah, then, at that time, the day will come that it must needs be expedient that they should believe these things.

2 Nephi 10:17. And the Lord will set his hand again the second time to restore his people from their lost and fallen state. Wherefore, he will proceed to do a marvelous work and a wonder among the children of men.

Following are the personal declarations of Jesus Christ:

3 Nephi 20:29-31. And I will remember the covenant which I have made with my people, and I have covenanted with them, that I would gather them together in mine own due time; that I would give unto them again the land of their fathers, for their inheritance, which is the land of Jerusalem, which is the promised land unto them forever, saith the Father.

And it shall come to pass that the time cometh, when the fullness of my gospel shall be preached unto them,

And they shall believe in me, that I am Jesus Christ, the Son of God, and shall pray unto the Father in my name.

There are numerous other passages in the Book of Mormon, that simply refer to the future gathering of the Jews, without making any direct reference to their belief or unbelief in the Redeemer.

There are other passages which indicate that there will be two classes of Jews who will gather to Palestine. The following is a sample:

2 Nephi 30:7. And it shall come to pass that the Jews which are scattered, also shall believe in Christ; and they shall begin to gather in upon the face of the land; and as many as shall believe in Christ, shall also become a delightsome people.

Some have taken the ground that the full unbelief situation is supported by the following from Section 45 of the Doctrine and Covenants:

D&C 45:51-52. And then shall the Jews look upon me and say, What are these wounds in thine hands and in thy feet?

Then shall they know that I am the Lord; for I will say unto them, These wounds are the wounds with which I was wounded in the house of my friends. I am he who was lifted up. I am Jesus that was crucified. I am the Son of God.

Isolated from other inspired statements, this would seem to bear out the complete unbelief theory. Another passage in the same section, however, dispels it:

D&C 45:43-44. And the remnant shall be gathered unto this place,

And then they shall look for me, and, behold, I will come; and they shall see me in the clouds of heaven, clothed with power and great glory, with all the holy angels; and he that watches not for me shall be cut off.

Those who look for Christ close to the time of his coming must certainly be believers in him. Therefore, when he comes down to his people, the latter will be divided into two classes—believers and unbelievers in the Savior.

The 45th section is largely a reiteration of what Jesus told his ancient disciples regarding his second coming and events which were to precede it. Among these is the coming in of the times of the Gentiles—the restoration of the gospel to them. The times of the Gentiles are to be fulfilled within the same generation in which they are ushered in. Then will come the opportunity of the remnant of Jews, as the gospel will then go exclusively to them, and their gathering be accomplished. The gospel is "first to the Gentiles and then to the Jews."

In the accomplishment of the purposes of God, the principle of preparation, or graduation, is always manifested. Many people in this dispensation have been prepared in advance for the declaration of the gospel in its fullness to them, and they have consequently accepted the glad tidings as soon as their ears were saluted by the divine message.

The Jewish Mind is Being Prepared for the Acceptance of Christ

So it is in every special movement inaugurated by the Almighty among the hosts of men. The fulfillment of the wonderful promise of the God of Israel concerning the remnant of his ancient people in the last days must, being of far-reaching importance, be no exception to the rule. Hence the preparation of the Jewish mind for the acceptance of Christ and his gospel is now in its initial stage.

The International Zionist Movement is Fulfilling its Objectives

The attention of the Hebrew race must be directed toward the land of their fathers, as an initiatory preparation for their gathering. This is already in progress. It is a function of what is called the Zionist Movement, inaugurated several years ago, by Dr. Herzl, and has had a steady and rapid growth. It is international, and has among its adherents and supporters a majority of the leading and most influential Jews of the world. This organization has a large and increasing fund to be used in carrying out the object of its existence—the colonizing of Palestine by the Jewish people and their re-establishment in a national capacity. The nature of this movement is such that it must attract the interest of all intelligent Hebrews, whose eyes are thus directed to the former home of their race.

The yearning toward the ancient home of the Jews must be associated by an appreciation of the character and teachings of Jesus Christ. It is preparing them to receive the fullness of his gospel. This preparatory process is shown in their increased activity.

What is the Jewish Thought About Jesus of Nazareth Today?

"...a large number of Jewish scholars and Rabbis responded to a request to answer the following question: "What is the Jewish thought today of Jesus of Nazareth?"

Dr. Isadore Singer, managing editor of the Jewish Encyclopedia:

"I regard Jesus of Nazareth as a Jew of Jews; one whom all Jews are learning to love. His teaching has been an immense service to all the world in bringing Israel's God to the knowledge of hundreds of millions of mankind.

"The great change in Jewish thought concerning Jesus of Nazareth, I can not better illustrate than by this fact: When I was a boy, had my father, who was a very pious man, heard the name of Jesus uttered from the pulpit of our synagogue, he and every other man would have left the building, and the Rabbi would have been dismissed at once. Now it is not strange in many synagogues to hear sermons preached eulogistic of this Jesus, and nobody thinks of protesting. In fact, we are all glad to claim Jesus as one of our people."

Dr. Emil G. Hirsch, of the Sinai congregation, and professor of Rabbinical literature in the University of Chicago:

"The gospel Jesus, the Jesus who teaches so superbly the principles of Jewish ethics, is revered by all the expounders of Judaism. His words are studied; the New Testament forms a part of Jewish literature. Among the great preceptors that have worded the truths of which Judaism is the historical guardian, none, in our estimation, takes precedence of the Rabbi of Nazareth. To impute to us suspicious sentiments concerning him does us great injustice. We know him to be among our greatest and purest."

Dr. Max Nordau, critic and philosopher:

"Jesus is soul of our soul, and he is flesh of our flesh. Who then would think of excluding him from the people of Israel."

Dr. Kaufman, Rabbi of Temple Beth-ell, New York:

"As a veritable prophet, Jesus, in such striking manner, disclaimed allegiance and asked for no other authority but that of the living voice within, while passing judgment on the law, in order to raise life to a higher standard. * * * All this modern Judaism gladly acknowledges, reclaiming Jesus as one of its greatest sons."

Jesus of Nazareth a Jew of Jews

If such expressions did not justly represent the modern Jewish thought, in relation to Jesus of Nazareth, surely there would have been a Jewish protest on the subject, yet apparently none has appeared. If they are accepted, tacitly or otherwise, what do such enunciations mean? Simply this: That a considerable body of that race have reached the brink of the acceptance of Jesus of Nazareth as the Redeemer of Israel. If he be "a Jew of Jews," whom "all Jews are learning to love," if, "among the great preceptors none take precedence of the Rabbi of Nazareth;" if he be "among the greatest and purest," he was all he announced himself to be—the Son of God, the Messiah. No being of that description could appear in the capacity of a pretender. The only ultimate logical position of those who take this view is their acceptance of him as the Messiah!

These statements are evidences that the Jews are "beginning to believe in Christ," and are therefore being prepared for complete conversion. The process by which this will be brought about has been clearly revealed.

In the Doctrine and Covenants there are numerous statements to the effect that the gospel is to be carried "first to the Gentiles, and secondly unto the Jews." In this connection, reference is now made to page 387, verses 33, 34, 35 [Section 107:33-35], Doctrine and Covenants in which the express duties, in that regard, of the "traveling presiding High Council" of the Twelve, and of the Seventy, are declared.

When the servants of the Lord withdraw from the Gentiles and proclaim the fullness of the gospel to the Jews, it is unreasonable to presume that they will, as a body, reject the divine message. Such a position would bring upon them severe divine condemnation. Doubtless there will be a class of those who gather to Palestine who will be unbelievers, but it will probably be proportionately small.

Many Jews Will Gather to their Homeland With a Belief in Jesus Christ

A considerable number of the references in the foregoing are clear upon the point that, when the times of the Jews are ushered in, many of them will gather in upon the land of Palestine in a condition of belief in Jesus Christ. Other passages refer merely to the future fact of the gathering, while others indicate that they will consist of two classes—believers and unbelievers. It is safe to accept of both as correct, as they do not conflict.

Existing conditions foreshadow that the believers in Christ will preponderate also from the following indications:

1st. The turning of the desire and attention of the Jews toward the land of Palestine.

2nd. The wonderful change in the intelligent Hebrew mind in favor of an exalted estimate of Jesus of Nazareth, as a great teacher, a pure character, and an inspired prophet of God.

3rd. The prospective and positive duty, sure to be fulfilled—of the Elders of The Church of Jesus Christ of Latter-day Saints, when the set time is reached, to declare the fullness of the gospel to the Jews. Just as sure as this glorious duty shall be performed, so is it that the labors of the servants of the Most High shall not be fruitless. Present events are leading up to that final preparatory process for the gathering of the remnants of Judah, that when Christ shall appear he will find faith among his ancient people. (John Nicholson, *Improvement Era,* 5:628-633, June 1902.)

Total Darkness Will Cover the Face of the Earth

If you want to know about the time when the sun and moon are to be darkened, and when the stars will no longer give any light, and when there will be a total darkness over all the face of the earth, here is an event predicted so that you can not mistake. When you see the nations of the earth, especially the heathen nations, and also those north of Jerusalem—the great nation of Russia and other nations on the continent of Asia, together with many in Europe, gather up against Jerusalem after the Jews have returned and rebuilt their city and Temple, and when their armies become exceeding great multitudes in the valley of decision, then you may look for the Lord to come down with his mighty ones, and for the constellations of heaven to be darkened.

The LORD also shall roar out of Zion, and utter his voice from Jerusalem; and the heavens and the earth shall shake; but the LORD *will be* the hope of his people, and the strength of the children of Israel.

Israel and Judah Will Trust in God

The children of Israel as well as Judah will put their trust in the Lord God of their fathers in that day, and they will look for deliverance from his hand. They will know that they can not stand without the aid of the Lord against all those from the north quarters—Gog and Magog, all the hosts of Russia and of the various nations round about that come up there and cover the land like a cloud. They will know that unless God helps them they can not obtain a victory over this mighty host; but they will put their trust in the Lord, and he will "roar out of Zion and utter his voice from Jerusalem," and he will be the hope of his people and the strength of the children of Israel.

So shall ye know that I *am* the LORD your God dwelling in Zion, my holy mountain; then shall Jerusalem be holy, and there shall no strangers pass through here any more.

And it shall come to pass in that day, *that* the mountains shall drop down new wine, and the hills shall flow with milk, and all the rivers of Judah shall flow with waters, and the fountain shall come forth of the house of the LORD, and shall water the valley of Shittim.

Egypt shall be a desolation, and Edom shall be a desolate wilderness, for the violence *against* the children of Judah, because they have shed innocent blood in their land.

But Judah shall dwell for ever, and Jerusalem from generation to generation.

For I will cleanse their blood *that* I have not cleansed: for the LORD dwelleth in Zion.

The Lord Will Come to the Temple of Zion Before He Comes to the Temple of Jerusalem

The difference between Zion and Jerusalem; Zion will be favored with the presence of the Lord before the Jews are permitted to behold him. The Lord will come to the Temple of Zion before he comes to the Temple at Jerusalem. Before he comes in the clouds of heaven with power and great glory, he will manifest himself in the city and Temple of Zion; or in other words all the pure in heart who are permitted in those days to enter into the Lord's Temple in Zion, which will be built on this continent, the Lord will reveal his face unto them, they will see him and he will dwell in the midst of Zion. His throne will be there. This land—the land given to the children of ancient Joseph, now called the American continent—will be the land of Zion, and the great central capital on this land will be the New Jerusalem; and the inhabitants of that city and their habitations and Temple will be overshadowed by the glory of God. But after he has come to and roared out of Zion, after he has "suddenly come to his Temple," and visited his people there in the character of a Shepherd, and dwelt in their midst for a long space of time, he then goes with all his Saints to visit old Jerusalem, the last work before the day of rest shall come being to visit those nations that are gathered together in the great winepress to be trodden without the city on the east side of the city, and there the blood of horses, camels and men will be mingled together, and in those small valleys, so great will be the number slain that the blood will reach to the horses' bridles, for a certain distance, according to the word of the Lord. (Orson Pratt, *JD* 15:337-338, January 26, 1873.)

Jews Will Recognize that Jesus is the Messiah

Zechariah, in his 14th chapter, has told us much concerning the great battle and overthrow of the nations who fight against Jerusalem, and he has said, in plain words, that the Lord shall come at the very time of the overthrow of that army, yes, in fact, even while they are in the act of taking Jerusalem, and have already succeeded in taking one-half the city, and spoiling their houses, and ravishing their women. Then behold their long-expected Messiah, suddenly appearing, shall stand upon the Mount of Olives, a little east of Jerusalem, to fight against those nations and deliver the Jews. Zechariah says the Mount of Olives shall cleave in twain, from east to west, and one-half of the mountain shall remove to the north, while the other half falls off to the south, suddenly forming a very great valley, into which the Jews shall flee for protection from their enemies as they fled from the earthquake in the days of Uzziah, king of Judah, while the Lord cometh and all the saints with him. Then will the Jews behold that long, long-expected Messiah, coming in power to their deliverance, as they always looked for him. He will destroy their enemies, and deliver them from trouble at the very time they are in the utmost consternation, and about to be swallowed up by their enemies. But what will be their astonishment when they are about to fall at the feet of their Deliverer, and acknowledge him their Messiah! They discover the wounds which were once made in his hands, feet, and sides, and, on inquiry, at once recognize Jesus of Nazareth the King of the Jews, the man so long rejected. Well did the Prophet say, they shall mourn and weep, every family apart, and their mourning, for he will forgive their iniquities and cleanse them from uncleanness. Jerusalem shall be a holy city from that time forth, and all the land shall be turned as a plain from Geba to Rimmon, and she shall be lifted up and inhabited in her place, and men shall dwell there, and there shall be no more utter destruction of Jerusalem, "And in that day there shall be one Lord, and his name one, and he shall be King over all the earth." (Zech. 14:9.)

Two Prophets Among the Jews Will Prophesy and Work Mighty Miracles

John in his 11th chapter of Revelation, gives us many more particulars concerning this same event. He informs us that, after the city and temple are rebuilt by the Jews, the Gentiles will tread it under foot forty and two months, during which time there will be two prophets continually prophesying and working mighty miracles. And it seems that the Gentile army shall be hindered from utterly destroying and overthrowing the city, while these two prophets continue. But, after a struggle of three years and a half, they at length succeed in destroying these two prophets, and then overrunning much of the city, they send gifts to each other because of the death of the two prophets, and in the meantime will not allow their dead bodies to be put in graves, but suffer them to lie in the streets of Jerusalem three days and a half, during which the armies of the Gentiles, consisting of many kindreds, tongues and nations, passing through the city, plundering the Jews see their dead bodies lying in the street. But after three days and a half, on a sudden, the spirit of life from God enters them, and they will arise and stand upon their feet, and great fear will fall upon them that see them. And then they shall hear a voice from heaven in a cloud, and their enemies beholding them. And having described all these things, then comes the shaking, spoken of by Ezekiel, and the rending of the Mount of Olives, spoken of by Zechariah. John says, "The same hour was there a great earthquake, and the tenth part of the city fell, and in the earthquakes scenes that follows is the sound of voices saying, "The kingdoms of this world are become the kingdom of our Lord, and of his Christ; and he shall reign forever and ever." Now, having summed up the description of these great events spoken of by these prophets,...there is no difficulty in understanding them all to be perfectly plain and literal in their fulfillment.

The Messiah Comes to Deliver the Jews and Cleanses Jerusalem

Suffice it to say, the Jews gather home, and rebuild Jerusalem. The nations gather against them in battle. Their armies encompass the city, and have more or less power over it for three years and a half. A couple of Jewish prophets, by their mighty miracles, keep them from utterly overcoming the Jews, until at length they are slain, and the city is left in a great measure to the mercy of their enemies for three days and a half, the two prophets rise from the dead and ascend up into heaven. The Messiah comes, convulses the earth, overthrows the army of the Gentiles, delivers the Jews, cleanses Jerusalem—cuts off all wickedness from the earth, raises the saints from the dead, brings them with him, and commences his reign of a thousand years, during which time his Spirit will be poured out upon all flesh, men and beasts, birds and serpents, will be perfectly harmless and peace and the knowledge and glory of God shall cover the earth as the waters cover the sea; and the kingdom and the greatness of the kingdom under the whole heaven shall be given to the saints of the Most High. (P.P. Pratt, *Voice of Warning,* pp. 40-42, 1957 edition.)

The Temple Will be Built and the Nations Near Jerusalem Will Come to Worship the King and Keep the Feast of Tabernacles

When Jesus shall have raised all the righteous from their graves,...he will descend with all the hosts of heaven accompanying him, and will stand upon the Mount of Olives, and he will go out of Jerusalem, and the Jews will go out to the mount to meet him and will acknowledge him as their Messiah and King; and then it shall come to pass, that the heathen nations will also more fully recognize him as the true and only God. Then will be fulfilled that which is written in the last chapter of Zechariah, that every nation round about Jerusalem, shall come up from year to year, to worship the King, the Lord of hosts, at Jerusalem, and also to keep the Feast of Tabernacles. There will be a great many of those solemn assemblies and feasts that were commanded in ancient times, that will be re-established in the midst of Israel when they shall return. And the Lord Jesus will be there. His Twelve Apostles who wandered about will be there; and they sit upon twelve thrones, and assist our Lord and Savior in judging the twelve tribes of Israel. But Jesus will have a throne as well as these twelve disciples. Where will be his throne? A temple is to be reared in ancient Palestine where it formerly stood. Ezekiel saw it in vision, and he describes the building of that house when it shall be complete, and he saw the glory of God coming by the way of the East, and this glorious personage entered through the East Gate of that temple, and entered into the temple; and Ezekiel, being full of the Spirit of God, was picked up and carried into that court, where Jesus had entered, and he heard a voice speaking unto him, Behold the peace of my throne, where I will dwell in the midst of the children of Israel for ever, and they shall no more defile my name, but I will dwell with them for ever. (Orson Pratt, *JD* 20:153-154, March 9, 1879.)

Great Effort to Christianize the Jews in the Last Days

...Both the Old and New Testatments have been published in Hebrew, and in the various modern languages of the nations among whom the Jews reside. Missionaries have been sent...into many places. The result is, that a few thousand have turned away from the religion of their ancestors, and embraced what is called Christianity. It is said, that these converts now believe that Jesus Christ is the true Messiah. However corrupt modern Christianity may be, it is certainly a good thing to place within the reach of the Jew, the New Testament as well as the Old; it is also a blessing to the Jew to be convinced that the person whom their fathers crucified was indeed the great Prophet, so clearly foretold by Moses. It would also prove a great blessing to the Jews, if he would strictly observe the great moral precepts, so forcibly portrayed in the ancient Gospel. (Orson Pratt, *MS* 28:681, October 27, 1866.)

Change in the Hearts of the Jews Toward Jesus

President McKay said: During the few moments that I occupy this position, I desire to say something regarding this significant prophecy with a view of reaching the young men and the young women of Israel, that they might do two things, the first of which is to stop amidst their pleasures, to pause in the midst of the rush of this Twentieth Century and think—think of the significance and mission of the Church of Jesus Christ; to try to realize even in a slight degree, the significance of the world changes that are now taking place, and measure them by the standard of righteousness as taught by their parents and the authorities of the Church.

...Brethren, isn't it a significant thing that today there is a change in the hearts of the descendants of Israel in regard to the Holy One of Israel?

Rabbi Denounced the Holy One, Jesus the Jew

In 1918, while visiting the California Mission with President Robinson, he put in my hand a book entitled, *Jesus the Jew,* written by a prominent Jew of Sacramento. In the first chapter of that book we get a picture of the enmity and bitterness of the Jews when the author was a boy. Their hearts were not turned, even at that late date, much toward the Holy One, but most bitterly against him. He said in substance: "I remember when a boy that one of my classmates brought into the class a book containing the name of Jesus. I remember how wrought up and excited the Rabbi became when he was made aware of its presence in the schoolroom. 'Sacrilege! Sacrilege!' he indignantly cried. Then the Rabbi proceeded to denounce the Holy One. He said: 'How can any Jew who realizes what that name has brought upon his people even touch a book containing the name of Jesus? He told how the Jews had been persecuted, how they had [been] made outcasts and wanderers [and] ever been driven from pillar to post, [upon] the face of the earth; how their beards had been torn from their roots, their teeth drawn from their jaws; how they had been whipped at the post, put upon the rack, and their bones drawn joint from joint; how they had been outraged, ravished, and killed, all on account of Jesus"—and by the Christians, President Smith adds. That is one picture, when that man was but a boy—when you were boys, my fellow workers in the priesthood. Here is another picture given by a prominent Jew. Isadore Singer, the editor of the Jewish Encyclopedia: "When I was a boy, had my father, who was a very pious man, heard the name of Jesus uttered from the pulpit of our synagogue, he and every other man in the congregation would have left the building, and the rabbi would have been dismissed at once." That is illustrative of the spirit among the descendants of Israel when this Book of Mormon came forth among the children of men. Even at that time no man, it seems to me, acting upon his ordinary judgment, would dare say that the time would come when they would accept that Holy One, but here, two thousand years before, a prophet of God said the day would come when they, would no more turn their hearts aside from the Holy One, and that then he would remember the promises he made to their fathers.

Is the Messiah Yet to Come?

Now the question is: Has that day come? That same man who heard his teacher say, "Sacrilege, Sacrilege!" because a boy happened to bring a book containing the name of Jesus, said:

> I began to study his teachings. I found what his teachings were—purity, humility; 'Blessed are the poor in spirit.' 'Blessed are they that mourn.' 'Blessed are the pure in heart, for they should see God.' 'Blessed are the meek, for they shall inherit the earth.' 'Blessed are they that hunger and thirst after righteousness, for they shall be filled.'

And then he proceeds to show how Israel today is indebted to Jesus the Jew. In one chapter entitled, "Is the Messiah yet to come?" he says: "The enlightened Jew says no, but the Messianic age is what the Jews today are looking forward to."

And here in that connection let me just read one verse from that same Mr. Singer: "I regard Jesus of Nazareth as a Jew of the Jews, one whom all Jewish people"—all Jewish people!—"are learning to love. His teaching has been an immense service to the world in bringing Israel's God to the knowledge of hundreds of millions of mankind. The great change in Jewish thought concerning Jesus of Nazareth I cannot better illustrate than by this fact—" and then he relates the instance of his childhood, as I have read it.

"Now it is not strange in many synagogues to hear sermons preached eulogistic of this Jesus, and nobody thinks of protesting. In fact, we are all glad to claim Jesus as one of our people."

Boys of latter-day Israel, does it not seem that the time has come when, "their hearts no more turn against the Holy One?" It seems to me that it has. (David O. McKay, *CR,* pp. 44-46, October 4, 1918.)

The Mormon Missionaries Will Teach the Jews About Jesus

The time will soon come when the Elders of The Church of Jesus Christ of Latter-day Saints will be sent with glad tidings of great joy to the Jews, for when the Gospel was restored to the earth through the revelations of God to the Prophet Joseph Smith, the Elders of the Church were commanded to go first to the Gentiles and then to the Jews.... (B.H. Roberts, *MS* 50:88, February 6, 1888.)

Chapter 12

The Lord Shall Be Their God

I will take the children of Israel from among the heathen, whither they be gone, and will gather them on every side, and bring them into their own land:

And I will make them one nation in the land upon the mountains of Israel; and one king shall be king to them all: and they shall be no more two nations, neither shall they be divided into two kingdoms any more at all:

Neither shall they defile themselves anymore with their idols, nor with their detestable things, nor with any of their transgressions; but I will save them out of all their dwelling places, wherein they have sinned, and will cleanse them: so shall they be my people, and I will be their God.

And David my servant shall be king over them; and they all shall have one shepherd: they shall also walk in my judgments, and observe my statutes, and do them.

And they shall dwell in the land that I have given unto Jacob my servant, wherein your fathers have dwelt; and they shall dwell therein, even they, and their children, and their children's children for ever: and my servant David shall be their prince for ever.

Moreover I will make a covenant of peace with them; it shall be an everlasting covenant with them: and I will place them, and multiply them, and will set my sanctuary in the midst of them for evermore.

My tabernacle also shall be with them; yea, I will be their God, and they shall be my people.

And the heathen shall know that I the Lord do sanctify Israel, when my sanctuary shall be in the midst of them for evermore. (Ezekiel 37:21-28.)

The brightness is dazzling, now, as we envision the final triumph of the Jews. The great procession is joined by the lost tribes of

Israel as they pass through the glistening gates of the Holy City and march toward the temple. Christ reigns in the House of the Lord and his glory within the temple courts gives luster to the jewelled ornaments and golden walls. Peace is established in all the world. There is no more war nor disease nor pain. The Jewish saga has reached an end, and a beginning, and all of Abraham's dreams are fulfilled.

Prophecies of the Ancient Prophets are Being Fulfilled Today

Their situation since their rejection of the Messiah, although painful to contemplate, is full of interest, and shows to a demonstration, that all those things have come upon them, which were spoken by the prophets and by the Savior, respecting their degradation and overthrow. From the historians who have written since the death of the Savior, many facts are related, which show that the predictions of the ancient prophets, have been fulfilled, and likewise many things respecting their history which are worthy of being handed down from generation to generation. We...will illustrate their peculiar attachment to their ancient faith, their ardent love for the land of their fathers, their bravery and indomitable spirit in war, and likewise their unwavering belief of their final restoration to the land of Canaan.

Jews Will Rise From the Dust and Re-build the Temple

In whatever light the Jews may be looked upon by the world, it is evident, that they will ere long assume an important attitude. That they will "rise from the dust," gather up from their long dispersions, return to their much loved lands, re-build the Temple, and again take the lead among the nations of the earth, is abundantly proven from the word of God.

The assurance of these things are calculated to raise feelings of no ordinary kind in the bosom of every Saint of God. It was the anticipation of the glorious events connected with the return of the Jews, and the building of the Temple, that caused the sweet singer of Israel to tune to sweetest harmony, and strike his golden lyre in praises to the Lord, and which called forth the unrivaled eloquence of Isaiah, and the pathos of Jeremiah, who, while contemplating the scenes which are now about to be fulfilled upon the heads of the Jews, broke forth into such sublime and delightful strains; which have a powerful effect upon every mind, and carry conviction, that the writers were then under the operation of the spirit of Him who hath said, "I am a Father to Israel and Ephraim is my first born."

Not only have we "the more sure word of prophecy," but the events which have recently transpired, on the old continent, have been gradually preparing the way for Israel to gather to the places where their fathers once flourished, and which are endeared to them by unnumbered pleasing and interesting associations, calculated to raise and give scope to the most lively feelings of the heart.

Glory of the Lord to Rest Upon the Jews

But it is not their mere gathering together, that awakens such interest in the bosom of the saint of God, but the glorious events which necessarily grow out of the same. We not only contemplate the ancient covenant people of the Lord, restored to happiness, and in the enjoyment of power, wealth, and immense influence, but the much more sublime and glorious spectacle of the glories of Heaven's King resting down upon them, the veil which has long shrouded them in darkness, for ever rent assunder, the spirit of grace and supplication poured out upon them, the Savior appearing in their midst, shewing his hands, his feet, and side, while twice ten thousand tongues, in one commingling strain and glorious exhaltation sing, *"Blessed is he that cometh in the name of the Lord. Hosanna, hosanna in the highest, Amen and Amen."*

"Come thou glorious day of promise,
Come and spread they cheerful ray
When the scattered sheep of Israel
  Shall no longer go astray;
    When Hosannas
With united voice they cry.

Lord, how long wilt thou be angry?
  Shall thy wrath for ever burn?
Rise, redeem thine ancient people,
  Their transgressions from them turn.
    King of Israel
  Come and set thy people free.

O that soon thou would'st to Jacob
  Thine enliv'ning spirit send;
Of their unbelief and misery
  Make, O Lord, a speedy end.
    Lord, Messiah,
Prince of Peace, o'er Israel reign.

Glory, honour, praise and power,
Be unto the Lamb for ever;
Jesus Christ is our Redeemer,
Hallelujah! Hallelujah!
Praise ye the Lord!
Hallelujah! Praise the Lord."

(Anonymous, *TS* 2:407-408, May 15, 1841.)

God Will Fight the Battles of His People Against the Gentiles

The Lord has decreed that the Jews should be gathered from all the Gentile nations where they have been driven, into their own land, in fulfillment of the words of Moses their law-giver...O house of Judah,...it is true that after you return and gather your nation home and rebuild your city and temple, that the Gentiles may gather together their armies to go against you to battle, to take you a prey and to take you as a spoil, which they will do, for the words of your prophets must be fulfilled; but when this affliction comes, the living God that led Moses through the wilderness will deliver you, and your Shiloh will come and stand in your midst and will fight your battles; and you will know Him, and the afflictions of the Jews will be at an end, while the destruction of the Gentiles will be so great that it will take the whole House of Israel who are gathered about Jerusalem seven months to bury the dead of their enemies, and the weapons of war will last them seven years for fuel, so that they need not go to any forest for wood. These are tremendous sayings—who can bear them? Nevertheless they are true and will be fulfilled, according to the sayings of Ezekiel, Zechariah, and other prophets. Though the heavens and the earth pass away, not one jot or tittle will fall unfulfilled. (Wilford Woodruff, "Wilford Woodruff" by Matthias F. Cowley, pp. 509-510, February 22, 1879.)

Elder Taylor's Conversation on Temples with Baron Rothschild, a Jew

In looking still forward we find that there are other things ahead of us. One thing is the building of Temples, and that is a very important item, and ought to rest with force upon the minds of all good Saints. I remember, some time ago, having a conversation with Baron Rothschild, a Jew. I was showing him the Temple here, and said he—"Elder Taylor, what do you mean by this Temple? What is the object of it? Why are you building it?" Said I, "Your fathers had among them Prophets, who revealed to them the mind and will of God; we have among us Prophets who reveal to us the mind and will of God, as they did. One of your Prophets said—"The Lord whom ye seek shall suddenly come to his Temple, but who may abide the day of his coming? For he shall sit as a refiner's fire and a purifier of silver." "Now," said I, "Sir, will you point me out a place on the face of the earth where God has a Temple?" Said he, "I do not know of any." "You remember the words of your Prophet that I have quoted?" Said he—"Yes, I know the Prophet said that, but I do not know of any Temple anywhere. Do you consider that this is that Temple?" "No, sir, it is not." "Well, what is this Temple for?" Said I, "The Lord has told us to build this Temple so that we may administer therein baptisms for our dead (which I explained to him), and also to perform some of the sacred matrimonial alliances and covenants that we believe in, that are rejected by the world generally, but which are among the purest, most exalting and ennobling principles that God ever revealed to man." "Well, then, this is not our Temple?" "No, but," said I, "You will build a Temple, for the Lord has shown us, among other things, that you Jews have quite a role to perform in the latter days, and that all the things spoken by your old prophets will be fulfilled, that you will be gathered to old Jerusalem, and that you will build a Temple there; and when you build that Temple, and the time has arrived, 'the Lord whom you seek will suddenly come to his Temple.' (John Taylor, *JD* 18:199-200, April 6, 1876.)

Orson Pratt's Description of the Temple to be Built in Jerusalem

By and by there will be a Temple built at Jerusalem. Who do you think is going to build it? You may think that it will be the unbelieving Jews who rejected the Savior. I believe that that which is contained on the 77th page of the Book of Mormon, as well as in many other places, in that same book, will be literally fulfilled. The Temple at Jerusalem will undoubtedly be built, by those who believe in the true Messiah. Its construction will be, in some respects different from the Temples now being built. It will contain the throne of the Lord, upon which he will, at times, personally sit, and will reign over the house of Israel for ever. It may also contain twelve other thrones, on which the twelve ancient Apostles will sit, and judge the twelve tribes of Israel. It will, very likely, have an apartment, with a table, on which food and drink will be prepared, such as are suitable to the taste and happiness of immortal resurrected beings, thus fulfilling the words of Jesus—"Ye that have followed me in the regeneration shall eat and drink at my table, and sit upon twelve thrones, judging the twelve tribes of Israel. Amen." (Orson Pratt, *JD* 19:19-20, May 20, 1877.)

The Righteous of all Tribes to be Gathered Together

...If there are any people of God upon any detached part of this world, they with it will also be gathered into one, and His people and the Jews will hear the words of the Nephites, and the Ten Tribes must hear the words of the Jews and Nephites, and God's people be gathered and be one. All things will be gathered in one, and Zion be redeemed, the glory of God be revealed, and all flesh see it together. God's dominion will be established on the earth, the law go forth from Zion, and the word of the Lord from Jerusalem, and the kingdoms of this world will become subject to God and His Christ. (John Taylor, *JD* 1:230, April 8, 1853.)

The Ten Tribes Will Return from the North Country and the Jews will Return to Jerusalem

...Then will commence the gathering of the Jews to old Jerusalem; then the ten tribes in the northern regions, wherever they may be, after having been concealed from the nations for twenty-five hundred years, will come forth and will return, as Jeremiah has said, from the north country. A great company will come, and they will sing in the height of Zion, and "flow together for the goodness of the Lord, for wine and for oil, and for the young of the flock; and their souls shall be as a watered garden, and they shall not sorrow any more at all." What a happy time for them, when they come from their cold quarters in the north! The Jews dispersed among the Gentiles will not come and sing in the height of Zion, or but very few of them, they will go to Jerusalem. Some of them will believe in the true Messiah, and thousands of the more righteous, whose fathers did not consent to the shedding of the blood of the Son of God, will receive the Gospel before they gather from among the nations. Many of them, however, will not receive the Gospel, but seeing that others are going to Jerusalem they will go also; and when they get back to Palestine, to the place where their ancient Jerusalem stood, and see a certain portion of the believing Jews endeavoring to fulfill and carry out the prophecies, they also will take hold and assist in the same work. At the same time they will have their synagogues, in which they will preach against Jesus of Nazareth, "that impostor," as they call him, who was crucified by their fathers.

Surrounding Nations Attempt to Destroy Jerusalem but Prevented by Two Prophets Possessing God's Power

After awhile, when tens of thousands of them have gathered and rebuilt their Temple, and re-established Jerusalem upon its own heap, the Lord will send forth amongst them a tremendous scourge. What will be the nature of that scourge? The nations that live in the regions round about Jerusalem will gather up like a cloud, and cover all that land round about Jerusalem. They will come into the Valley of Jehoshaphat, east of Jerusalem, and they will lay siege to the city. What then? The Lord will raise up two great Prophets, they are called witnesses, in the Revelations of St. John. Will they have power? Yes, during the days of their prophesying they will have power to smite those who undertake to destroy them, and until their testimonies are fulfilled they will be able to keep at bay all those nations besieging Jerusalem, so that they will not have power to take that city. How long will that be? Three and a half years, so says John the Revelator. If any man hurt them they shall have power to bring upon that man, nation or army, the various plagues that are there written. They will have power to smite the earth with plague and famine, and to turn the rivers of water into blood. And when they have fulfilled their prophecy, then the nations that have been lying before Jerusalem so long, waiting for an opportunity to destroy the city, will succeed in killing these two Prophets, and their bodies, says John's revelations, will lie in the streets of Jerusalem three days and a half after they are killed. What rejoicing there will be over the death of these men! Those who have been waiting so long and anxiously for this to take place, will no doubt send gifts one to another, and if the telegraph wires are not destroyed, they will telegraph to the uttermost parts of the earth that they have succeeded in killing the two men who had so long tormented them with plagues, turning the waters into blood, etc. But by and by, right in the midst of their rejoicing, when they think the Jews will not certainly fall a prey to them, behold there is a great earthquake, and in the midst of it these two Prophets rise from the dead, and they hear a voice up in the heavens saying—"Come up hither;" and they immediately ascend in the sight of their enemies.

The Savior Appears During the Destruction of Jerusalem

What next? Notwithstanding all this, those nations will be so infatuated, and so determined to persecute the people of God—as much so as Pharoah and his army in ancient days—that they will say—"Come, now is the time to pitch into the Jews and destroy them." And they will commence their work of destruction, and they will succeed so far as to take one half the city, and while they are in the very act of destroying Jerusalem, behold the heavens are rent, and the Son of God with all the heavenly hosts appears, and he descends and rests upon the summit of Mount Olives, which is before Jerusalem on the east. And so great will be the power of God that will then be made manifest, that the mountain will divide asunder, half going towards the south, and half towards the north, producing a great valley going east and west, from the walls of Jerusalem eastward.

Jews Astonished Upon Beholding their Deliverer

What next? The Jews that are not taken captive by these nations, will flee to the valleys of the mountains, says the Prophet Zechariah; and when they get into that great valley, where these personages are who have descended, they expect to find the Deliverer which their Prophets have spoken of so long. But they do not for a moment suppose that it is Jesus, oh no, Jesus was an impostor. The personage they have been looking for some eighteen hundred years is the true Messiah, and now, say they—"He has come to deliver us." But how great will be their astonishment when, while looking at their Deliverer, they see that his hands are marred considerably! Say they, one to another—"There are large scars in his hands; and there is another large scar in his side, and behold his feet, they are scarred also!" And, as the Prophet Zechariah has said, they will begin to inquire of him—"What are these wounds with which thou art wounded?" And he replied—"These are the wounds with which I was wounded in the house of my friends."

When Jews are Convinced that Jesus is the Messiah, They Begin to Mourn

What then? Then they begin to believe, then the Jews are convinced, I mean that portion of them who formerly despised Jesus of Nazareth, and being convinced they begin to mourn, and they mourn every family apart, and their wives apart. The family of the house of Levi apart and their wives apart; the family of the house of David and their wives apart, and there will be such mourning in Jerusalem as that city never experienced before. What is the matter? What are they mourning about? They have looked upon him whom their fathers pierced, they behold the wounds, they are now convinced that they and their fathers have been in error some eighteen hundred years, and they repent in dust and ashes.

A Fountain Opened Up for Baptism on the East Side of the Temple

The next step for them will be baptism for the remission of their sins. They look upon him whom their fathers pierced and they mourn for him as one who mourns for his only son, and, as Zechariah says, they are in bitterness for him. But repentance alone would not be sufficient, they must obey the ordinances of the Gospel; hence there will be a fountain opened at that time on purpose for baptism. Where will it be opened? On the east side of the Temple. A stream will break out from under the threshold of the Temple, says the Prophet, and it will run eastward, and will probably pass directly through the deep valley made by the parting of the Mount of Olives. It will run eastward, and as you go down from the Temple a few thousand cubits it increases so rapidly that it becomes a great river that cannot be forded.

From that day forward there shall be written upon the bells of the horses and upon the vessels of the house of the Lord—"Holiness to the Lord;" and thenceforth all the people who are spared from the nations round about, will have to go up to Jerusalem year by year to worship the King, the Lord of Hosts. (Orson Pratt, *JD* 18:64-67, July 25, 1875.)

Peace and Righteousness Established and People Become One Mind with God

The following is a beautiful description of the establishment of peace, and this great rest of the saints: "Awake, awake; put on thy strength, O Zion; put on thy beautiful garments, O Jerusalem, the holy city: for henceforth there shall no more come unto thee the uncircumcised and the unclean. Shake thyself from the dust; arise, and sit down, O Jerusalem: loose thyself from the bands of thy neck, O captive daughter of Zion. For thus saith the Lord, ye have sold yourselves for naught; and ye shall be redeemed without money." "Therefore, my people shall know my name: therefore, they shall know in that day that I am he that doth speak; behold it is I. How beautiful upon the mountains are the feet of him that bringeth good tidings, that publisheth peace; that bringeth good tidings of good, that publisheth salvation; that saith unto Zion that God reigneth! Thy watchman shall lift up the voice; with the voice together shall they sing: for they shall see eye to eye, when the Lord shall bring again Zion. Break forth into joy, sing together, ye waste places of Jerusalem: for the Lord hath made bare his holy arm in the eyes of all nations; and all the ends of the earth shall see the salvation of our God." (Isaiah 52:1-10.) Isaiah in another place speaking of this work says: "O thou afflicted, tossed with tempest, and not comforted, behold, I will lay thy stones with fair colors, and lay thy foundations with sapphires. And I will make thy windows of agates, and thy gates of carbuncles, and all thy borders of pleasant stones. *And all thy children shall be taught of the Lord;* and great shall be the peace of thy children. In righteousness shalt thou be established: thou shalt be far from oppression; for thou shalt not fear: and from terror; for it shall not come near thee." (Isaiah 54:11-14.) We learn from the foregoing quotations that the watchman of Zion, shall see eye to eye; or in other words, be of one mind with regard to the things of God; and also that all their children shall be taught of the Lord.

Purity of the Saints that Shall Dwell in Zion

Isaiah says in another chapter: "Violence shall no more be heard in thy land, wasting nor destruction within thy borders: but thou shalt call thy walls salvation and thy gates praise. The sun shall be no more thy light by day; neither for brightness shall the moon give light unto thee: but the Lord shall be unto thee an everlasting light, and thy sun shall no more go down; neither shall thy moon withdraw itself; for the Lord shall be thine everlasting light, and the days of thy mourning shall be ended. Thy people also shall be *all* righteous; they shall inherit the land forever, the branch of my planting, the work of my hands, that I may be glorified. A little one shall become a thousand, and a small one a strong nation: I the Lord will hasten it in his time." (Isaiah 60:18-22.) The above is not only a description of the majesty of the Lord when he will reign over his people in Mount Zion; but of the purity of the saints: for says the prophet, "Thy people also shall be all righteous: they shall inherit the land forever." The reader will also remember, that the prophet is here speaking of those that shall dwell in Zion.

Prophets Describe the Future Reign of the Lord

Isaiah in another place says: "For behold, I create new heavens, and a new earth: and the former shall not be remembered, nor come into mind. But be ye glad and rejoice forever in that which I create: for behold, I create Jerusalem a rejoicing and her people a joy. And I will rejoice in Jerusalem, and joy in my people; and the voice of weeping shall be no more heard in her, nor the voice of crying. There shall be no more thence an infant of days, nor an old man that hath not filled his days, for the child shall die an hundred years old: but the sinner, being an hundred years old shall be accursed. And they shall build houses, and inhabit them; and they shall plant vineyards, and eat the fruit of them. They shall not build, and another inhabit; they shall not plant, and another eat: for as the days of a tree are the days of my people, and mine elect shall long enjoy the work of their hands. They shall not labour in vain, nor bring forth for trouble: for they are the seed of the blest of the Lord, and their offspring with them. And it shall come to pass, that before they call, I will answer: and while they are yet speaking, I will hear. The wolf and the lamb shall feed together, and the lion shall eat straw like the bullock: and dust shall be the serpent's meat. They shall not hurt nor destroy in all my holy mountain, saith the Lord." (Isaiah 65:17-25.) We learn first, from the above that the earth will be restored; second, that there shall be no wasting nor destruction, nor sorrow or mourning; but that the people of God shall dwell in peace and quietude, and long enjoy the work of their hands; third, that the Lord will give them an abundance of revelations; for says Isaiah, "before they call, I will answer: and while they are yet speaking I will hear;" fourth, the wild beasts will become peaceable and harmless and eat vegetable food. The prophet says in another place; that the Lord will cause peace to flow like a river to his people.

Zepheniah writes thus: "Therefore, wait ye upon me, saith the Lord, until the day that I rise up to the prey; for my determination is to gather the nations, that I may assemble the kingdoms, to pour upon them mine indignation, even all my fierce anger: for all the earth shall be devoured with the fire of my jealousy. For I will turn to the people a pure language, that they may all call upon the name of the Lord, to serve him with one consent. From beyond the rivers of Ethiopia my suppliants, even the daughter of my dispersed [the

American Indians], shall bring mine offering. In that day shalt thou not be ashamed for all thy doings, wherein thou hast transgressed against me: for then I will take away out of the midst of thee them that rejoice in thy pride; and thou shalt no more be haughty because of mine holy mountain. I will also leave in the midst of thee an afflicted and poor people, and they shall trust in the name of the Lord. The remnant of Israel shall not do iniquity, nor speak lies; neither shall a deceitful tongue be found in their mouth: for they shall feed and lie down, and none shall make them afraid. Sing, O daughter of Zion; shout O Israel; be glad and rejoice with all the heart, O daughter of Jerusalem. The Lord hath taken away thy judgments, he hath cast out thine enemy: the King of Israel, even the Lord, is in the midst of thee; thou shalt not see evil any more. In that day it shall be said to Jerusalem, fear thou not; and to Zion, let not thine hands be slack. The Lord thy God in the midst of thee is mighty; he will save, he will rejoice over thee with joy; he will rest in his love; he will joy over thee with singing. (Zeph. 3:8-17.) It is evident from the above—first, that when the nations are assembled the Lord will destroy them with the fire of his jealousy; second, that he will restore to his people a pure language that they may become of one heart and of one mind; third, that so glorious will be the work that the Lord's dispersed people upon this continent shall bring him an offering; fourth, that the House of Israel will not do iniquity any more; fifth, that their enemies shall be cast out, and their judgments taken away, that they should not be afflicted any more; sixth, that the Lord, the King of Israel, shall be in the midst of them, and that he will rest in the arms of his love, and joy over them with singing. Surely, this will be a *rest* for the people of God in earnest, and this will be the time that the House of Israel will enjoy that *rest,* so often spoken of in the Bible, that the Lord has in store for them.

Spirit of God Will be Poured Out Upon All Flesh

Joel after speaking of the restoration of the house of Israel and the manner that they shall be blessed with temporal blessings, says: "And ye shall eat in plenty, and be satisfied, and praise the name of the Lord your God, that hath dealt wonderously with you: and my people shall never be ashamed. And ye shall know that I am in the midst of Israel, and that I am the Lord your God, and none else: and my people shall never be ashamed. And it shall come to pass afterward, that I will pour out my Spirit upon all flesh; and your sons and your daughters shall prophesy, your old men shall dream dreams, your young men shall see visions. And also upon the servants and upon the handmaids in those days will I pour out my Spirit." (Joel 2:26-29.) From this we learn that the Spirit of God will be poured out upon all flesh, and that it will cause the people of God to prophesy. And it is evident that by this, the words of Isaiah, and Jeremiah will be fulfilled: "The knowledge of God shall cover the earth, as the waters cover the sea." "All shall know the Lord from the least to the greatest." The Spirit of God is the Spirit of knowledge and revelation, and when so generally diffused among the saints, it will enable them to know God alike. Jeremiah says in another place, that the Lord will cause the captivity of Israel to return, and he will build them as at first, and then he will reveal unto them the abundance of peace and truth. When this Spirit is poured out upon all flesh, it will of course effect the beasts of the forest, and thus bring to pass the singular change of their disposition:—"The wolf also shall dwell with the lamb, and the leopard shall lie down with the kid; and the calf, and the young lion, and the fattling together; and a little child shall lead them. And the cow and the bear shall feed; their young ones shall lie down together: and the lion shall eat straw like the ox. And the sucking child shall play on the hole of the asp, and the weaned child shall put his hand on the cockatrice's den. *They shall not hurt* nor destroy in all my holy mountain." Thus the beasts will cease to be ferocious, that the child can perform its wanderings among them unmolested. The prophet says, that all this shall be done in the Lord's holy mountain. (Anonymous, *TS* 3:687-690, February 15, 1852.)

Chapter 13

Summary Statements and Some Closing Observations

> We have also a more sure word of prophecy; whereunto ye do well that ye take heed, as unto a light that shineth in a dark place, until the day dawn, and the day star arise in your hearts:
>
> Knowing this first, that no prophecy of the scripture is of any private interpretation.
>
> For the prophecy came not in old time by the will of man: but holy men of God spake as they were moved by the Holy Ghost. (2 Peter 1:19-21.)

I am grateful for the experience this work has provided. My witness is that God the Eternal Father lives and is the father of our spirits. He loves his children and wants them to be obedient and follow the ordained plan of salvation which will bring happiness now and eternal joy in the eternities to come. Jesus Christ is his Son, and we join with Peter when he ceclared to the people in Jerusalem:

> And when they had set them in the midst, they asked, By what power, or by what name, have ye done this?
>
> Then Peter, filled with the Holy Ghost, said unto them, Ye rulers of the people, and elders of Israel,
>
> If we this day be examined of the good deed done to the impotent man, by what means he is made whole;
>
> Be it know unto you all, and to all the people of Israel, that by the name of Jesus Christ of Nazareth, whom ye crucified, whom God raised from the dead, even by him doth this man stand here before you whole.
>
> This is the stone which was set at nought of you builders, is become the head of the corner.
>
> Neither is there salvation in any other: for there is none other name under heaven given among men, whereby we must be saved. (Acts 4:7-12).

Someone has written, "Nothing is as important in anyone's life as a sincere faith in Jesus Christ, the Savior of the world."

Guided by Prophets

The Church of Jesus Christ of Latter-day Saints is "guided by revelation through modern prophets." Joseph Smith said, "...the spirit of prophecy...is the testimony of Jesus...and that constitutes a prophet." (*HC* 5:215.)

"Behold, the Lord's hand is not shortened, that it cannot save; neither his ear heavy, that it cannot hear." (Isaiah 59:1.)

Our Heavenly Father loves us and he is kind and cares about all his children, so he sent his prophets. "...one of the chief manifestations of his goodness is his communication with mankind, which always comes through His prophets."

Much of the material that has been presented for the reader is prophecy, and the manuscript has explored primarily the relationships between the Mormons (of Joseph) and the closely-knit ties of the Jews (of Judah), a member of the House of Israel, with whom the Lord entered into sacred covenants. To appreciate and more clearly comprehend these relationships, the material selected was carefully researched and viewed through the brilliantly luminated windows of prophecy and revelation.

Two Thousand Years of Wandering

By prophetic clarity it appears..."the Jewish people are near the completion of their nearly two thousand years of wandering." Their colorful, courageous and painful existence since their rejection of the Messiah dramatically portrays the fulfillment of the warning voices of the prophets and the Savior regarding their persecution, loss of political power, homeland, and destruction of their sacred temple.

The End is Better Than the Beginning

Known unto the Lord are all the conditions, circumstances, and challenges which man will be confronted with here in his mortal state. From previous intimate experiences and associations with his children in a pre-existent state, the Lord knew how they would conduct their lives here on earth. The great prophet Isaiah commented on this subject:

> Remember the former things of old: for I am God, and there is none else: I am God, and there is none like me.
>
> Declaring the end from the beginning, and from ancient times the things that are not yet done, saying, My counsel shall stand, and I will do all my pleasure: (Isaiah 46:9-10.)

Through the window of prophecy the future events in the lives of the Jewish people have been revealed by the prophets as promised by Amos, the prophet, who said:

> Surely the Lord God will do nothing, but he revealeth his secret unto his servants the prophets. (Amos 3:7.)

This is a Day of Fulfillment and Restoration

The restoration of the gospel by the Prophet Joseph Smith and the message of the Book of Mormon..."shall make known to all kindreds, tongues, and people, that the Lamb of God is the Son of the Eternal Father, and the Savior of the world; and that all men must come unto him or they cannot be saved." (I Nephi 13:40.)

President Kimball said: "Many people tend to forget that the Book of Mormon was written not only to the Lamanites but also to the convincing of the Jew and Gentile that Jesus is the Christ, the Eternal God, manifesting himself unto all nations."

The material presented in this volume is convincing evidence that the period of history in which we are living is a day of restoration and fulfillment. Israel is being gathered, the Jews have returned to Israel, their promised homeland. The future glory prophesied in Holy Writ that awaits the Lord's covenant people in the last days is nigh at hand if only they will accept and "worship the God of their fathers." Perhaps the time is not too far distant when by appointment of the Lord through his prophet, elders of The Church of Jesus Christ of Latter-day Saints will carry the gospel to the Jews. Armed with the Book of Mormon, many of the Jews will accept their message as prophecied. Perhaps there will be many who will also reject their witness that Jesus is the Christ. However, in my opinion circumstances may not be much different among the Jewish populace from what they were during His first ministry. At that time historians may have overestimated their claim that the inhabitants of Palestine as a nation of Jews, rejected Jesus of Nazareth. This conclusion was not entirely true. Were not Christ's twelve apostles faithful and valiant believers? Surely there must have been hundreds and perhaps thousands of converts during the lives and ministry of these dedicated men. They knew he was the Savior and the redeemer of mankind. As many knew who he was then, so many of Judah will recognize him when he comes again. This must be so, for the prophets have so predicted. This will be preparatory to the building of the temple in Jerusalem. Surely a temple to worship the God of their fathers would not be built by a people in unbelief, who refuse to accept Jesus Christ.

In this work an effort was made to present certain of the latter-day events prophesied; some in the past, some present, and some yet to be fulfilled in the future. The last days are upon us and the signs of the times—preparatory to the Advent of the Lord are nigh. We read in the Doctrine and Covenants:

> Ye look and behold the fig trees, and ye see them with your eyes, and ye say when they begin to shoot forth, and their leaves are yet tender, that summer is now nigh at hand;
>
> Even so it shall be in that day when they shall see all these things, then shall they know that the hour is nigh.
>
> And it shall come to pass that he that feareth me shall be looking forth for the great day of the Lord to come, even for the signs of the coming of the Son of Man. (D&C 45:37-39.)

Someone has written: "We are living in a day of fulfillment. We are seeing the culmination of many great and glorious things and the beginning of other things whose culmination will be vastly more glorious than the things of the present time."

Prophecies uttered many centuries ago in the land of Palestine before the birth of Christ and some that have been reiterated in America are being fulfilled. The membership of the Church now living "are...on the very threshold of [witnessing] the fulfillment of great and mighty prophecy. Truly God has revealed his secrets to the prophets and the prophecies they utter fail not."

The inhabitants of the world are confronted with numerous calamities, pestilences, and desolating wars. These perils are sweeping the earth with devastating consequences. The Lord has decreed that peace would be taken from the earth and wars, great hailstorms, famines, and earthquakes are but "a divine disclosure of future events."

Perhaps, Elder Orson F. Whitney envisioned our day when he wrote,

> Earth's long week is now drawing to a close, and we stand at the present moment in the Saturday Evening of Time, at or near the end of

the sixth day of human history. Is it not a time for thought, a season for solemn meditation? Morning will break upon the Millennium, the thousand years of peace, the Sabbath of the World!" *Saturday Night Thoughts,* rev. ed. [Salt Lake City: Deseret Book Co., 1927], p. 12).

The Times of the Gentiles are Approaching Their End

More recently, in our day, President Joseph Fielding Smith emphasized:

"Many things have taken place during the past one hundred and thirty-six years to impress faithful members of the Church with the fact that the coming of the Lord is near. The gospel has been stored. The Church has been fully organized. The priesthood has been conferred upon man. The various dispensations from the beginning have been revealed and their keys and authorities given to the Church. Israel has been and is being gathered to the land of Zion. The Jews are returning to Jerusalem. The gospel is being preached in all the world as a witness to every nation. Temples are being built, and ordinance work for the dead, as well as for the living, is performed in them. The hearts of the children have turned to their fathers, and the children are seeking after their dead. The covenants which the Lord promised to make with Israel in the latter days have been revealed, and thousands of gathered Israel have entered into them. Thus the work of the Lord is advancing, and all these things are signs of the near approach of our Lord."

Jesus said the Jews would be scattered among all nations and Jerusalem would be trodden down by the Gentiles until the times of the Gentiles were fulfilled. (Luke 21:24.) The prophecy in Section 45, verses 24-29, of the Doctrine and Covenants regarding the Jews was literally fulfilled. Jerusalem, which was trodden down by the Gentiles, is no longer trodden down but is made the home for the Jews. They are returning to Palestine, and by this we may know that the times of the Gentiles are near their close.

The Great and Dreadful Day of the Lord is Near

The words of the prophets are rapidly being fulfilled, but it is done on such natural principles that most of us fail to see it. Joel promised that the Lord would pour out his spirit upon all flesh: the sons and daughters should prophesy, old men should dream dreams, and young men should see visions. Wonders in heaven and in the earth would be seen, and there would be fire, blood, and pillars of smoke. Eventually the sun is to be turned into darkness and the moon as blood, and then shall come the great and dreadful day of the Lord. Some of these signs have been given; some are yet to come. The sun has not yet been darkened. We are informed that this will be one of the last acts just preceding the coming of the Lord.

One wonders if we are not now seeing some of the signs in heaven—not all, for undoubtedly some of them will be among the heavenly bodies, such as the moon and the sun, the meteors and comets, but in speaking of the heavens, reference is made to that part which surrounds the earth and which belongs to it. It is in the atmosphere where many of the signs are to be given. Do we not see airships of various kinds traveling through the heavens daily? Have we not had signs in the earth and through the earth with the radio, railroad trains, automobiles, submarines, and satellites, and in many other ways? There are yet to be great signs: the heavens are to be shaken, the sign of the Son of Man is to be given, and then shall the tribes of the earth mourn.

An Increase of Learning

Among the signs of the last days was an increase of learning. Daniel was commanded to "...shut up the words, and seal the book [of his prophecy], even to the time of the end: [and in that day] many shall run to and fro," said he "and knowledge shall be increased." [Dan. 12:4.) Are not the people "running to and fro" today as they never did before in the history of the world? Go to the Bureau of Information and ask there how many tourists visit Temple Square each year. Make inquiry at the various national parks, at the bus, railroad, and steamship companies; learn how many are running to Europe, Asia, and all parts of the earth.

Are we not, most of us, running to and fro in our automobiles seeking pleasure? Is not knowledge increased? Was there ever a time in the history of the world when so much knowledge was poured out upon the people? But sad to say, the words of Paul are true—the people are "ever learning and never able to come to the knowledge of the truth." (2 Tim. 3:7.)

Have you ever tried to associate the outpouring of knowledge, the great discoveries and inventions during the past 136 years, with the restoration of the gospel? Do you not think there is some connection? It is not because we are more intelligent than our fathers that we have received this knowledge, but because God has willed it so in our generation! Yet men take the honor unto themselves and fail to recognize the hand of the Almighty in these things.

America was discovered because the Lord willed it. The gospel was restored in America, rather than in some other land, because the Lord willed it. This is the land "shadowing with wings" spoken of by Isaiah that today is sending ambassadors by the sea to a nation scattered and peeled, which at one time was terrible in the beginning. (Isaiah 18:1-2.) Now that nation is being gathered, and once again they shall be in favor with the Lord.

Signs of the Last Days

Have we not had numerous rumors of wars? Have we not had wars, such wars as the world never saw before? Is there not today commotion among the nations, and are not their rulers troubled? Have not kingdoms been overturned and great changes been made among nations? The whole earth is in commotion. Earthquakes in divers places are reported every day. I took the liberty to call Dr. Melvin Cook and have him get for me some facts about how many earthquakes we have now. He quotes from a recent book (Earthquakes and Earth Structure) by John H. Hodgson (who is chief, Division of Seismology, Dominion Observatory, Ottawa) the following: "The way the numbers [of earthquakes] go up as the magnitude goes down makes it easy for us to accept the estimate that, if all earthquakes down to zero magnitude could be detected, the number would be between one and ten million each year." Then he goes on to say that there are about 2,000 earthquakes each year with the magnitude between 5 and 6 and about 20,000 between 4 and 5; therefore it looks as if there are around 20,000 earthquakes a year that could be damaging if they occurred in populated areas. The other signs given by the Lord have been seen or are at our doors. We know this to be the case both from observation and from the predictions of the prophets. Elijah, 130 years ago, told Joseph Smith that the great and dreadful day of the Lord was near, "...even at the doors." (D&C 110:16.)

Yet the old world goes on about its business paying very little heed to all the Lord has said and to all the signs and indications that have been given. Men harden their hearts and say "...that Christ delayeth his coming until the end of the earth." (D&C 45:26.)

They are "...eating and drinking, marrying and giving in marriage..." according to the customs of the world, not of God, without one thought that the end of wickedness is near. Pleasure and the love of the world have captured the hearts of the people. There is no time for such people to worship the Lord or give heed to his warnings; so it will continue until the day of destruction is upon them.

At no time in the history of the world has it been more necessary for the children of men to repent. We boast of our advanced civilization, of the great knowledge and wisdom with which we are possessed; but in and through it all, the love of God is forgotten! The Lord, as well as Elijah, gave us warning, as did also Joseph Smith. The Lord said: "For behold, verily, verily, I say unto you, the time is soon at hand that I shall come in a cloud with power and great glory.

"And it shall be a great day at the time of my coming, for all nations shall tremble.

"But before that great day shall come, the sun shall be darkened, and the moon be turned into blood; and the stars shall refuse their shining, and some shall fall, and great destructions await the wicked." (D&C 34:7-9.)

If the great and dreadful day of the Lord were near at hand when Elijah came 130 years ago, we are just one century nearer it today. But some will say: "But no! Elijah, you are wrong! Surely 130 years have passed, and are we not better off today than ever before? Look at our discoveries, our inventions, our knowledge, and our wisdom! Surely you made a mistake!" So many seem to think and say, and judging by their actions they are sure, that the world is bound to go on in its present condition for millions of years before the end will come. Talk to them; hear what they have to say—these learned men of the world. "We have had worse times," they say. "You are wrong in thinking there are more calamities now than in earlier times. There are not more earthquakes, the earth has always been quaking, but now we have facilities for gathering the news which our fathers did not have. These are not signs of the times; things are not different from former times." And so the people refuse to heed the warnings the Lord so kindly gives to them, and thus they fulfill the scriptures. Peter said such sayings would be uttered, and he warned the people. (2 Pet. 3:3-7.) In this warning Peter calls attention to the destruction of the world in the flood and says that at the coming of Christ—which scoffers would postpone or deny—there shall come another cleansing of the earth, but the second time by fire. Is not the condition among the people today similar to that in the days of Noah? Did the people believe and repent then? Can you make men, save with few exceptions, believe today that there is any danger? Do you believe the Lord when he said almost 135 years ago: "For I am no respecter of persons, and will that all men shall know that the day speedily cometh; the hour is not yet, but is nigh at hand, when peace shall be taken from the earth, and the devil shall have power over his own dominion." (D&C 1:35.)

"And behold, and lo, I come quickly to judgment, to convince all of their ungodly deeds which they have committed against me, as it is written of me in the volume of the book." (D&C 99:5.)

"Prepare ye, prepare ye for that which is to come, for the Lord is nigh

"And the anger of the Lord is kindled, and his sword is bathed in heaven, and it shall fall upon the inhabitants of the earth." (D&C 1:12-13.)

"Verily, I say unto you, this generation, in which these things shall be shown forth, shall not pass away until all I have told you shall be fulfilled." (Joseph Smith 1:34.)

Shall we slumber on in utter oblivion or indifference to all that the Lord has given us as warning? I say unto you, "Watch therefore: for ye know not what hour your Lord doth come.

"But know this, that if the good man of the house had known in what watch the thief would come, he would have watched, and would not have suffered his house to be broken up.

"Therefore be ye also ready: for in such an hour as ye think not the Son of Man cometh." (Matt. 24:42-44.)

May we heed this warning given by the Lord and get our houses in order and be prepared for the coming of the Lord. (Joseph Fielding Smith, *CR,* April, 1966, pp. 12-15.)

How Should Latter-day Saints Prepare for the Last Days?

The prophets have taught and prophesied of conditions during the dispensation of the fullness of times, when "all things would be gathered together in one." Much of what the Lord has told his prophets has been fulfilled. The evidence and magnitude of numerous events that are presently taking place are a witness that these are the last days. An awareness of these happenings are testified to by the scriptures. Latter-day Saints must study, pray, and listen to the spoken and written word. The scriptures contain a record of the past and future events that have been carefully identified. In addition they contain the revelations and commandments, which point out the only acceptable and true way of life.

Latter-day Saints living in this day and time have been favorably rewarded by the Lord, who through his prophets have described events and circumstances on earth during the last days. The many tribulations described in D&C 45:26-31, 33 are noteably apparent in our day. We read:

> And in that day shall be heard of wars and rumors of wars, and the whole earth shall be in commotion, and men's hearts shall fail them, and they shall say that Christ delayeth his coming until the end of the earth.
>
> And the love of men shall wax cold, and iniquity shall abound.
>
> And when the times of the Gentiles is come in, a light shall break forth among them that sit in darkness, and it shall be the fulness of my gospel;
>
> But they receive it not; for they perceive not the light, and they turn their hearts from me because of the precepts of men.
>
> And in that generation shall the times of the Gentiles be fulfilled.
>
> And there shall be men standing in that generation, that shall not pass until they shall see an overflowing scourge; for a desolating sickness shall cover the land.
>
> And there shall be earthquakes also in divers places, and many desolations; yet men will harden their hearts against me, and they will take up the sword, one against another, and they will kill one another.

Coming of the Son of Man is Near

The fulfillment of the prophecies and the signs of the time indicate that the coming of the Son of Man is nigh at hand. This is evident from Joseph Smith 1:33-39, which says:

> And immediately after the tribulation of those days, the sun shall be darkened, and the moon shall not give her light, and the stars shall fall from heaven, and the powers of heaven shall be shaken.
>
> Verily, I say unto you, this generation, in which these things shall be shown forth, shall not pass away until all I have told you shall be fulfilled.
>
> Although, the days will come, that heaven and earth shall pass away; yet my words shall not pass away, but all shall be fulfilled.
>
> And, as I said before, after the tribulation of those days, and the powers of the heavens shall be shaken, then shall appear the sign of the Son of Man in heaven, and then shall all the tribes of the earth mourn; and they shall see the Son of Man coming in the clouds of heaven, with power and great glory;

And whoso treasureth up my word, shall not be deceived, for the Son of Man shall come, and he shall send his angels before him with the great sound of a trumpet, and they shall gather together the remainder of his elect from the four winds, from one end of heaven to the other.

Now learn a parable of the fig-tree—When its branches are yet tender, and it begins to put forth leaves, you know that summer is night at hand;

So likewise, mine elect, when they shall see all these things, they shall know that he is near, even at the doors;...

The Spirit of Prophecy Manifested by Joseph Smith and Oliver Cowdery

Nearly a year before the Church was organized a most significant event relative to prophecy was revealed by Joseph Smith.

...It was on the fifteenth day of May, 1829, that we were ordained under the hand of this messenger, and baptized.

Immediately on our coming up out of the water after we had been baptized, we experienced great and glorious blessings from our Heavenly Father. No sooner had I baptized Oliver Cowdery, than the Holy Ghost fell upon him, and he stood up and prophesied many things which should shortly come to pass. And again, so soon as I had been baptrized by him, I also had the spirit of prophecy, when, standing up, I prophesied concerning the rise of this Church, and many other things connected with the Church, and this generation of the children of men. We were filled with the Holy Ghost, and rejoiced in the God of our salvation.

Our minds being now enlightened, we began to have the scriptures laid open to our understandings, and the true meaning and intention of their more mysterious passages revealed unto us in a manner which we never could attain to previously, nor ever before had thought of. In the meantime we were forced to keep secret the circumstances of having received the Priesthood and our having been baptized, owing to a spirit of persecution which had already manifested itself in the neighborhood. (Joseph Smith 2:72-74.)

Latter-day Saints Commanded to Understand Prophecy and Its Fulfillment

Nearly three years after the Church was organized the Lord said:

And I give unto you a commandment that you shall teach one another the doctrine of the kingdom.

Teach ye diligently and my grace shall attend you, that you may be instructed more perfectly in theory, in principle, in doctrine, in the law of the gospel, in all things that pertain unto the kingdom of God, that are expedient for you to understand;

Of things both in heaven and in the earth, and under the earth; things which have been, things which are, things which must shortly come to pass; things which are at home, things which are abroad; the wars and the perplexities of the nations, and the judgments which are on the land; and a knowledge also of countries and of kingdoms—

That ye may be prepared in all things which I shall send you again to magnify the calling whereunto I have called you, and the mission with which I have commissioned you. (D&C 88:77-80.)

Prophecy Emphasized in the Principle of Gathering by the Prophet Joseph Smith

He said,

> It is a principle [gathering] I esteem to be of the greatest importance to those who are looking for salvation in this generation, or in these, that may be called, "the latter times," All that the prophets that have written, from the days of righteous Abel, down to the last man that has left any testimony on record for our consideration, in speaking of the salvation of the gathering. (*HC* 2:260.)

Orson Pratt Commanded by the Lord to Prophesy

In D&C 34:10 we read:..."lift up your voice and spare not, for the Lord God hath spoken; therefore prophesy, and it shall be given by the power of the Holy Ghost." Orson did as the Lord commanded and in consequence he is one of the frequently quoted individuals in this project. Orson's admonition to the Latter-day Saints on the principle of prophecy is most relevant to all Church members, who are striving to obtain the spirit of prophecy in order to comprehend the signs of the times:

> But the Latter-day Saints are not in darkness; they are the children of light, although many of us will actually be asleep. We shall have to wake up and trim up our lamps, or we shall not be prepared to enter in; for we shall all slumber and sleep in that day, and some will have gone to sleep from which they will not awake until they awake up in darkness without any oil in their

> lamps. But as a general thing, the Saints will understand the signs of the times, if they do lie down and get to sleep. Others have their eyes closed upon the prophecies of the ancient Prophets; and not only that, but they are void of the spirit of prophecy themselves. When a man has this, though he may appeal to ancient Prophets to get understanding on some subjects he does not clearly understand, yet, as he has the spirit of prophecy in himself, he will not be in darkness; he will have a knowledge of the signs of the times; he will have a knowledge of the house of Israel, and of Zion, of the ten tribes, and of many things and purposes and events that are to take place on the earth; and he will see coming events, and can say such an event will take place, and after that another, and then another; and after that the trumpet shall sound, and after that certain things will take place, and then another trump shall sound, &c., &c.; and he will have his eye fixed on the signs of the times, and that day will not overtake him unawares... (*JD* 7:189.)

The Zionist Movement

President Charles W. Penrose was a great scholar and student of the scriptures. He was a dedicated friend and advocate of the Jewish people and in complete sympathy with the purposes of Zionism. He recognized through the spirit of prophecy that the Zionist movement was a forerunner, "opening the way for the occupation of the Holy Land by the children of Jacob." His assessment of the Zionist movement and its contributions are an excellent summarization of those events that have been fulfilled and others which seem near at hand.

The Ancient Order of Maccabaeans and the Inspired Zionist Movement

"...An important meeting was held in Liverpool which...took place in the Tivoli Theatre, and there was a large attendance. It was in the interest of what is called the Zionist Movement, and was under the auspices of "The Ancient Order of Maccabaeans." A number of notable speakers addressed the audience, Rabbi S. J. Rabinowitz spoke in Hebrew. The principal speaker, however, was Mr. Herbert Bentwich, LL.B., of London, who offered the following resolution: "That this meeting of sympathizers with the Maccabaean Zionist Movement declares its loyal adherence to the Jewish National Cause, gratefully welcomes the foundation of constitutional government in the Turkish Empire as an aid to the securing of the legally assured House in Palestine, which is the immediate object of all Zionist endeavors, and pledges itself to support the Shekel Fund and all other institutions authorized by the International Bureau to further these objects."

The great change that has taken place in Turkish affairs by the overthrow of the dominion of Abdul Hamid as Sultan of the Ottoman Empire, and the establishment of constitutional government therein, has naturally stimulated the supporters of the movement in which the Order of Maccabaeans is an active factor. The Zionist organizations embrace large numbers of Jewish people in all the leading nations of the world. While it is true that many millions of the children of Judah scattered upon the face of the earth take little or no interest in the land of their fathers, but are engrossed in their business affairs where they live and move and have their being, nevertheless there are large numbers of Hebrews who keep in view the promises made of old, as to the restoration of their nation to Palestine and the re-establishment of the Kingdom of Israel.

Zionism—A Universal Movement and Sign of the Last Days

Many wealthy persons, Gentiles as well as Jews, are moved upon by a spirit of faith and hope for the fulfillment of the prophecies in Holy Writ, concerning the gathering of Israel and the return of Judah and the glory that is to attend the covenant people of the Lord in the latter days. There are some divisions of opinion in regard to the manner in which the Zionist movement is to be carried on, and different organizations among its promoters, yet the grand purpose and object are the same, namely, the building up of that Zion which was the subject of poetic and prophetic song and service in olden times. It is not surprising, then, that the people who are looking and working toward that end should perceive, in the recent upheaval of Turkish affairs, the likelihood of an advancement to their cause and its probable success under the more liberal condition of affairs that is now entered upon. The Holy Land is under the dominion of the Turk. Before the great events desired and expected can come to pass that land will have to be liberated, at least to the extent that the Jews who wish to gather there can be free to worship the God of their fathers and prepare the way for the fulfilment of ancient prophecies.

The meeting to which we have briefly referred is only one of the signs of activity among the promoters of the gathering of Judah. As was stated at the Liverpool gathering by H. S. Lewis, M.A., of

Manchester, in seconding the above resolution, which was unanimously carried, "Zionism is becoming a universal movement, and wherever were found centres of Jewish population, there are to be found Zionists. The great bulk of Jewish populations reside in countries where they are persecuted. To them there is no fatherland so appropriate and so possible as the home of their fathers." Other speakers also maintained that "Palestine and Palestine only is the solution of the Jewish question," and that there is but one goal for them—"the acquisition of the fatherland for the children of Israel."

Mormon Elders to Carry the Gospel to the Jews

...According to the revelations of God in these latter days, the great Zion to which the Lord will come and from which His law will go forth to the world, is to be built up on the western hemisphere. To this will be gathered the remnants of the House of Israel scattered among the nations. The children of Judah will gather to Jerusalem, where the House of God is to be rebuilt and its former glory restored and increased, and the Savior is to appear there also, standing on the Mount of Olives, from which He ascended into heaven over two thousand years ago, and where He will be received as the Messiah. His word will go forth from Jerusalem, and the sayings of the prophets concerning His advent will all be fulfilled.

The gathering of Israel from the four quarters of the earth is part of the work of this dispensation and devolves upon the servants of God in The Church of Jesus Christ of Latter-day Saints. As Judah has been scattered abroad according to ancient prophecy, so the seed of Israel has been dispersed among the Gentiles and has been mingled with them, but they are of the blood of Abraham and are known to the Lord, and He is bringing them from afar "saying to the north give up, and to the south keep not back, bring my sons from far and my daughters from the ends of the earth." The Zion which once was on the little hill near Jerusalem is being built up in the western mountains, the House of the Lord is exalted above the hills," and His people are flowing to it from many nations, as predicted by Isaiah and Micah. The movement called "Zionism," which is making headway in the world, is for the gathering of Judah to the land of their fathers and in due time will be accomplished, for the elders of this Church will go forth, specially, at the appointed time to carry the gospel to the Jews and help in their gathering home to Palestine.

The Messiah Will Reign in Mount Zion and in Jerusalem

We regard the Zionist Movement, as it is called, as a sign of the times. It is a precursor of the general agitation which will ensue among the sons of Judah. It is not that marvelous work which will yet be accomplished, but a forerunner thereof. It is a step in the right direction. The change already taking place in the Turkish Empire we view as the beginning of the modifications that will take place in the dominions of the Moslem, opening the way for the occupation of the Holy Land by the children of Jacob. The Lord is moving among the nations for the accomplishment of His great purposes, as foreshadowed by the prophets of old and as revealed through the great Seer of the nineteenth century, Joseph Smith.

God will gather Israel from afar and bring them to Zion. He will call for the sons of Judah and gather them from the ends of the earth to Palestine and establish them again in Jerusalem, and in due time Jesus of Nazareth, the Christ, the Messiah, will "reign in Mount Zion and in Jerusalem and before His ancients gloriously." His saints can now behold the signs which He foretold as plainly as they can see the opening of the buds in this glorious springtime, betokening the advent of summer, and they are making ready for the work that is before them to aid in the consummation of all things. We wish success to the promoters of the Zionist movement, and are watching for the great restoration which is an essential feature of the glorious kingdom of our Redeemer that is near at hand. (Charles W. Penrose, *MS* 71:296-299, May 13, 1909.)

The Jews Have Returned to Jerusalem

Students of the scriptures acknowledge the fulfillment of a modern miracle in the creation of a homeland for the Jewish people. In spite of intense hatred, war and political opposition the Jews are deeply rooted in their new nation of Israel. Their survival under such difficult and challenging circumstances is not particularly surprising to the Latter-day Saint people. To them it is the fulfillment of ancient and modern prophecy for hadn't the Lord revealed to his servants Amos and others that the Jews would eventually return to their ancient promised land? From Amos we read:

> And I will bring again the captivity of my people of Israel, and they shall build the waste cities, and inhabit them; and they shall plant vineyards, and drink the wine thereof; they shall also make gardens, and eat the fruit of them.

And I will plant them upon their land, and they shall no more be pulled up out of their land which I have given them, saith the Lord thy God." (Amos 9:14-15.)

Orson Pratt wrote:

The Jews, or many of them will gather back to Jerusalem in a state of unbelief in the true Messiah, believing in the prophets but rejecting the New Testament, and looking for the Messiah to come, honest-hearted no doubt, many of them. And they will re-build Jerusalem after the times of the Gentiles are fulfilled. (*JD* 14:352, March 10, 1872.)

Elder Charles W. Penrose and George Q. Cannon are in agreement with Orson Pratt as to the state of unbelief of the Jews when they return to Jerusalem. Penrose wrote:

The gathering of Judah is to be accomplished in this dispensation of the fulness of times. Their gathering place is Jerusalem. They will return to the land of their fathers chiefly in unbelief. A few of that race will begin to believe that Jesus of Nazareth is the Christ, but the masses of that people will not believe Him in that light until He comes and His feet shall stand again on the Mount of Olives. He will then appear as their deliverer...[they will] acknowledge Him as their Messiah, their redeemer, and their King. They will then receive His Gospel, the only plan of salvation: "A nation will be born in a day unto the Lord," and in the Temple that will be reared to His name they will officiate for their dead until all the links in the chain of their ancestry, back to the time when the Gospel was on the earth previous to the enunction of the Mosaic code are made complete. *Rays of Living Light,* Pamphlet No. 11 (Salt Lake City, Utah: Deseret News, n.d.), p. 3.

The Book of Mormon States That the Main Part of the Jews Will Accept Christ While Scattered

From Orson Pratt we read:

Then, when the Gentile nations shall reject the Gospel, and count themselves unworthy of eternal life, as the Jews did before them, the Lord will say—"It is enough, come away from them, my servants, I will give you a new commission, and you shall go to the scattered remnants of the house of Israel. (*JD* 18:177.)

By and by, after you have fulfilled your mission to the nations of the Gentiles, and there will not any more of them repent—that is, when you have fully accomplished all that is required of you in relation to them, you will have another mission, and so will the Twelve, and that is to the house of Israel that may be among those nations; I mean literal descendants of Jacob—the Jews, and the descendants of the other tribes that may be scattered among those nations. There are some from the ten tribes among them, but the body of the ten tribes are in the north country. You will find a few among all these Gentile nations: you will have to direct your attention to them after you have fulfilled your mission among the Gentiles, and their times are fulfilled. You will have something to do among the Jews, and then will be a time of great power such as you and I have not dreamed of. Indeed, we could not, with our narrow comprehensions of mind, perceive the power that will come then follow....

Then many of the Jews will believe, although many of that nation will gather to Jerusalem in unbelief. But the Book of Mormon has told us that the main part of them will believe while yet scattered. They will receive your testimony and gather to Jerusalem. (*JD* 7:187-188.)

God to Help Restore the Jews and Will Go Forth to Battle in Their Behalf

Israel will rise from the abject position which he has so long occupied. He is destined to be the head and not to serve. He is again to be the favored of God. But, though the Lord has given these cheering promises of future glory, prosperity, and independence, when the Jews are once more restored to the inheritances and lands of their fathers, yet he has made it easy to be understood by the words of the prophets, that they will be gathered to their own lands in unbelief. Many societies of Christendom, overlooking this fact, or, if seeing it, not believing that it would be so, are making strenuous efforts to convert the Jews, flattered no doubt with the hope that they will be successful. The testimony of the Scriptures goes to prove that after they have inhabited Jerusalem and the surrounding nations, tempted by cupidity, attack them, Jesus will make his appearance—"The Lord my God shall come and all the saints with thee"—and deliver them from their enemies by going forth to battle in their behalf. They will recognize him as their long-expected Messiah, whose appearance they had so ardently desired; but they will not recognize him as Jesus of Nazareth whom their fathers crucified, the Being whom they had been taught to believe was an impostor; therefore, they shall ask with surprise, "What are these wounds in thy hands?" And he shall answer, "Those with which I was wounded in the house of my friends." Such a question and such an answer would be meaningless, if they already believed him to be the Being whom their fathers had crucified. (George Q. Cannon, *Writings from the "Western Standard,"* Liverpool: pub. by George Q. Cannon, 42 Islington, 1864, Pub. in San Francisco, California, pp. 216-217.)

A Great and Glorious Zion to be Built Up in the Last Days

Orson Pratt emphasized that:

> ...Zion...will be built upon the great western hemisphere in North America, and become a righteous people long before the Jews will gather home. Zion will be built up by the gathering of the Saints from all the nations and kingdoms of the earth. Zion will be built up, her habitations will be reared, her Temple will be built and the glory of God will rest upon them long before these great events in connection with the house of Israel will be fulfilled. Hence there is a difference between Zion and Jerusalem in the latter days.
>
> We will now read something more about this Zion. Isaiah, as I have already quoted in the second chapter, has told us about the house of the Lord, and the great peace that should come, the beating of swords into ploughshares, &c., and then he goes on to portray the blessings that are to come upon Zion. He says, "In that day seven women shall take hold of one man, saying, We will eat our own bread and wear our own apparel, only let us be called by thy name to take away our reproach. In that day shall the branch of the Lord be beautiful and glorious, and the fruit of the earth shall be excellent and comely." Thus we see that Zion is to become glorious. The branch of the Lord, the branch of his own planting, established by his own power, the building up of a people and city by his own instructions and administration, by the inspiration of his servants, the establishing of Zion no more to be thrown down. And the Lord will create upon every dwelling place of Mount Zion and upon her assemblies a cloud and smoke by day, and a shining flaming fire by night; and upon all the glory shall be a defence; and there shall be a tabernacle for a shadow in the day time from the heat, and for a place of refuge and for a covert from storm and from rain. How often I have quoted this passage! I am not tired of quoting it yet. It is among the great events of the latter days; it is among those marvels and wonders that are just at hand. A Zion to be built up; a city of Zion having habitations, and upon these

habitations a supernatural light by night, and a supernatural cloud by day. No such event has happened since this prophecy was uttered by the Prophet Isaiah, it remains to be fulfilled in the latter days. No wonder then that the Lord said to Joseph Smith in the year 1831, that is, before we were a great people, while we were only a few hundreds, well did the Lord inspire him to say that Zion should become great and glorious and the day should come that the nations of the earth should tremble because of her, and should fear because of her terrible ones; for the glory of God shall be there, and the power of the Lord shall be there when the day comes that the city of Zion is clothed upon with the glorious appendage that is herein predicted; when the branch of the Lord becomes beautiful and glorious, and the fruit of the earth excellent and comely, when that day shall come that seven women shall take hold of one man, saying, "We will eat our own bread and wear our own apparel, only let us be called by thy name to take away our reproach," when that day shall come that the Lord God shall show forth his power in Zion—upon her Tabernacle, upon her Temple, her meeting places, her residences, palaces, towers, walls and gates, when that day shall come it will astonish the nations even unto the ends of the earth. (*JD* 14:353.)

President Penrose Commented About the Appearances of Jesus Christ to the Temple Prepared for Him

"We may consider the inhabitants of the earth at the time immediately preceding the coming of Christ under three general divisions:—

"First, the Saints of God gathered to one place on the western continent, called Zion, busily preparing for his appearance in their midst as their Redeemer, who had shed his blood for their salvation, now coming to reign over them and to reward them for their labours in establishing his government.

"Second, the Jews gathered to Jerusalem and also expecting the Messiah, but not believing that Jesus of Nazareth was the Son of God, and being in danger of destruction from their Gentile enemies:

"Third, the corrupt nations and kingdoms of men, who, rejecting the light of the Gospel, are unprepared for the Lord's advent and are almost ripe for destruction.

"Among the first-mentioned of these three classes of men the Lord will make his appearance first; and that appearance will be unknown to the rest of mankind. He will come to the Temple prepared for him, and his faithful people will behold his face, hear his voice, and gaze upon his glory. From his own lips they will receive further instructions for the development and beautifying of Zion and for the extension and sure stability of his kingdom.

"His next appearance will be among the distressed and nearly vanquished sons of Judah. At the crisis of their fate, when the hostile troops of several nations are ravaging the city and all the horrors of war are overwhelming the people of Jerusalem, he will set his feet upon the Mount of Olives, which will cleave and part asunder at his touch. Attended by a host from heaven, he will overthrow and destroy the combined armies of the Gentiles, and appear to the worshipping Jews as the mighty Deliverer and Conqueror so long expected by their race; and while love, gratitude, awe, and admiration swell their bosoms, the Deliverer will show them the tokens of his crucifixion and disclose himself as Jesus of Nazareth, whom they had reviled and whom their fathers put to death. Then will unbelief depart from their souls, and 'the blindness in part which has happened unto Israel' be removed. 'A fountain for sins and uncleanness shall be opened to the house of David and the inhabitants of Jerusalem,' and 'a nation will be born' unto God 'in a day.' They will be baptized for the remission of their sins, and will receive the gift of the Holy Ghost, and the government of God as established in Zion will be set up among them, no more to be thrown down for ever.

"The great and crowning advent of the Lord will be subsequent to these two appearances; but who can describe it in the language of mortals? The tongue of man falters, and the pen drops from the hand of the writer, as the mind is rapt in contemplation of the sublime and awful majesty of his coming to take vengeance on the ungodly and to reign as King of the whole earth.

"He comes! the earth shakes, and the tall mountains tremble; the mighty deep rolls back to the north as in fear, and the rent skies glow like molten brass. He comes! The dead Saints burst forth from their tombs, and 'those who are alive and remain' are 'caught up' with them to meet him. The ungodly rush to hide themselves from his presence, and call upon the quivering rocks to cover them. He comes! With all the hosts of the righteous glorified. The breath of his lips strikes death to the wicked. His glory is a consuming fire. The proud and rebellious are as stubble; they are burned and 'left neither root nor branch.' He sweeps the earth 'as with the besom of destruction.' He deluges the earth with the fiery floods of his wrath, and the filthiness and abominations of the world are consumed. Satan and his dark hosts are taken and bound—the prince of the power of the air has lost his dominion, for He whose right it is to reign has come, and "the kingdoms of this world have become the kingdoms of our Lord and of his Christ." (Charles W. Penrose, "The Second Advent," *Millennial Star,* 10 September 1859, pp. 582-583.)

The Jews Will Gather to Israel Prior to the Second Coming of Christ

Isaiah's comments about the second coming of the Savior makes it definite that the Jews will have returned to their homeland prior to his arrival:

> Arise, shine; for thy light is come, and the glory of the Lord is risen upon thee.
>
> For, behold, the darkness shall cover the earth, and gross darkness the people: but the Lord shall arise upon thee, and his glory shall be seen upon thee.
>
> And the Gentiles shall come to thy light, and kings to the brightness of thy rising.
>
> Lift up thine eyes round about, and see: all they gather themselves together, they come to thee: thy sons shall come from far, and thy daughters shall be nursed at thy side.
>
> Then thou shalt see, and flow together, and thine heart shall fear, and be enlarged; because the abundance of the sea shall be converted unto thee, the forces of the Gentiles shall come unto thee.
>
> Who are these that fly as a cloud, and as the doves to their windows?
>
> Surely the isles shall wait for me, and the ships of Tarshish first, to bring thy sons from far, their silver and their gold with them, unto the name of the Lord thy God, and to the Holy One of Israel, because he hath glorified thee.
>
> And the sons of strangers shall build up thy walls, and their kings shall minister unto thee: for in my wrath I smote thee, but in my favour have I had mercy on thee.
>
> Therefore thy gates shall be open continually; they shall not be shut day nor night; that men may bring unto thee the forces of the Gentiles, and that their kings may be brought.
>
> For the nation and kingdom that will not serve thee shall perish; yea, those nations shall be utterly wasted.
>
> The glory of Lebanon shall come unto thee, the fir tree, the pine tree, and the box together, to beautify the place of my sanctuary; and I will make the place of my feet glorious.
>
> The sons also of them that afflicted thee shall come bending unto thee; and all they that despised thee shall bow themselves down at the soles of thy feet; and they shall call thee, The City of the Lord, The Zion of the Holy One of Israel.

> Whereas thou hast been forsaken and hated, so that no man went through thee, I will make thee an eternal excellency, a joy of many generations.
>
> Thou shalt also suck the milk of the Gentiles, and shalt suck the breast of kings: and thou shalt know that I the Lord am thy Saviour and thy Redeemer, the mighty One of Jacob.
>
> For brass I will bring gold, and for iron I will bring silver, and for wood brass, and for stones iron: I will also make thy officers peace, and thine exactors righteousness.
>
> Violence shall no more be heard in thy land, wasting nor destruction within thy borders; but thou shalt call thy walls Salvation, and thy gates Praise.
>
> The sun shall be no more thy light by day; neither for brightness shall the moon give light unto thee: but the Lord shall be unto thee an everlasting light, and thy God thy glory.
>
> Thy sun shall no more go down; neither shall thy moon withdraw itself: for the Lord shall be thine everlasting light, and the days of thy mourning shall be ended. (Isaiah 60:1-5, 8-20.)

Note the following remarkable words of Jesus Christ, which read..."And they [the Jews] shall believe in me, that I am Jesus Christ, the Son of God:...

> And I will remember the covenant which I have made with my people; and I have covenanted with them that I would gather them together in mine own due time, that I would give unto them again the land of their fathers for their inheritance, which is the land of Jerusalem, which is the promised land unto them forever, saith the Father.
>
> And it shall come to pass that the time cometh, when the fulness of my gospel shall be preached unto them;
>
> And they shall believe in me, that I am Jesus Christ, the Son of God, and shall pray unto the Father in my name.
>
> Then shall their watchmen lift up their voice, and with the voice together shall they sing; for they shall see eye to eye.
>
> Then will the Father gather them together again, and give unto them Jerusalem for the land of their inheritance.
>
> Then shall they break forth into joy—Sing together, ye waste places of Jerusalem; for the Father hath comforted his people, he hath redeemed Jerusalem. (3 Nephi 20:29-34.)

And in some future time, perhaps not too far distant, a magnificent temple will be built within the walls of Jerusalem.

> And there was given me a reed like unto a rod: and the angel stood, saying, Rise, and measure the temple of God, and the altar, and them that worship therein.
>
> But the court which is without the temple leave out, and measure it not; for it is given unto the Gentiles: and the holy city shall they tread under foot forty and two months. (Revelations 11:1-2.)

Jews Will Build a Temple in Jerusalem as Predicted in Holy Writ

Some events have taken place and others are presently being fulfilled and will continue to be as the time scale of the restoration of Israel is completed in accordance "to the favor and blessings of God."

The Prophet Joseph Smith spoke of the final winding-up scene:

"Judah must return, Jerusalem must be rebuilt, and the temple, and water come out from under the temple, and the waters of the Dead Sea be healed. It will take some time to rebuild the walls of the city and the temple, &c.; and all this must be done before the Son of Man will make His appearance." (Joseph Smith, Jr., *HC* 5:337, April, 1843.)

In 1971, a most interesting and informative conference, attended by "fourteen hundred Protestants from various parts of the world," convened in Jerusalem, Israel. One of the primary items on the conference agenda for discussion was to "help rebuild the temple" in Jerusalem. The topic was a source of considerable misunderstanding and controversy, however, the delegates recognized the rebuilding of the temple was "a necessary part of the fulfillment of prophecy."

Through the direction of the Lord unto one of His appointed leaders in the Restored Church of Jesus Christ of Latter-day Saints a true and acceptable temple will be built in the old capitol city of Jerusalem. Under divine guidance the ordinances of salvation will be performed by the properly ordained priesthood authorities. Here in His temple, "they will officiate for their dead until all the links in the chain of ancestry,...are made complete."

Blessings Associated with the Building of a New Temple in Jerusalem

A temple building people are a happy and blessed people. The spiritual and temporal blessings are numerous and many people are rewarded for their sacrifice and faithfulness in contributing to the erection of a house of the Lord. President Charles W. Penrose gave some interesting insights in regards to the Mosque of the Moslems, which is located where the future temple will be built in Jerusalem:

> Then the Gospel...will be preached to the Jews. The way is now being prepared for this. The work is moving on for the gathering of the Jews to their own land that they may build it up as it was in former times; that the temple may be rebuilt and the mosque of the Moslem which now stands in its place may be moved out of the way; that Jerusalem may be rebuilt upon its original site; that the way may be prepared for the coming of the Messiah, who shall be seen in the midst of those whose ancestors nailed him to the cross, and who, when they see the marks in His hands, shall say in answer to their inquiries, "These are the wounds with which I was wounded in the house of my friends." (*JD* 24:215.)

Wars and Rumors of War Before the End Comes

The persual of almost any current newsmagazine or newspaper makes one cognizant of the critical world situation and the delicate georgaphical position of the Jews. The nation of Israel is literally surrounded by hostile nations. The Russian fleet is in the Mediterranean and Israel's borders are flanked on either side by menacing countries, many of whom seem ready and anxious to wage a war of extermination.

The winding up scene and the future destiny of Judah's people is one frought with war. The prophet Joseph Smith wrote of these scenes:

> There will be wars and rumors of wars, signs in the heavens above and on the earth beneath, the sun turned into darkness and the moon to blood.... (*HC* 5:337, April 1843.)

Again the Prophet Joseph Smith warned:

> For then, in those days, shall be great tribulation on the Jews, and upon the inhabitants of Jerusalem, such as was not before sent upon Israel, of God, since the beginning of their kingdom until this time; no, nor ever shall be sent again upon Israel.
>
> Behold, I speak these things unto you for the elect's sake; and you also shall hear of wars, and rumors of wars; see that ye be not troubled, for all I have told you must come to pass; but the end is not yet.

> And they shall hear of wars, and rumors of wars.
>
> Behold I speak for mine elect's sake; for nation shall rise against nation, and kingdom against kingdom; there shall be famines, and pestilences, and earthquakes, in divers places. (Joseph Smith 1:18, 23, 28-29.)

Gog and Magog—Before the Millennium

A careful study of the 38th and 39th chapters of Ezekiel reveals an impending war between the Jews and the Gentile nations! The prophet Ezekiel describes this terrible battle and the participants as he received it from the Lord:

> And the word of the Lord came unto me saying,
>
> Son of man, set thy face against Gog, the land of Magog, the chief prince of Meshech and Tubal, and prophesy against him,
>
> And say, Thus saith the Lord God; Behold, I am against thee, O Gog, the chief prince of Meshech and Tubal:
>
> And I will turn thee back, and put hooks into thy jaws, and I will bring thee forth, and all thine army, horses and horsemen, all of them clothed with all sorts of armour, even a great company with bucklers and shields, all of them handling swords:
>
> Persia, Ethiopia, and Libya with them; all of them with shield and helmet:
>
> Gomer, and all his bands; the house of Togarmah of the north quarters, and all his bands: and many people with thee.
>
> Thou shalt ascend and come like a storm, thou shalt be like a cloud to cover the land, thou, and all thy bands, and many people with thee.
>
> And thou shalt come from thy place out of the north parts, thou, and many people with thee, all of them riding upon horses, a great company, and a mighty army:
>
> And thou shalt come up against my people of Israel, as a cloud to cover the land; it shall be in the latter days, and I will bring thee against my land, that the heathen may know me, when I shall be sanctified in thee, O Gog, before their eyes, (Ezekiel 38:1-6, 9, 15-16.)

Gog and Magog Will be Destroyed

> And I will turn thee back, and leave but the sixth part of thee, and will cause thee to come up from the north parts, and will bring thee upon the mountain of Israel:

And I will smite thy bow out of thy left hand, and will cause thine arrows to fall out of thy right hand.

Thou shalt fall upon the mountains of Israel, thou, and all thy bands, and the people that is with thee: I will give thee unto the ravenous birds of every sort, and to the beasts of the field to be devoured.

And they that dwell in the cities of Israel shall go forth, and shall set on fire and burn the weapons, both the shields and the bucklers, the bows and the arrows, and the handstaves, and the spears, and they shall burn them with fire seven years:

So that they shall take no wood out of the field, neither cut down any out of the forests; for they shall burn the weapons with fire: and they shall spoil those that spoiled them, and rob those that robbed them, saith the Lord God.

And seven months shall the house of Israel be burying of them, that they may cleanse the land. (Ezekiel 39:2-4, 9-10, 12.)

Orson Pratt Also Wrote of Some of the Causes and Terrible Consequences of War:

...While in that state of unbelief Gog and Magog, the inhabitants of Russia and all those nations in northern Europe and northern Asia, a great multitude, will gather against the Jews before Jesus comes, and they will fill up the great valley of Armageddon, the great valley of Jehosaphat and all the surrounding valleys; they will be like a cloud covering the land. Horses and chariots and horsemen, a very great army, will gather up there to take a spoil. For you know when the Rothschilds and the great bankers among the Jewish nation shall return back to their own land to rebuild the city of Jerusalem, carrying their capital with them, it will almost ruin some of the nations, and the latter will go up against Jerusalem to take a spoil. And they will succeed in taking half the city captive; and when they are in the act of destroying that city, behold the Lord will come with all his Saints, and he shall stand his feet on the Mount of Olives, "And in that day" says the Prophet Zechariah "shall the Lord go forth and fight against all those nations that have fought against Jerusalem, and their flesh shall consume away upon their bones, their eyes in their sockets. This great calamity comes upon the Jewish nation in consequence of their unbelief in the true Messiah. (*JD* 14:352-353, March 10, 1872.)

Orson Pratt foresaw the day when many nations would unite in waging a large scale war against Israel after she had returned to her homeland. The Prophet Ezekiel prophesied of Israel's prosperity and the determination of other nations to destroy her.

Satan will gain power and influence over the unrepentant inhabitants of the world and because of their wickedness, Israel will nearly be destroyed. Orson adds that Palestine will be encompassed by millions of hostile enemies:

> After the kingdom of God has spread upon the face of the earth, and every jot and tittle of the prophecies have been fulfilled in relation to the spreading of the Gospel among the nations,—after signs have been shown in the heavens above, and on the earth beneath, blood, fire, and vapour of smoke,—after the sun is turned into darkness, and the moon shall have the appearance of blood, and the stars have apparently been hurled out of their places, and all things have been in commotion, so great will be the darkness resting upon Christendom, and so great the bonds of priestcraft with which they will be bound, that they will not understand, and they will be given up to the hardness of their hearts. Then will be fulfilled that saying, "That the day shall come when the Lord shall have power over his Saints, and the Devil shall have power over his own dominion. He will give them up to the power of the Devil, and he will have power over them, and he will carry them about as chaff before a whirlwind. He will gather up millions upon millions of people into the valleys round about Jerusalem in order to destory the Jews after they have gathered. How will the Devil do this? He will perform miracles to do it. The Bible says the kings of the earth and the great ones will be deceived by these false miracles. It says there shall be three unclean spirits that shall go forth working miracles, and they are spirits of devils. Where do they go? To the kings of the earth; and what will they do? Gather them up to battle unto the great day of God Almighty. Where? Into the valley of Armageddon. And where is that? On the east side of Jerusalem.
>
> When he gets them gathered together, they do not understand any of these things; but they are given up to that power that deceived them, by miracles that had been performed, to get them to go into that valley to be destroyed. Joel, Zephania, Zechariah, Isaiah, Ezekiel, and nearly all of the ancient Prophets have predicted that the nations shall be gathered up against Jerusalem, in the valley of Jehoshaphat and the valley of Megiddo,—that there the Lord shall fight for his people, and smite the horse and his rider, and send plagues on these armies, and their flesh shall be consumed from their bones, and their eyes from their sockets. They will actually fulfil these prophecies, with all their pretension to Bible and prophetic learning. (JD 7:188-89.)

The Battlefield of Armageddon

It appears from the words of Ezekiel and Zechariah that Jerusalem and most of Israel will be encompassed by the hostile armies from "all nations" to destroy her. The main thrust of the invasion will be centered in the valley of Armageddon. While the numerous hosts of invading soldiers are gathered and locked in mortal combat the Savior will suddenly appear. He will deliver the remaining hosts of Israel from the clutches of impending destruction. A most descriptive account of the fate of those who fight against the children of Israel is recorded in the Doctrine and Covenants. We read:

> ...the sun shall be darkened, and the moon shall be turned into blood, and the stars shall fall from heaven, and there shall be greater signs in heaven above and in the earth beneath;
>
> And there shall be weeping and wailing among the hosts of men;
>
> And there shall be a great hailstorm sent forth to destroy the crops of the earth.
>
> And it shall come to pass, because of the wickedness of the world, that I will take vegeance upon the wicked, for they will not repent; for the cup of mine indignation is full; for behold, my blood shall not cleanse them if they hear me not.
>
> Wherefore, I the Lord God will send forth flies upon the face of the earth, which take hold of the inhabitants thereof, and shall eat their flesh, and shall cause maggots to come in upon them;
>
> And their tongues shall be stayed that they shall not utter against me; and their flesh shall fall from off their bones, and their eyes from their sockets;
>
> And it shall come to pass that the beasts of the forest and the fowls of the air shall devour them up. (D&C 29:14-20.)

The magnitude and severity of the wars and events that will transpire at the second coming of Christ are almost beyond the comprehension of the human imagination. We read:

> ...they shall see an overflowing scourge; for a desolating sickness shall cover the land.
>
> But my disciples shall stand in holy places, and shall not be moved; but among the wicked, men shall lift up their voices and curse God and die.
>
> And there shall be earthquakes also in divers places, and many desolations; yet man will harden their hearts against me,

and they will take up the sword, one against another, and they will kill one another.

Then shall the arm of the Lord fall upon the nations.

And then shall the Lord set his foot upon this mount, and it shall cleave in twain, and the earth shall tremble, and reel to and fro, and the heavens also shall shake.

And the Lord shall utter his voice, and all the ends of the earth shall hear it; and the nations of the earth shall mourn, and they that have laughed shall see their folly.

And calamity shall cover the mocker, and the scorner shall be consumed; and they that have watched for iniquity shall be hewn down and cast into the fire.

And then shall the Jews look upon me and say: What are these wounds in thine hands and in thy feet?

Then shall they know that I am the Lord; for I will say unto them: These wounds are the wounds with which I was wounded in the house of my friends. I am he who was lifted up. I am Jesus that was crucified. I am the Son of God.

And then shall they weep because of their iniquities; then shall they lament because they persecuted their king. (D&C 45: 31-33, 47-53.)

President Charles W. Penrose spoke about the time when Christ would appear on the Mount of Olive:

His next appearance will be among the distressed and nearly vanquished sons of Judah. At the crisis of their fate, when the hostile troops of several nations are ravaging the city and all the horrors of war are overwhelming the people of Jerusalem, he will set his feet upon the Mount of Olives, which will cleave and part asunder at his touch. Attended by a host from heaven, he will overthrow and destroy the combined armies of the Gentiles, and appear to the worshiping Jews as the mighty Deliverer and Conqueror so long expected by their race. (*Millennial Star,* 21:583, September 10, 1859.)

A Final State of Happiness for Redeemed Israel and David Their King

The Jews will accept Christ as their Redeemer and from Ezekiel we read of the happiness, peace and glory that await the redeemed of Israel:

...Thus saith the Lord God; Behold, I will take the children of Israel from among the heathen, whither they be gone, and will gather them on every side, and bring them into their own land:

And I will make them one nation in the land upon the mountains of Israel; and one king shall be king to them all; and they shall be no more two nations, neither shall they be divided into two kingdoms any more at all:

Neither shall they defile themselves any more with their idols, nor with their detestable things, nor with any of their transgressions: but I will save them out of all their dwelling-places, wherein they have sinned, and will cleanse them: so shall they be my people, and I will be their God.

And David my servant shall be king over them; and they all shall have one shepherd: they shall also walk in my judgments, and observe my statutes, and do them.

And they shall dwell in the land that I have given unto Jacob my servant, wherein your fathers have dwelt; and they shall dwell therein, even they, and their children, and their children's children for ever: and my servant David shall be their prince for ever.

Moreover I will make a covenant of peace with them; it shall be an everlasting covenant with them: and I will place them, and multiply them, and will set my sanctuary in the midst of them for evermore.

My tabernacle also shall be with them: yea, I will be their God, and they shall be my people.

And the heathen shall know that I the Lord do sanctify Israel, when my sanctuary shall be in the midst of them for evermore. (Ezekiel 37:21-28.)

Zechariah observes:

Yea, many people and strong nations shall come to seek the Lord of hosts in Jerusalem, and to pray before the Lord.

...In those days it shall come to pass, that ten men shall take hold of all languages of the nations, even shall take hold of the skirt of him that is a Jew, sayng, We will go with you. (Zechariah 8:22-23.)

Isaiah promises:

The sons also of them that afflicted thee shall come bending unto thee; and all they that despised thee shall bow themselves down at the soles of thy feet; and they shall call thee, The city of the Lord, The Zion of the Holy One of Israel. (Isaiah 60:14.)

The children of Israel shall be:

...sanctified in holiness before the Lord, to dwell in his presence day and night, forever and ever. (D&C 133:35.)

May these happy and blessed events soon be fulfilled and the redeemed of Israel praise the Lord for their triumphant victory.

Who is This King David and What Will be His Role When He Appears Among the Redeemed of Israel?

According to the prophets the name of this king shall be David; not the patriarch David who was the son of Jesse; but a literal descendant of his. Some suppose that the Psalmist David will be raised from his tomb, and again reign over Israel; but we consider this one of the most unreasonable ideas that could be advanced. He no doubt will be in the Lord's own due time raised from the dead, but not to act the part of a prince in the midst of Israel who remain in the flesh. Neither will any of the patriarchs act the part of an earthly king; although they will reign with Christ. Indeed, we have no reason to believe that Christ himself will act the part of an earthly king, or priest, to any great extent. It is inconsistent for us to suppose that the immortal saints, who are glorified, will be perpetually confined in the midst of the mortal ones. Because it is said, they shall reign on the earth, is no reason why we should say they shall be constantly among the mortal saints. The idea is that the earth will be under the control of Christ and the glorified saints, and Christ will virtually reign over the whole earth, and this David will be subject to him. The redeemed saints will reign on earth, and perhaps have in many respects, authority over the mortal ones. We do not wish to be understood, that there will be a total or entire separation between the mortal, and immortal; but the object of the foregoing remarks is to show the distinction of privilege. The prophet says, that the Lord shall reign in Mount Zion, and in Jerusalem, and before his ancients gloriously; hence, when the redeemed saints dwell on earth, they will dwell in Mount Zion, and in Jerusalem which places the Lord will fully prepare for them. (Anonymous, Isaiah 3: 687-691, February 15, 1842.)

The Prophet Joseph Smith and Others Have Written About David in These Words:

Although David was a king, he never did obtain the spirit and power of Elijah and the fullness of the Priesthood; and the Priesthood that he received, and the throne and kingdom of David is to be taken from him and given to another by the name of David in the last days, raised up out of his lineage. (HC 6:253.)

It is of particular interest that Orson Hyde also mentioned this second David in his dedicatory prayer of Palestine on October 24, 1841.

> Let them know that it is Thy good pleasure to restore the kingdom unto Israel—raise up Jerusalem as its capital, and constitute her people a distinct nation and government, with David Thy servant, even a descendant from the loins of ancient David to be their king. (HC 4:457.)

This same king David spoken about is also referred to in the Old Testament by several prophets in this manner:

Jeremiah:

> But they shall serve the Lord their God, and David their king, whom I will raise up unto them. (Jeremiah 30:9.)

Ezekiel:

> And David my servant shall be king over them; and they all shall have one shepherd: they shall also walk in my judgments, and observe my statutes, and do them. (Ezekiel 37:24.)

Hosea:

> Afterward shall the children of Israel return, and seek the Lord their God, and David their king; and shall fear the Lord and his goodness in the latter days. (Hosea 3:5.)

These statements are comforting and reassuring. The Priesthood of Jesus Christ and the will of the Lord will be exercised in righteousness, and Judah will be redeemed in the due time and will of the Lord.

There Was a Divine Intervention For a Jewish Homeland In the Twentieth Century

The second coming of Christ is nigh and the fulfillment of many of the prophecies of Isaiah, Joel, Ezekiel, Amos, Moses, Daniel, Zephaniah, Zechariah and others are literally becoming historical facts. The Jewish State of Israel has received the friendship and assistance from various Gentile nations. History has recorded the role of Great Britain during World War I "in the liberation of Palestine from Turkish rule...[and] the issuance of the Balfour Declaration on November 2, 1917." Orson Hyde was convinced that God had intervened to prepare the way for the return of the Jews to Palestine.

From Jacob's prophecy, we read:

> ...and the nations of the Gentiles shall be great in the eyes of me, saith God, in carrying them [the Jews] forth to the lands of their inheritance. Yea, the kings of the Gentiles shall be nursing fathers unto them, and their queens shall become nursing mothers. (2 Nephi 10:8-9.)

The victory of the Jewish army in 1948 was viewed by some as a military miracle, when they successfully withstood the attack of "seven converging armies of the Arabs." Within a relatively short period of time the poorly equipped and ill prepared troops of Judah had miraculously defeated and driven the invading Arab armies from her borders. Several years later, Elder LeGrand Richards, a member of the Quorum of The Twelve spoke of this event during the April General Conference of the Church. Elder Richards believed as Orson Hyde and others that God intervened in these miraculous victories. He referred to an article which described the appearance "of three bearded men," who were dressed in white robes. Their leadership and activities among the Jewish soldiers intimidated and eventually caused some of the Arab armies to surrender. (*The Improvement Era,* June, 1954, p. 406.)

It shouldn't be difficult for Latter-day Saints to recognize the influence and instrumentality of the Lord in this momentous event. Jesus promised..."whosoever shall gather together against thee (the Jews) shall fall for thy sake." (3 Nephi 22:15-17.)

Who Were the Three Bearded Strangers That Appeared Unto the Jewish Army and Rendered Them Assistance?

The question may be asked, "Who were the three bearded men dressed in white robes?" They could possibly be the three Nephites, for Jesus said:

> And behold they will be among the Gentiles, and the Gentiles shall know them not. They will also be among the Jews, and the

Jews shall know them not. And it shall come to pass, when the Lord seeth fit in his wisdom that they shall minister unto all the scattered tribes of Israel, and unto all nations, kindreds, tongues and people, and shall bring out of them unto Jesus many souls, that their desire may be fulfilled, and also because of the convincing power of God which is in them. And they are as the angels of God, and if they shall pray unto the Father in the name of Jesus they can show themselves unto whatsoever man it seemeth them good. Therefore, great and marvelous works shall be wrought by them, before the great and coming day when all people must surely stand before the judgment seat of Christ; (3 Nephi 28:27-31.)

Israel to Become a Fruitful and Productive Land

Ezekiel also teaches that the desolate land will become tillable and beautiful "like the garden of Eden," which it is becoming. Some other statements from Ezekiel are yet to be fulfilled as we read the promised word of the Lord through His great faithful servant:

> Thus saith the Lord God; In the day that I shall have cleansed you from all your iniquities I will also cause you to dwell in the cities, and the wastes shall be builded.
>
> And the desolate land shall be tilled, whereas it lay desolate in the sight of all that passed by.
>
> And they shall say, This land that was desolate is become like the garden of Eden; and the waste and desolate and ruined cities are become fenced, and are inhabited.
>
> Then the heathen that are left round about you shall know that I the Lord build the ruined places, and plant that that was desolate: I the Lord have spoken it, and I will do it. (Ezekiel 36:33-36.)

The Miracle of the Jews

As the curtain falls on this phase of Jewish history and the stage of life is cleared and reset with new props and scenery for the final scene, one is brought to a realization that what has gone on before has been a melodrama. Yet through it all, the Jews were subjected to war, disease, plagues, torture, driven from their homes like captive fugitives into foreign lands, their sacred holy places destroyed, and other undescribable sufferings cast upon them by their enemies who occupied their lands and took possession of their places of worship. The future is much, much better than the beginning. The final scene of this world-wide drama has been beautifully described, and made crystal clear as viewed through the window of prophetic utterances. A compassionate and forgiving Heavenly Father has promised this nation of miraculous survivors a millennia of peace and prosperity, as her people become "Christianized and all thy children shall be taught of the Lord;" her homeland will be fruitful and productive. All of this and more will be given them when they in truth worship the Savior and Redeemer, Jesus of Nazareth, the God of their fathers, Abraham, Isaac and Jacob.

The Message

Through the window of inspiration, this book has shown Joseph's devotion to his brother Judah. The message offered to his kin and all the descendants of Abraham, Isaac and Jacob is the gospel of Jesus Christ, restored by Joseph Smith, the prophet, who was the Lord's spokesman in this dispensation, and by whom the new covenant with Israel was restored.

We invite you to read, study, and pray about the promise of the Book of Mormon. It is God's word to the Jews, the Gentiles and all of the house of Israel, and it is true.

Many Records Will be Revealed Unto the Jews

> And also that ye may believe the gospel of Jesus Christ, which ye shall have among you; and also that the Jews, the covenant people of the Lord, shall have other witnesses besides him whom they saw and heard, that Jesus, whom they slew, was the very Christ and the very God. (Mormon 3:21.)

> And behold, they shall go unto the unbelieving of the Jews; and for this intent shall they go—that they may be persuaded that Jesus is the Christ, the Son of the living God; that the father may bring about, through his most Beloved, his great and eternal purpose, in restoring the Jews, or all the house of Israel, to the land of their inheritance, which the Lord their God hath given them, unto the fulfilling of his covenant; (Mormon 5:14.)

> Wherefore, because that ye have a Bible ye need not suppose that it contains all my words; neither need ye suppose that I have not caused more to be written.
>
> For I command all men, both in the east and in the west, and in the north, and in the south, and in the islands of the sea, that they shall write the words which I speak unto them; for out of the

> books which shall be written I will judge the world, every man according to their works, according to that which is written.
>
> For behold, I shall speak unto the Jews and they shall write it; and I shall also speak unto the Nephites and they shall write it; and I shall also speak unto the other tribes of the house of Israel, which I have led away, and they shall write it; and I shall also speak unto all nations of the earth and they shall write it.
>
> And it shall come to pass that the Jews shall have the words of the Nephites, and the Nephites shall have the words of the Jews; and the Nephites and the Jews shall have the words of the lost tribes of Israel; and the lost tribes of Israel shall have the words of the Nephites and the Jews.
>
> And it shall come to pass that my people, which are of the house of Israel, shall be gathered home unto the lands of their possessions; and my word also shall be gathered in one. And I will show unto them that fight against my word and against my people, who are of the house of Israel, that I am God, and that I covenanted with Abraham that I would remember his seed forever. (2 Nephi 29:10-14.)

In the due time of the Lord the records of the lost tribes of Israel will be brought forth as promised.

A Latter-day Prophet Spoke to Judah

Apostle Wilford Woodruff spoke to the Jews of the Savior's divinity and mission and of the events to transpire when they return to their promised land:

> ...all that Jesus said concerning the Jews has had its fulfillment to the present day. This should be a strong testimony to the whole infidel world of the truth of Christ's mission and divinity. Let them look at the Jewish nation and the state of the world, in fulfillment of the words of the Savior eighteen hundred years ago in Jerusalem. It is one of the strongest testimonies in the world of the fulfillment of revelation, the truth of the Bible and the mission of Jesus Christ. The Jews have fulfilled the words of Moses, the prophets and Jesus, up to the present day. They have been dispersed and trampled under the feet of the Gentile world now for eighteen hundred years. When Pontius Pilate wished to release Jesus Christ, saying that he found no fault in that just man, the high priests, scribes, pharisees and other Jews present on that occasion cried, "Crucify him, and let his blood be upon us and upon our children." Has it not followed them to this day, and been

manifest in their dispersion, persecution and oppression through the whole Gentile world for eighteen hundred years? It has. And they have to fulfill the words of the Lord still further. As I have been reading to you to-day, the Jews have got to gather to their own land in unbelief. They will go and rebuild Jerusalem and their temple. They will take their gold and silver from the nations and will gather to the Holy Land, and when they have done this and rebuilt their city, the Gentiles, in fulfillment of the words of Ezekiel, Jeremiah and other prophets, will go up against Jerusalem to battle and to take a spoil and a prey; and then when they have taken one-half of Jerusalem captive and distressed the Jews for the last time on the earth, their Great Deliverer, Shiloh, will come. They do not believe in Jesus of Nazareth now, nor ever will until he comes and sets his foot on Mount Olivet and it cleaves in twain, one part going towards the east, and the other towards the west. Then, when they behold the wounds in his hands and in his feet, they will say, "Where did you get them?" And he will reply, "I am Jesus of Nazareth, King of the Jews, your Shiloh, him whom you crucified." Then, for the first time will the eyes of Judah be opened. They will remain in unbelief until that day. This is one of the events that will transpire in the latter day." (Wilford Woodruff, *JD* 15:277-278.)

The Savior Shall Appear on the Mount of Olives at His Second Coming

The Lord Jesus Christ will appear on the Mount of Olives to reign in love, justice, and glory. There will be but one fold and one shepherd as revealed through another look into the window of prophecy. Israel shall be brought home to Zion; and the sons of Judah will have returned to Jerusalem. The colorful events to follow are in fulfillment of prophecy:

> And his feet shall stand in that day upon the mount of Olives, which is before Jerusalem on the east, and the mount of Olives shall cleave in the midst thereof toward the east and toward the west, and there shall be a very great valley and half of the mountain shall remove toward the north, and half of it toward the south. (Zechariah 14:4.)

The signs revealed on the Mount of Olives will be conclusive and Judah will recognize that this Jesus is the Christ, the Messiah and the Savior of the world. Now He will reign in love and justice "over the whole earth, and this David will be subject to him." He is the God of Israel, and the God of the whole world. He is Jehovah of the ancient scriptures, and God, the Savior of the new scriptures.

Into his hands God has placed all things, and given him power over the nations—all flesh, and he is exercising that power." (George Q. Morris, *CR*:102, April 6, 1960.)

The First and Great Commandment of Love Must Prevail in the Hearts of Mankind as They Come Unto Christ

At the Last Supper Jesus said:

> A new commandment I give unto you, that ye love one another; as I have loved you, that ye also love one another.
>
> By this shall all men know that ye are my disciples, if ye have love one to another. (John 13:34-35.)

The Great Book of Mormon Prophet, Moroni Counseled:

> ...I would exhort you that ye would come unto Christ, and lay hold upon every good gift, and touch not the evil gift, nor the unclean thing.
>
> And awake, and arise from the dust, O Jerusalem; yea, and put on thy beautiful garments, O daughter of Zion; and strengthen thy stakes and enlarge thy borders forever, that thou mayest no more be confounded, that the covenants of the Eternal Father which he hath made unto thee, O house of Israel may be fulfilled.
>
> Yea, come unto Christ, and be perfected in him, and deny yourselves of all ungodliness; and if ye shall deny yourselves of all ungodliness and love God with all your might, mind and strength, then is his grace sufficient for you, that by his grace ye may be perfect in Christ; and if by the grace of God ye are perfect in Christ, ye can in nowise deny the power of God.
>
> And again, if ye be the grace of God are perfect in Christ and deny not his power, then are ye sanctified in Christ by the grace of God, through the shedding of the blood of Christ, which is in the covenant of the Father unto the remission of your sins, that ye become holy, without spot. (Moroni 10:30-33.)

May the spirit of the Lord touch the hearts of all mankind, so that love and understanding will replace hatred and envy, and brotherhood prevail throughout the world through Jesus Christ our Savior.

We conclude with these words spoken by a present day prophet, "To you, our friends of Modern Judah, we declare, we are Joseph, your brothers. We claim kinship with you as descendants from our fathers, Abraham, Isaac, and Jacob. We belong to the same family. We, too, are the house of Israel."

Appendices

Appendix 1

A Few Selected Quotes Chosen From Among the Numerous Statements Relative to the Jews by Some of the Presidents of The Church of Jesus Christ of Latter-day Saints

Surely the Lord God will do nothing but he revealeth his secret unto his servants the prophets. (Amos 3:7.)

Through the window of inspiration it is readily apparent that the prophets of the Lord were inspired. Through the vantage point of time we are privileged to see the fulfillment of some of these prophecies.

To the alert reader of these scriptures, it will be evident that the following statements are in various stages of fulfillment; some past, others present, and some yet future.

From Joseph Smith, Jr.

The Prophet Joseph Smith spoke of the final winding-up scene:

> Judah must return, Jerusalem must be rebuilt, and the temple, and water come out from under the temple, and the waters of the Dead Sea be healed. It will take some time to rebuild the walls of the city and the temple, etc.; and all this must be done before the Son of Man will make His appearance. There will be wars and rumors of wars, signs in the heavens above and on the earth beneath, the sun turned into darkness and the moon to blood, earthquakes in divers places, the seas heaving beyond their bounds; then will appear one grand sign of the Son of Man in heaven. But what will the world do? They will say it is a planet, a comet, etc. But the Son of Man will come as the sign of the coming of the Son of Man, which will be as the light of the morning cometh out of the east. (*HC*, 5:337, April, 1843.)

At the Kirtland Temple Dedication of March 27, 1836:

> O Lord...thou knowest that thou has a great love for the children of Jacob, who have been scattered upon the mountains for a long time...

> We therefore ask thee to have mercy upon the children of Jacob, that Jerusalem, from this hour, may begin to be redeemed;
>
> And the yoke of bondage may begin to be broken off from the house of David;
>
> And the children of Judah may begin to return to the lands which thou didst give to Abraham, their father. (D&C 109:60-64.)

Gathering of Israel

> One of the most important points in the faith of the Church of the Latter-day Saints, through the fullness of the everlasting gospel is the gathering of Israel (of whom the Lamanites constitute a part)—that happy time when Jacob shall go up to the House of the Lord, to worship Him in spirit and in truth, to live in holiness; when the Lord will restore His judges as at first and His counselors as at the beginning; when every man may sit under his own vine and fig tree, and there will be none to molest or make afraid; when He will turn to them a pure language, and the earth will be filled with sacred knowledge, as the waters cover the great deep; when it shall no longer be said, the Lord lives that brought up the children of Israel out of the land of Egypt, but the Lord lives that brought up the children of Israel from the land of the north and from all the lands whither He has driven them. That day is one, all important to all men. (Joseph Smith, Jr., *HC* 2:357, January 6, 1836.)

> What was the object of gathering the Jews or the people of God in any age of the world?...The main object was to build unto the Lord a house whereby He could reveal unto His people the ordinances of His house, and the glories of His kingdom and teach the people the way of salvation; for there are certain ordinances and principles that, when they are taught and practiced, must be done in a place or house built for that purpose. (Joseph Smith, Jr., *HC* 5:423, June 11, 1843.)

> The time has at last arrived when the God of Abraham, of Isaac, and of Jacob has set His hand again the second time to recover the remnants of His people....and with them to bring in the fullness of the Gentiles and establish that covenant with them, which was promised when their sins should be taken away. (Joseph Smith, Jr., *HC* 1:313, January 4, 1833.)

The following information was obtained from the sermons and writings of President Brigham Young.

Jerusalem Not to be Redeemed by Proselyting Them

Jerusalem is not to be redeemed by our going there and preaching to the inhabitants. It will be redeemed by the high hand of the Almighty. It will be given into the possession of the ancient Israelites by the power of God, and by the pouring out of His judgments. The ground where you can sow the good seed, and where it will yield crops that you can gather, is outside of that where the ancient Apostles and Prophets labored. They had the light and power of God with them; and made manifest the hand of the Almighty in delivering the people and working miracles, and saving those that were redeemed; and the people who are the most ready to receive the Gospel are those who have lived without it from the days of Noah to this time. (Brigham Young, *JD,* 2:141, December 3, 1854.)

Jews Will be the Last to Receive the Gospel

Jerusalem is not to be redeemed by the soft still voice of the preacher of the Gospel of peace. Why? Because they were once the blessed of the Lord, the chosen of the Lord, the promised seed. They were the people from among whom should spring the Messiah; and salvation could be found only through that tribe. The Messiah came through them, and they killed him; and they will be the last of all the seed of Abraham to have the privilege of receiving the New and Everlasting Covenant. You may hand out to them gold, you may feed and clothe them, but it is impossible to convert the Jews, until the Lord God Almighty does it. (Brigham Young, *JD*, 2:142, December 3, 1854.

When the Jews Acknowledge the True Messiah

When the Savior visits Jerusalem, and the Jews look upon him, and see the wounds in his hands and in his side and in his feet, they will then know that they have persecuted and put to death the true Messiah, and then they will acknowledge him, but not till then. They have confounded his first and second coming, expecting his first coming to be as a mighty prince instead of as a servant. They will go back by and by to Jerusalem and own their Lord and Master. (Brigham Young, *JD,* 11:279, December 23, 1866.)

Every Tongue Confess That Jesus is The Christ

The kingdom that Daniel saw will push forth its law, and that law will Protect the Methodists, Quakers, Pagans, Jews, and every other creed there ever was or ever will be, in their religious rights. At the same time the Priesthood will bear rule, and hold the government of the Kingdom under control in all things, so that every knee will bow, and every tongue confess, to the glory of God the Father, that Jesus is the Christ. Every one must bow to the Savior, and acknowledge and confess him with their mouths. Can they still be Methodists? Yes. Presbyterians? Yes.

...I most assuredly expect that the time will come when every tongue shall confess, and every knee shall bow, to the Savior, though the people may believe what they will with regard to religion. (Brigham Young, *JD*, 2:189, February 18, 1855.)

From Writings and Sermons of President John Taylor

Do You Believe in Christ?

Do you think the Jews today would want to publish things pertaining to Jesus, describing the manner in which he would come? I should think not. In a conversation I once had with Baron Rothschild he asked me if I believe in the Christ? I answered him, "Yes, God has revealed to us that he is the true Messiah, and we believe in him." I further remarked "Your Prophets have said, 'They shall look upon him whom they have pierced, and they shall mourn for him, as one mourneth for his only son, and shall be in bitterness for him as one that is in bitterness for his first born,' 'And one shall say unto him, What are these wounds in thy hands? Then he shall answer, Those with which I was wounded in the house of my friends.' "Do you think the Jewish Rabbies would refer you to such scripture as that? Said Mr. Rothschild, "Is that in our Bible?" "That is in your Bible, sir."

Abraham Saw Christ' Day

The Book of Mormon and the Bible refer to many other similar passages referring to the same event, as well as passages referring to the Savior's birth. "Behold," says Isaiah, "a virgin shall conceive, and bear a son, and shall call his name Immanuel." Again the Savior says, "Abraham saw my day and was glad. Ancient people of God, in whose hearts was enkindled the flame of inspiration, looked forward to that memorable event when the Lamb was slain from before the foundation of the world would offer himself as a sacrifice, whilst we look back to the same thing. We break bread and eat, and we drink water in the presence of each other every Sabbath day, and we do it in remembrance of the broken body and shed blood of our Lord and Savior Jesus Christ; and this we will continue to do until he comes again. When he does come, the Latter-day Saints expect to be among that favored number that will eat and drink with him at his own table in our Father's kingdom. I expect this just as much as I expect to eat my supper tonight. (John Taylor *JD,* 18:329, December 31, 1876.)

The Gathering of Israel

Why is it that you are here today? And what brought you here? Because the keys of the gathering of Israel from the four quarters of the earth have been committed to Joseph Smith, and he has conferred those keys upon others that the gathering of Israel may be accomplished, and in due time the same thing will be performed to the tribes in the land of the north. It is on this account, and through the unlocking of this principle and through these means, that you are brought together as you are today. (John Taylor, *JD,* 25:179, May 18, 1884.)

There will be a literal Zion, or gathering of the Saints to Zion, as well as a gathering of the Jews to Jerusalem. (John Taylor, *The Government of God,* p 104, August, 1852.)

Promises to Abraham Will Yet Be fulfilled

Abraham will yet realize the fulfillment of the promises made to him and will stand in his proper place and position as their father and the proper representative of his seed in the grand jubilee in this earth, when the purposes of God shall be accomplished pertaining thereunto....Jesus, you will remember, in speaking of Abraham, said, "Abraham saw my day and was glad." Abraham had promises made to him pertaining to the land of Palestine, that were not really fulfilled in his time; and Stephen, soon after the Savior of the world died, in talking about Abraham, said that God had promised it to his seed; says Stephen, the Lord "gave him none inheritance in it; no not so much as to set his foot on; yet he promised that he would give it to him for a possession, and his seed after him, when as yet he had no child." There are men now living among the descendants of Abraham, who expect to see that promise fulfilled, when his descendants will again inherit that land of promise, and when all things spoken of by the mouth of the Prophets will be accomplished. The measuring line will yet go forth again in Jerusalem, and Jerusalem will yet be inhabited on its own place, even in Jerusalem. (John Taylor, *JD,* 18:325, December 31, 1876.)

President Wilford Woodruffs' Statements About the Jews:

The Gathering to America and Jerusalem

When God commanded Noah to build an ark, he saved himself with his family by gathering into it. When the angels commanded

Lot to flee to Zoar, he saved himself by fleeing thence....And as the Lord has said by the ancient prophets, in the last days there should be deliverance in Jerusalem and in Mount Zion; and by the mouth of the modern prophet, seer and revelator, (he) pointed out the location of Zion and commanded the Saints among the Gentiles to gather thereunto and build it up, while the Jews gather to Jerusalem. The safety of the Saints depends as much upon their fulfilling His commandments as the safety of Noah and Lot depended upon their obedience to the commands of God in their day and generation. (Wilford Woodruff, *MS* 6:3, June 15, 1845.

Jews Commanded to Return to Palestine

A command is also given to the Jews among all nations, to prepare to return to Jerusalem in Palestine, and to Re-build that city and temple unto the Lord. Thus, America and Jerusalem are set forth as two places of gathering for the nations, that they may escape the judgements about to overtake the world, as the prophets have testified, that in Mount Zion and in Jerusalem shall be deliverance. (Wilford Woodruff, *MS*, 6:136, October, 1845.)

Jews Will Recognize Shiloh As Their King

"And this is the will of your great Elohim, O house of Judah, and whenever you shall be called upon to perform this work, the God of Israel will help you. You have a great future and destiny before you and you cannot avoid fulfilling it; you are the royal chosen seed, and the God of your father's house has kept you distinct as a nation for eighteen hundred years, under all the oppression of the whole Gentile world. You may not wait until you believe on Jesus of Nazareth, but when you meet with Shiloh your king, you will know him; your destiny is marked out, you cannot avoid it. It is true that after you return and gather your nation home, and rebuild your City and Temple, that the Gentiles may gather together their armies to go against you to battle....; but when this affliction comes, the living God, that led Moses through the wilderness, will deliver you, and your Shiloh will come and stand in your midst and will fight your battles; and you will know him, and the afflictions of the Jews will be at an end, while the destruction of the Gentiles will be so great that it will take the whole house of Israel who are gathered about Jerusalem seven months to bury the dead of their enemies, and the weapons of war will last them seven years for fuel, so that they need not go to any forest for wood. These are tremendous sayings—who can bear them? Nevertheless they are true, and will be fulfilled, according to the sayings of Ezekiel, Zechariah, and other prophets.

Though the heavens and the earth pass away, not one jot or tittle will fall unfulfilled." (Matthias F. Cowley, *Wilford Woodruff,* Bookcraft, 1964, pp. 509-510.)

When Will Jews Believe in Jesus Christ?

You cannot convert a Jew. They will never believe in Jesus Christ until He comes to them in Jerusalem, until these fleeing Jews take back their gold and silver to Jerusalem and rebuild their city and temple, and they will do this as the Lord lives. Then the Gentiles will say, "Come let us go to Jerusalem; let us go up and spoil her. The Jews have taken our gold and silver from the nations of the earth—come let us go up and fight against Jerusalem." Then will the prophecies that are before you be fulfilled. (Wilford Woodruff, *JD* 22:173, June 12, 1881.)

The Jews have got to gather to their own land in unbelief. They will go and rebuild Jerusalem and their temple. They will take their gold and silver from the nations and will gather to the Holy Land, and when they have done this and rebuilt their city the Gentiles... will go up against Jerusalem to battle and to take a spoil and a prey; and then, when they have taken one-half of Jerusalem captive and distressed the Jews for the last time on the earth, their Great Deliverer, Shiloh, will come. They do not believe in Jesus of Nazareth now, nor ever will until He comes and sets His foot on Mount Olivet and it cleaves in twain, one part going towards the east and the other towards the west. Then, when they behold the wounds in His hands and in His feet, they will say, "Where did you get them?" And he will reply, "I am Jesus of Nazareth, King of the Jews, your Shiloh, Him whom you crucified." Then, for the first time will the eyes of Judah be opened. They will remain in unbelief until that day. This is one of the events that will transpire in the latter day. (Wilford Woodruff, *JD* 15:277-278, January 12, 1873.)

Watch for the Signs of the Times

We are approaching some of the most tremendous judgments God ever poured out upon the world. You watch the signs of the times, the sign of the coming of the Son of Man. They are beginning to be manifest both in heaven and on earth. As has been told by the apostles, Christ will not come until these things come to pass. Jerusalem has got to be rebuilt. The temple has got to be built. Judah has got to be gathered and the House of Israel. And the Gentiles will go forth to battle against Judah and Jerusalem before the coming of the Son of Man. These things have been revealed by the prophets; they will have their fulfillment. (Wilford Woodruff, *MS* 52:740, October 6, 1890.)

Comments About the High Priests and Other Jews who Crucified Jesus by President Lorenzo Snow

High Priests of the Jewish Faith and Other Jews Believed They Had Accomplished Their Purpose in Putting Jesus to Death

It may appear through our ignorance in not understanding fully the ways of the Lord and His purposes, that in our onward march in carrying out the programme before us, we sometimes come to a stopping place for the time being, but the fact is, there is no such thing in the programme, and there cannot be providing the people continue their labors putting their trust in the promises of God. The Apostles, notwithstanding the opportunities they had of acquainting themselves with the purposes of the Almighty, through personal converse with the Son of God, thought there was a time when they would have to stand still, and cease their labors as ministers of God. When they saw the Savior hanging upon the cross in the agonies of death, their hearts failed them, and they concluded that all was over with them. They had thought that Jesus was to be king of Israel, and deliver them from the Gentile yoke, but now their hopes seemed vain and all was lost; now said their leader, let us go a fishing. Was there a cessation of the work of God, when Jesus was suffering upon the cross? No, the work was still going on, but the Apostles did not understand it; they did not seem to comprehend the fact that the purposes of God were being carried out when He was suffering upon the cross; but when Jesus appeared to them after He arose from the tomb, He gave them to understand that in His suffering and death the words of the prophets were being fulfilled; and He opened their understanding that they might understand the Scriptures. But the High Priests of the Jewish faith, and all those who were foremost in the crucifixion of the Savior, believed they had accomplished their purpose in putting to death Him whom they feared would take away their name and nation, and doubtless felt satisfied with their work, especially as He failed to come down from the cross when they cried out, If He be the Son of God, let Him come down from the cross. (Lorenzo Snow, *JD* 23:152, April 7, 1882.)

The Dedication of the Manti Temple by President Lorenzo Snow on May 21, 1888

Have thou mercy upon Judah and Jerusalem; hasten the going forth of this sacred record to the Hebrews of all nations; raise up men and means to carry the glad tidings of thy returning favor to that afflicted people. Wilt thou hear and answer the prayers of thy servants and turn away the barrenness of their land? Make it very fertile as in days of old; turn the hearts of the exiles to thy promises made to their fathers, and let the land of Jerusalem become inhabited as towns without walls for the multitude of men and cattle therein, that they may rebuild their city and temple, that the glory of the latter house may be greater than that of the former house. (Lorenzo Snow, *Millennial Star* 50:385-392, June 18, 1888.)

Statements Pertaining to the Jews by President Joseph F. Smith

Jewish Desire to Establish Homeland

With the Jews, it is the more vital question. There is a very strong hope among them that they may sooner or later acquire some governmental hold upon the country of their fathers. Zionists for many years have advocated a republic through colonization in that land. They have hoped that they might retain their Jewish peculiarities and religion in a stricter life and activity. Thousands and thousands of them have no higher ambition than to return to Jerusalem, that they may be buried somewhere on the Mount of Olives within the shadow of the walls of the Holy City.

This thrilling event has aroused great enthusiasm, not only throughout Europe, but also in the United States, and especially in the city of New York, where there are so many Jews gathered on the so-called "East side." They are already speculating in their minds as to the future events of that land. It is to be hoped, and it is believed, that Palestine will continue to rebuild and receive something of its ancient glory. The Jews have the disposition and the money to make of it one of the most attractive cities of the world. It could be the center of the new Jewish life, if not of a Jewish republic under the protectorate of some one of the great powers; but which one?

There is none of them that is perhaps so well qualified to take over the control of that country as the United States; and it may be almost certainly predicted, if the war ends in favor of the Allies, which appears to be inevitable, that the United States will be asked to take over the administration of Palestine. It is the one country that could have positively no selfish ends in view.

The Fulfilment of Ancient and Modern Prophecy

As to the view of the Latter-day Saints concerning the present fall of Jerusalem, they look upon it as one of the steps in the foretold gathering of the Jews in the latter days, and as the beginning of the fulfilment of ancient and modern prophecy. The restored gospel of Jesus Christ is to be preached to the gathered Jews, and the Saints are glad to behold the signs of the coming day. Perhaps no plainer exposition of the subject could be given than that contained in one of the revelations, of which there are many on the subject, to the Prophet Joseph Smith, in 1831 (Doc. & Cov. 45), concerning Jerusalem and the Jews:

And this I have told you concerning Jerusalem, and when that day shall come, shall a remnant be scattered among all nations;

But they shall be gathered again, but they shall remain until the times of the Gentiles be fulfilled.

And in that day shall be heard of wars and rumors of wars, and the whole earth shall be in commotion, and men's hearts shall fail them, and they shall say that Christ delayeth his coming until the end of the earth.

And the love of men shall wax cold, and iniquity shall abound;

And when the times of the Gentiles is come in, a light shall break forth among them that sit in darkness, and it shall be the fulness of my gospel. * * * And in that generation shall the times of the Gentiles be fulfilled. (Joseph F. Smith *Improvement Era,* 21: 259-261, January, 1918.)

President Heber J. Grant, Friend of the Jewish people Commented as Follows:

In Due Time the Jews Shall Be in the Favor of God Again

Some of you may be familiar with the agitation that is going on at the present time, in the publications, against the Jewish people. There should be no ill-will, and I am sure there is none, in the heart of any true Latter-day Saint, toward the Jewish people. By the authority of the Holy Priesthood of God, that has again been restored to the earth, and by the ministration, under the direction of the Prophet of God, Apostles of the Lord Jesus Christ have been to the Holy Land and have dedicated that country for the return of the Jews: and we believe that in the due time of the Lord they shall be in the favor of God again. And let no Latter-day Saint be guilty of taking any part in any crusade against these people. I believe in no other part of the world is there as good a feeling in the hearts of mankind towards the Jewish people as among the Latter-day Saints. (Heber J. Grant, *Conference Report,* p. 124, April 5, 1921.)

Time of the Gentiles Near Fulfillment

When the British General with his army entered the City of Jerusalem I felt that the time of the Gentiles was very close to being fulfilled. At my request the choir will sing a song written by a converted Jew, the father of our faithful Latter-day Saint, Sister Rebecca Neibaur Nibley—"Come thou glorious day of promise!" By special request the choir sang, "Come, thou glorious day of promise." (Neibaur.)

Come thou glorious day of promise,
Come and spread thy cheerful ray,

When the scattered sheep of Israel
Shall no longer go astray;
When Hosannas,
With united voice they'll cry.

Lord, how long wilt Thou be angry;
Shall Thy wrath forever burn?
Rise, redeem Thine ancient people,
Their transgressions from them turn.
King of Israel,
Come and set Thy people free.

O, that soon Thou wouldst to Jacob,
Thy enlivening Sprit send!
Of their unbelief and mis'ry
Make, O Lord, a speedy end.
Lord, Messiah!
Prince of Peace o'er Israel reign.

(Heber J. Grant, *Conference Report,* pp. 106-107, October, 1921.)

Prayer Offered at the Dedication of the Alberta Temple, at Cardston, Canada, August 26, 1923 by President Heber J. Grant—

We thank thee, O God, our Eternal Father, that the land of Palestine, the land where our Savior and Redeemer ministered in the flesh, where he gave to the world the plan of life and salvation, is now redeemed from the thralldom of the unbeliever, and is now under the fostering care of the great, enlightened and liberty-loving empire of Great Britain. We acknowledge thy hand, O God, in the wonderful events which have led up to the partial redemption of the land of Judah, and we beseech thee, O Father, that the Jews may, at no far distant date, be gathered home to the land of their fathers.

We thank thee that thy servants, the Prophets Joseph Smith and Brigham Young, were moved upon to send Apostles to Jerusalem to dedicate that land for the return of the Jews.

We acknowledge thy hand, O God, our Heavenly Father, in the fact that one of the benefits of the great world war, through which the nations of the earth have recently passed, is the opportunity afforded the Jews to return to the land of their fathers.

We beseech thee, our Father in heaven, that the victory which came to the cause of the Allies may lead to increased liberty and peace throughout all the nations of the earth.

We pray that thy blessings may be upon kings, rulers and nobles, in all nations, that they may minister in justice and righteousness and give liberty and freedom to the peoples over whom they rule.

We thank thee that the spirit of justice and righteousness has characterized the rulers in the British Empire, and we humbly beseech thee that the people of this great nation and the peoples of the world may overcome selfishness and refrain from strife, contention, and all bitterness, and that they may grow and increase in the love of country, in loyalty and patriotism, and in a determination to do that which is right and just. (Heber J. Grant, *Improvement Era* 26:1075-1081, October, 1923.)

President George Albert Smith Spoke About the Jews

The Return of the Jews to Jerusalem

The gospel has been offered to the Gentiles for almost a hundred years. The time is rapidly approaching when it will be preached to the Jews, who are to gather in from their long dispersion, upon the land of their inheritance. Palestine is to be inhabited as a city without walls and the glory of the Lord will rest upon His chosen people, when they repent of their sins and turn unto Him. (George Albert Smith, *MS* 83:2, January, 1921.)

Dedication of the Idaho Falls Temple by President George Albert Smith on September 23, 1945—

Wilt thou, O Lord, have in remembrance the promises made by thee to Judah in his stricken and scattered condition. Hasten the time when he shall be restored to the land of his inheritance. Remove from him thy displeasure, and may the days of his tribulation soon cease, and Jerusalem rejoice, and Judah be made glad for the multitude of her sons and daughters, for the sweet voices of children in her streets, and for the manifold blessings thou wilt pour out upon them.

Remember, O Lord, thy promises to Israel, whom thou didst cause to be taken captive and scattered among the heathen and to be dispersed throughout all countries, that thou wouldst again gather them from among the nations whither they had been scattered. Wilt thou, O gracious Father, in thy wisdom and mercy, speedily fulfill thy promises unto Israel and cause that they may again be gathered and hearken unto the voice of thy servants, the prophets, and thereby merit the rich blessings thou hast promised them when they acknowledge Jesus Christ, thy Beloved Son, as their Redeemer. (George Albert Smith, *Improvement Era,* 48:562-565, October 1945.)

Look For the Good and Recognize the Virtues in Others

...Think of the condition the Jews find themselves in, whereever they are in all the world. I want to say to you that some of the best people that have ever lived were the Hebrew race and they were examples in many instances but they, in some cases, lost their faith and turned away. I want to say that some of the best men and women that we have had in Salt Lake City were Jews. I hope that the Latter-day Saints will not forget, will not fall into the habit that people have who hate the Jews because of their prosperity, and sometimes hate them for other reasons; that they will not fall into the habit of condemning a nation, condemning all of those people, without remembering a circumstance that happened in the British Parliament.

Disraeli's Answer

There was an argument going on between a great Hebrew, Benjamin Disraeli, who was Prime Minister of England, and a man who was a noted arguer in the House of Lords, and when he could no longer answer the Jew then he began to taunt him with being a Jew. He said: "Yes, you are only a Jew anyhow."

And then Disraeli arose and said: "This man has taunted me with being a Jew. I am a Jew and I am proud of it. And when the forebears of this man were fighting like wild beasts for their mates, my people were laying the foundation for the literature of the world." That was his answer.

And then one more, and I hope we will all remember it. "When this man and those he loves bow in prayer, everything they ask for, they ask for in the name of Jesus Christ, a Jew."

I am stressing that tonight, although I did not expect to when I got on my feet because of the hatred that sometimes grows in men's hearts and we fail to see the virtues of others. Brethren, in the midst of these political campaigns such as we are having now, for goodness' sake do not stoop to criticising and finding fault unfairly and unjustly with those who do not believe the same as you do in politics. Let us be real Latter-day Saints,—not make believes—and see the virtues of the others. There is virtue in both camps.

Think of Jerusalem tonight. Think of the predicament of that great people who have maintained their integrity as a nation, as individuals, as a race, as few others in the world have done. It has been marvelous to me, but see how pitiable their situation is now, and if all the people of the world were righteous and they were in transgression, there would be hope for them because our Heavenly Father has insisted, in his advice and counsel to the world, that "Jerusalem shall be redeemed." (George Albert Smith, *Conference Report,* October 1948, pp. 182-184.)

Ogden Temple Dedicatory Prayer By President Harold B. Lee on January 18, 1972

And now our Father, we thank thee for thy direction in building temples wherein the blessing of baptism and of celestial marriage and of eternal life may be made available to the living and the dead. And we thank thee that thou art gathering scattered Israel out of Babylon, into thy Church and kingdom, so they may receive the blessings promised in thy holy temples.

Wilt thou, O Lord, remember thy covenants with Abraham, Isaac, and Jacob concerning their seed; and with Lehi and Nephi and thy "other sheep" on the American continent; that their descendants should have the blessings of the gospel, "which are the blessings of salvation, even of life eternal." Cause that the scattered remnants of thine ancient chosen people may open their hearts to the message of those living prophets whom thou dost now send to them.

And hasten the day, O Lord of Hosts, when the scattered remnants of Judah, after their pain, shall be sanctified in holiness before thee and shall build again the waste places of Jerusalem, that they may once again be numbered with thy people; that the promises may be fulfilled, "for out of Zion shall go forth the law, and the word of the Lord from Jerusalem."

Let not the choice spirits whom thou hast sent to earth in the lineage of thy friend, Abraham our father, be led in paths where they transgress thy laws "and fight and quarrel one with another, and serve the devil, who is the master of sin." O may the spirit of love and of unity of service and of righteousness be in the homes of all Israel, that thy chosen people may truly be as a city set on a hill whose light cannot be hid. (Harold B. Lee, *The Ensign,* 2:8-13, March, 1972.)

New Temple in Washington D. C. Dedicated by President Spencer W. Kimball

Our Holy Father, we have watched with great concern our brethren of Judah. We have seen their persecutions and torture and sufferings, and we pray that the hour may speedily come when they will believe the gospel, accept Thy Son as their Savior, and be redeemed. (Spencer W. Kimball, *Church News*, November 23, 1974, pp. 47.)

Appendix 2

Lessons Readied for Jewish

Three missionary discussions, which bridge the distance between the culture and beliefs of the Jewish people and the basic missionary lessons, have been prepared by the Church.

And in conjunction with these discussions, a flip chart, five tracts or pamphlets, and a "Missionary Training Manual for Use in the Jewish Proselyting Program" have been prepared. A sixth pamphlet contains Jewish members' testimonies.

The discussions were prepared to answer a challenge issued by President Spencer W. Kimball in 1975 when he said that Jewish people must hear the gospel.

Working under the direction of the Missionary Department, a committee was called in November 1975. The discussions developed take a spiritual approach to the Church, rather than an intellectual approach which had been used commonly in the past, a committeeman said.

All the Jewish converts interviewed by the committee had had a distinct spiritual experience. The committee said it felt inspired that the gospel, not intellectual arguments, needed to be presented to the Jewish people. The discussions were designed to teach these points:

First, Joseph Smith is a prophet. His experience is consistent with the ancient prophets and their heavenly visitations.

Second, the Book of Mormon is a record of God's dealings with the nation of Israel. Third, Jesus Christ is the Messiah. There are five witnesses used to support this; the Old and New Testaments, the Book of Mormon, Joseph Smith's testimony and the testimony of the missionary. Fourth, there was both a Christian and an Israeli apostasy. This means that neither Christ nor Christianity was responsible for the persecution of the Jews. However, the true Church has been restored in our time and there is a living prophet.

The special tracts were written and 11 new paintings were created to illustrate various points for the flip chart.

A survey of Jewish non-members throughout the United States indicated that most did not know the scriptures well, and that Judaism leaves unanswered some of the most basic questions, such as the nature of God, what happens after death, and whether there is a living prophet. Because of the basic questions asked by the survey, two of those queried eventually became interested in the Church and were baptized.

The first discussion teaches that man is created in God's image, and that the ancient prophets received divine instructions. It tells of the calling and subsequent persecution of Joseph Smith, and of the translation of the Book of Mormon.

The second discussion reviews the story of Joseph Smith's calling and explains that the Book of Mormon is a second witness. The discussion then lists biblical prophecies of the Messiah and explains how Christ fills the prophecies.

The third discussion tells of the apostasy of the people from the teachings of the ancient prophets. It also tells of the apostasy from the Church organized by Christ.

After the three discussions have been completed, the missionaries are able to continue with the basic discussions.

Missionaries who are called to areas with a heavy Jewish population will receive special instruction at the Missionary Training Center in Provo, Utah. By reading the supplementary material in the manual, they will learn of the lives of the Jewish people. It also contains a brief biblical history and traces their religious and cultural development. It contains a dictionary of popular Jewish terminology and holidays. It also gives the results of the survey regarding their knowledge of religion and God. The manual also lists do's and don'ts for missionaries.

While well-intentioned, many LDS members, because of their unfamiliarity with Jewish culture, often accidentally offend investigators, a committee member explained. The missionary lessons have been designed specifically not to be offensive and at the same time, teach the basic principles. Missionaries in Jewish areas will need the assistance of members in contacting their Jewish neighbors.

"Before proselyting, the first thing to learn is the culture of the Jewish people," said a committee member. "Missionaries and members need to know that Jewish people are children in the gospel like anyone else who has not heard it."

He said there are three main bodies of religious thought among these people. The orthodox Jews believe in the coming of the Messiah and a resurrection. Among the conservatives, some hold the orthodox beliefs and some do not. The reformed Jews believe neither in the Messiah nor in resurrection.

The Jewish religous training ends at 13 years of age with the Bar Mitzvah for boys or Bas Mitzvah for girls.

The discussions will be used in all areas of large Jewish population.

By far the largest concentration of Jewish people in the world is in the United States. For example, there are more in Brooklyn than there are in Jerusalem. (John L. Hart, *Church News,* March 31, 1979, p. 6.)

Appendix 3

CHRONOLOGY OF ANCIENT JUDAH

(All dates are approximate)

		2022 —	Abraham born	
	2000			
		1922 —	Isaac born	
	1900			
	1800			
		1771 —	Joseph born	
	1700			
			EGYPTIAN BONDAGE	
	1600			
		1517 —	Moses leads Israel from Egypt	
	1500			
		1470 —	Joshua	
	1400			
			JUDGES	
	1300			
	1200			
	1100			
		1020 —	Saul crowned Israel's 1st King	
	1000	—	David	
		962 —	Solomon	
		922 —	Israel is divided	
	900			
	800		JUDAH	ISRAEL
		722 —		Israel Falls
	700			
	600			
		587 —	Judah Falls—BABYLONIAN CAPTIVITY	
		537 —	Judah Returns	
	500			
	400			
		332 —	Alexander the Great conquers Judea	
	300			
	200			
		170 —	Maccabean Revolt	
B.C.	100			
		63 —	Roman Rule	
			Birth of Christ	
		—	Jesus Christ	
A.D.		70 —	Fall of Jerusalem	

Appendix 4

MODERN JUDAH

1830 — Church of Jesus Christ of Latter-day Saints established
1836 — Kirtland Temple dedicated, Keys of Gathering returned
1837 — British Mission opened, 1st foreign mission
1841 — Orson Hyde dedicates Land of Palestine
1847 — Saints under Brigham Young enter Salt Lake Valley
1869 — 1st Transcontinental railroad completed—travel made easier
1878 — 1st agricultural settlement in Palestine in modern times

FIRST ALIYA

1896 — Theodor Herzl publishes *Der Judenstaat* (The Jewish State)
1897 — 1st World Zionist Congress at Basel

SECOND ALIYA

1917 — Balfour Declaration

THIRD ALIYA—BRITISH MANDATE

1933 — Hitler comes to power in Germany, the Holocaust begins

HOLOCAUST

1948 — State of Israel is declared, Ist armed conflict
1956 — Suez Crisis
1967 — Six-day War
1973 — Yom Kippur War
1977 — Peace Initiatives begun

Index

J

K

L

M

MC

N

O

P

R

S